The Nativist Movement in America

By the middle of the nineteenth century, anti-Catholicism had become a central conflict in America. Fueling the dissent were Protestant groups dedicated to preserving what they understood to be the Christian vision and spirit of the "founding fathers." Afraid of the religious and moral impact of Catholics, they advocated for stricter laws in order to maintain the Protestant predominance of America. Of particular concern to some of these native-born citizens or "nativists," were Roman Catholic immigrants whose increasing presence and perceived allegiance to the pope alarmed them.

Concentrating on the mid-19th century and examining the anti-Catholic violence that erupted along the East Coast, Katie Oxx historicizes the burning of an Ursuline convent in Charlestown, Massachusetts, the Bible Riots in Philadelphia, and the theft and destruction of the "Pope's Stone" in Washington D.C.

In four concise chapters, together with trial transcripts and newspaper articles, poems and personal narratives, the author introduces the nativist movement to students, illuminating the history of exclusion and a formative clash between religious groups.

Katie Oxx is Assistant Professor of Religious Studies at Saint Joseph's University.

Critical Moments in American History

Edited by William Thomas Allison, Georgia Southern University

The Nativist Movement in America

Religious Conflict in the Nineteenth Century

Katie Oxx

Routledge
Taylor & Francis Group

NEW YORK AND LONDON

First published 2013
by Routledge
711 Third Avenue, New York, NY 10017

Simultaneously published in the UK
by Routledge
2 Park Square, Milton Park, Abingdon, Oxon OX14 4RN

Routledge is an imprint of the Taylor & Francis Group, an informa business

Library of Congress Cataloging in Publication Data
Oxx, Katie.
  The nativist movement in America : religious conflict in the 19th century / by Katie
  Oxx.
    p. cm.
  Includes bibliographical references and index.
  1. United States—Church history—19th century. 2. Nativism. 3. Anti-Catholicism—
  United States. 4. Religious pluralism—United States. I. Title.
  BR525.O99 2013
  277.3'081—dc23
  012035635

ISBN: 978-0-415-80747-0 (hbk)
ISBN: 978-0-415-80748-7 (pbk)
ISBN: 978-0-203-08185-3 (ebk)

Typeset in Bembo and Helvetica
by EvS Communication Networx, Inc.

SUSTAINABLE
FORESTRY
INITIATIVE

Certified Sourcing
www.sfiprogram.org
SFI-00555
The SFI label applies to the text stock.

Printed and bound in the United States of America by
Walsworth Publishing Company, Marceline, MO.

Contents

Series Introduction

Welcome to the Routledge *Critical Moments in American History* series. The purpose of this new series is to give students a window into the historian's craft through concise, readable books by leading scholars, who bring together the best scholarship and engaging primary sources to explore a critical moment in the American past. In discovering the principal points of the story in these books, gaining a sense of historiography, following a fresh trail of primary documents, and exploring suggested readings, students can then set out on their own journey, to debate the ideas presented, interpret primary sources, and reach their own conclusions—just like the historian.

A critical moment in history can be a range of things—a pivotal year, the pinnacle of a movement or trend, or an important event such as the passage of a piece of legislation, an election, a court decision, a battle. It can be social, cultural, political, or economic. It can be heroic or tragic. Whatever they are, such moments are by definition "game changers," momentous changes in the pattern of the American fabric, paradigm shifts in the American experience. Many of the critical moments explored in this series are familiar; some less so.

There is no ultimate list of critical moments in American history—any group of students, historians, or other scholars may come up with a different catalog of topics. These differences of view, however, are what make history itself and the study of history so important and so fascinating. Therein can be found the utility of historical inquiry—to explore, to challenge, to understand, and to realize the legacy of the past through its influence of the present. It is the hope of this series to help students realize this intrinsic value of our past and of studying our past.

William Thomas Allison
Georgia Southern University

Figures

Acknowledgments

I have so many people to thank for their assistance, and I apologize ahead of time if I have neglected any individuals or institutions.

The Massachusetts Historical Society and the James Burns archives of Boston College supplied me with needed documents on the Ursuline convent burning, and my Uncle Jeff Oxx with hospitality and expert Boston history. My work on Philadelphia would not have been possible without the historians and professionals at the Library Company and Historical Society, (whom I also thank for financial support), as well as the staff of the Free Library and Presbyterian Historical Society of Philadelphia. Likewise the archivists and librarians at the National Archives and the Martin Luther King Jr. branch of the Washington Public Library were incredibly helpful. Shawn Weldon at the Philadelphia Archdiocese Historical Research Center and the late Bobby Burke at Old Saint Joe's deserve special mention.

I owe so much to all my friends, colleagues, and mentors in American religious and Catholic history as well as those at Saint Joseph's University, especially Shawn Krahmer and Randall Miller, who have both been a constant source of encouragement and counsel. Ann Taves deserves special thanks for her years of historical training and mentoring; if I am ever half the scholar she is, I will be a very, very good one, and it will be because of her.

I am extremely fortunate to have so many friends and family members who inspire me and challenge me and call my bluff and keep me warm, especially my father, Joe Oxx, my sister, Meghan Magamoll, and my California parents, Richard and Elaine Jacobsen. None of this would be possible without my life partner, Rick Jacobsen.

Lastly, my most sincere gratitude is due to editorial assistant Rebecca Novack for her guidance, patience, and support; she made my first experience producing a manuscript painless. I am also grateful to Kimberly

Guinta, Bill Allison, and everyone at Routledge for backing my work and seeing it through to the end.

This one's for Dad.

Timeline

1455	*Romanus Pontifex*, first papal bull of the Doctrine of Discovery issued.
1492	Christopher Columbus claimed the Americas for Spain.
1565	St. Augustine, Florida founded.
1607	Jamestown Settlement founded in Virginia, first Protestant Episcopal parish.
	First Anglican church established.
1619	First slaves arrived in Virginia.
1620	Plymouth, Massachusetts founded.
1628	Massachusetts Bay Colony founded by "Puritans."
1629	Charlestown, Massachusetts founded.
1634	The *Dove* and the *Ark* arrived in Maryland bringing the first Catholics to the British colonies.
1636	Roger Williams founded Rhode Island.
1649	Maryland Toleration Act.
1654	First Jewish colony established in New Amsterdam.
	Maryland Toleration Act repealed.
1655	First Quakers arrived in Boston.
1662	Halfway Covenant adopted.
1680	Pueblo Revolt.
1682	Pennsylvania founded.
1701	Society for the Propagation of the Gospel founded.
1718	San Antonio, Texas founded.
1727	Ursulines established orphanage hospital and school in New Orleans.
1730	First synagogue in colonies founded in New York.
1732	First public Catholic mass in colonies in Philadelphia.
1741	Jonathan Edwards preached "Sinners in the Hands of an Angry God."
1751	Georgetown founded.

1768	Qur'an portions translated.
	Franciscans founded missions in California.
1776	Declaration of Independence drafted.
1780	Battle of Springfield fought in New Jersey.
1784	Methodist Episcopal Church founded.
1789	George Washington elected.
1790	District of Columbia founded.
	Catholic population reached at least 30,000 in the United States.
	John Carroll appointed first Bishop.
	Muslims petition South Carolina for freedom.
1794	African Methodist Episcopal Church founded.
1796	John Adams elected.
1799	George Washington died.
1801	Thomas Jefferson elected.
1801	Cane Ridge Revival, Kentucky.
1803	Louisiana Purchase.
1804	New Jersey abolished slavery.
1808	James Madison elected; slave *trade* became illegal.
1812	War of 1812.
1816	James Monroe elected.
1820	Missouri Compromise.
1823	Monroe Doctrine.
1824	American Sunday School Union founded.
1825	John Quincy Adams elected.
1826	American Temperance Society founded.
1828	Andrew Jackson elected.
1830	Catholic population reached 600,000 in the United States.
	Indian Removal Act.
	The Protestant magazine founded, published.
	The Book of Mormon published by Joseph Smith.
1831	New York Protestant Association founded.
1833	Massachusetts is the last state to disestablish religion.
	Lourette, first captivity narrative published in the United States.
	Washington National Monument Society founded.
1834	Ursuline convent burned.
1835	Lyman Beecher's "Plea for the West" published.
	Texas War for Independence.
1836	*Awful Disclosures of the Hotel Dieu Nunnery* published.
	Martin Van Buren elected.
1837	Native American Association founded in New York.
1838	Trail of Tears, forced removal of Cherokees.

1840	William Henry Harrison elected.
1841	Harrison died; John Tyler became president.
1842	Bible Burning in Champlain, New York.
	Anti-Catholic riots in Newark, New Jersey.
	American Protestant Association founded, Philadelphia, Pennsylvania.
1843	American Republican Party formed in New York.
1844	Philadelphia Anti-Catholic Bible Riots.
	American Republican Party becomes the Native American Party.
	Native American Party wins decisive victories.
	James Polk elected president.
	Joseph Smith, founder of Church of Jesus Christ of Latter Day Saints, murdered.
	The Millerites' "Great Disappointment."
1845	Native American Party holds national convention.
	"Manifest Destiny" coined by John Sullivan.
	Texas annexed by the United States.
1846	Mexican-American War began.
1848	Zachary Taylor elected.
	Treaty of Guadalupe Hidalgo.
1849	Order of the Star Spangled Banner ("Know Nothings") formed.
1850	Catholics became largest religious denomination in the United States with over a million adherents.
	Taylor died; Willard Fillmore became president.
1851	Catholic priest tarred and feathered in Maine.
1852	Franklin Pierce elected president.
1854	Destruction of the "Pope's Stone" in Washington, DC.
	American Party formed from merger of various nativists and Know Nothings.
	Nativists John Tower and Robert Conrad elected mayors of Washington, DC and Philadelphia, respectively.
	Anti-Catholic riots in Maine.
1855	Anti-Catholic riots in Louisville, Kentucky.
1856	James Buchanan elected president.

CHAPTER 1

Creating a Christian America

Whether your news lands on a doorstep or in an inbox or on a Twitter feed in America, it is frequently an inventory of fear, resentment, and violent conflict, and a significant portion of it can be attributed to religion. Examples of this are ubiquitous. From before his election, the persistent falsity that President Barack Obama was not a Christian was suggested by conservative politicians and religious leaders alike. State senators and representatives have risen to renown by warning Americans of the threats immigrants and Muslims pose to the American "way of life." In the same twenty-four hour period in March of 2012, the Florida House of Representatives passed legislation allowing for school prayer and a bill banning Shari'a law, a move which not only illustrates the power of the conservative evangelical lobby, but also the ignorance of many regarding the most basic tenets of the Islamic religion. Current public debates ranging from immigration law to national security spending to education and health care reform betray a histrionics that tap into something much deeper and more elemental than those specific culture-war battles: the question of who is an American.

Unfortunately, much of this debate illustrates how much racial, ethnic, and religious discrimination exists against those who are not considered "American." Though some groups—like the Birthers and the League of the South—deploy overtly racist and xenophobic language, less explicit, quite subtle messages often slip undetected into the current public square.[1] Using coded language, or inventing new vocabularies altogether, public debates are framed by those who have the power to shape them. Immigrants become "aliens;" non-citizen residents become "illegals." Words like "cult" and "weird" fuse with "Mormon" into inseparable modifiers of the Church of Jesus Christ of Latter-Day Saints.[2] Terms like "patriot," "hero," and "true American" are shorthand for those who "belong."

This bigotry towards those not considered "American" is called "nativism," and it is not a new phenomenon. The contentious process of defining America and Americans has held widespread urgency in many historical periods, when those who considered themselves its native citizens attempted to exclude or eliminate outsiders. Though nativism often manifests as prejudice against people who are not U.S. citizens, the ideology encompasses a much broader, symbolic definition of national identity. Some aspects of it are necessarily ambiguous; all are **socially constructed.** What is "foreign" in one place or at one moment in history is common in another, for example. The dynamic nature of nativism allows it to adjust and adapt to those changing contexts.[3] Nativist outbreaks are cyclical and reoccur at various intervals in U.S. history, and it is imperative to thoroughly assess their appeal, power, and consequences.

> Something (ideas, institutions) is socially constructed if it emerges from and is shaped in the context of a particular society. In other words, it is not a "natural" or scientific or biological entity preexisting and external to that society.

Though racial, economic, and gender tensions are often intertwined in nativist conflict, the specifically religious aspects of it are crucial—even primary sometimes. Indeed, ascribing to a particular kind of Christianity has been a nearly universal requirement for being an American according to nativist thought and as historical events clearly demonstrate. In the early nineteenth century, for instance, as immigration and territorial expansion increased Catholic presence in the United States, native-born Protestants note a fear and dislike of Catholic religious practices more than they disparage ethnic traditions or foreign language usage. They worried about how the Pope—not the King of Germany—would influence American affairs. In their paranoia, they determined that Catholicism was a "cult" run by a despot, and that tyranny was its *modus operandi*. They believed and argued that the destruction of all things pure and free and democratic, all things deemed innately American, was its aim.

Three episodes in American history typify the religious anti-Catholic bigotry that undergirded the nativist movement, and the terrible violence and devastation that resulted. When these incidents are used to unpack the messiness of nativism, its religious roots become strikingly evident. Indeed, the victims of the violence had little in common except their religion.

First, in Charlestown, Massachusetts in 1834, a Protestant mob attacked a Catholic Ursuline convent and school from which one of the sisters had allegedly escaped. At the time a fairly robust anti-Catholicism was gaining momentum, and its supporters circulated polemics that articulated perceived threats Catholics posed to American institutions. Protestant ministers wondered what went on between priests and Catholic women behind the confessional door. Others questioned the school's curriculum and speculated that religious indoctrination was at its core. Still others ruminated on the "secrets" of cloistered convents, especially when rumors circulated that women were being held against their will and abused. That many of the young students were Protestant girls added to the panic. Even after a team of local men toured the convent and found nothing out of the ordinary, citizens remained convinced that at best, the convent was a site of Catholic evangelism, and at worst, a breeding ground of sexual depravity. On one hot August night, a large and agitated crowd gathered outside and demanded access to the private property. Unappeased, they burned the convent to the ground. The women and children fortunately escaped physical injury but the property damage was tremendous.[4]

Although the incident in Charlestown horrified many, anti-Catholic violence spread to Philadelphia, where riots shook the city from May to July of 1844. At the time, the Protestant King James Bible was standard curricular material in common—or public—schools. Catholic Bishop Francis Kenrick requested children of his flock be permitted to read from their authorized Douay translation or be excused from using the Bible altogether. His request was granted. In response, incensed Protestant politicians, ministers, and influential citizens rallied behind the Bible as symbol of American freedom and liberty over the foreign, allegedly despotic, Catholic Church. Before the summer was over, every Catholic church in the city was threatened, two were burned to the ground and one badly damaged, two libraries, two rectories, a schoolhouse, and multiple blocks of homes were burned, about thirty people killed, and hundreds injured. The Philadelphia Bible Riots were the worst violence in the city's history to that point and the first large-scale urban unrest in American history.[5]

Unfortunately, the violence spread further still. In the District of Columbia in 1854, citizens and politicians planned to honor the country's first president. Again, the explicit attempt to define America and, by extension, Americans, was being shaped, this time literally, in stone, in the Washington Monument. Following other international leaders, states, and civic organizations, Pope Pious IX sent a contribution on behalf of the Vatican. The D.C. nativist party members, the "Know Nothings," who had a significant presence in the monument society, did not consider the so-called "Pope's Stone" a gift for which to be thankful. One evening, a small group of them trespassed onto the construction site where materials for the monument were stored. They allegedly locked the guard in his look-out post and poisoned his dog. By nearly all accounts, the men found the stone, dragged it to the Potomac River, and hurled it into the dark water.[6]

Nativists did not just target Catholics. Native Americans, African Americans, Jews, Muslims, Hindus, and even adherents of indigenous American forms of Christianity like the Church of Jesus Christ of Latter-Day Saints were subject to religious persecution because their faith was considered "foreign."[7] However, the opposition to Catholicism and to the influence and presence of Catholics has been the most blatant and persistent in U.S. history. Some of this can be attributed to the comparative size and distribution of the Catholic population. Although some cities had sizable Jewish populations, for example, they were well outnumbered by Catholics. Catholic churches marked the urban landscape, and unlike Native or African Americans, whose otherness was almost always immediately apparent, Catholics mixed relatively freely in the public square.[8] In addition, though nativist fears of a papal overthrow of the American government were unfounded, Catholics were under the religious authority of the Bishop of Rome, the Pope. Until 1870, he was also the temporal ruler of the Papal States, and throughout nearly all of the nineteenth he campaigned for a sizeable extension and centralization of papal power.[9] Surely this served to protect them from genocidal impulses lurking in the American psyche. They could not be classified as property and worked or beaten to death, as most adherents of African religions and Islam were according to the legally sanctioned institution of slavery.[10] Nor could they be massacred or "removed" as followers of Native American religions were under official government policy. They could not be chased out or driven to unoccupied, easily ignored territories where, once corralled, they could be murdered with relative impunity as Joseph Smith, founder of the Church of Jesus Christ of Latter-Day Saints and his followers were. No, the "Catholic question" had to be answered, and the project of doing so was fundamental to the creation of America, its institutions, citizenry, and culture.

This text will examine anti-Catholicism as primary example of the religious bigotry that played (and plays) a significant—and at times, preeminent—role in nativism. This chapter will briefly sketch American history up to the early national period to provide context for the three episodes examined here. It will also summarize the historiography of nativism, religious conflict, and anti-Catholicism throughout that history.

COLONIAL AMERICA

The religious nativist movement that emerged in the nineteenth century was not a unique historical occurrence. From at least the fifteenth century, powerful political and religious leaders colluded to determine who belonged where and what constituted that belonging.

One of the earliest models for this was what scholars call the Doctrine of Christian Discovery, which married Christian theology with territorial possession.[11] The doctrine is culled from a number of primary sources in which the papacy divided global territories among Christian rulers. All people inhabiting the land were to be "subdued" and Christianized, and all resources (including human beings) were to be distributed to the Spanish and Portuguese in particular. The Doctrine laid the groundwork for an understanding of non-Christians as heathen property to be used at will by Christians, who were in turn given the power to take the land from those who were deemed unworthy of it. Although this Doctrine was formulated and enforced by Catholic popes, its ideology provided later imperialists and colonial powers with both a model and a justification for their land grabs, massacres, and strategies for domination.

In the colonial period of American history—from 1492 to 1776—Catholic presence and experience in what is now the United States was extraordinarily diverse and nearly impossible to generalize. In the West, South, and Southwest, Spanish Catholics were the original colonizers, representatives of the European empire who sent them to exploit human and natural resources and extend the power of the respective crowns under which they operated. On the ground though, this classification breaks down swiftly as humans encounter and influence one another, and a messy range of affinities and attributes leads to hybrid identities, and folks whose bodies betray religious privilege and racial subjugation at the same time, for instance.[12] The French controlled the Great Lakes and Midwest regions, and up and down the Mississippi River. In the thirteen British colonies of the Atlantic, Catholic presence was by and large limited to Maryland and Pennsylvania, due to the unique history of those colonies and a model of relative religious toleration, albeit a temporary and always tenuous one. Catholics were not free in any British possession to practice with impunity, with the brief exception of the first two decades of Maryland colonial history.[13]

Christopher Columbus set a precedent in the Americas when he interpreted their discovery as a religious act. From even before the first colonists' arrival, they followed his lead. Early settler's—both clergy and non—most often interpreted their experience(s) religiously and through an explicitly biblical lens that at once determined and conditioned those experiences. Their religious and scriptural archetypes circumscribed all social and political relationships. They also laid the groundwork for church-state models as well as understandings of self, citizenry, community, society, government, and nation in the emerging republic.

It is absolutely crucial to understand the history, development, and evolution of the relationship between "church" and "state" in the places under question here in order to understand how American Christianities developed and how religious intolerance was exercised in American history. In his famous tome, "A Model of Christian Charity," John Winthrop, Massachusetts's first governor, iterated defining principles for a theocratic society before he even reached the "New World." His model would survive for two centuries as the last vestige of a religious establishment in the United States.

Winthrop's **Puritans** intuited their world biblically and aimed to shape their new society to fit that understanding.

1.1 Puritans

Scholars and historians are divided on the utility of this word and categorization, because it has been used as both a catchall for a range of religious and moral positions and a term of derision. That said, we can note some general characteristics of those who have been called Puritans.[14] It is crucial to acknowledge, furthermore, the profound influence their ideologies and actions have had on American culture.

The Puritans have their origins in Elizabethan England in the mid-sixteenth century. They did not approve of the moderately Reformed church she advocated, but desired an aggressive Calvinist theocracy to purge the country of its Roman Catholicism. They were convinced the Reformation's aims—and thus, the perfection of society—had not yet been achieved, and a small group of extremists among them left England to establish the Massachusetts Bay Colony. Their radical zeal explains (to a certain extent) their persecution of communities and individuals they believed had impeded their progress: Catholics, witches, the unregenerate, etc. They displayed what has called a "white-hot moralism."[15] They were rigorously devoted to the Bible and imagined themselves and others through a lens that sorted (and sometimes distorted) the reality around them according to scriptural types. They demanded a conversion experience of church members and saw a strict line of demarcation between those who had had that experience and the rest of the society.

Puritans demanded a profession of faith, a conversion experience from each individual who sought membership in their community to illustrate the subscriber's understanding of the covenant with God and their elect status. Because religious and civil authority were effectively fused, this act joined the believer to the whole of society. Scholars have come to call this theocratic social and political model the "New England Way:" a compact that bound individuals to God, one another, the congregation, and the polis and where the regulations of church and state reinforced one another. The compulsion of the New England Way lay in this reciprocity, this collective dedication to the sacred pact.[16]

Anyone who did not understand or practice Christianity in the same way the Puritans did was a threat to their covenant, and the government of the Puritan colonies was responsible for rooting out and persecuting religious dissent. The Christian charity in Winthrop's model, it quickly became clear, did not extend far. The earliest examples of religious discrimination can be found in the treatment of the slaves the settlers transported to the Massachusetts Bay Colony as their property. To the Puritans, the transatlantic slave trade was not only morally justified, but many considered it more beneficial than the eternally damning consequences of the slaves' previous religious adherence. Most practiced an indigenous African religion or Islam, both of which, it should be noted, influenced later forms of African-American and Euro-American Christianity in the United States, though not without the Puritan's considerable attempts to eradicate the religions of the "Mohametans" and "fierce monsters."[17]

Encounters with Native Americans further illustrate the settlers' sense that they were on a divine mission to Christianize. The religious beliefs of the country's first inhabitants were discounted and the explicit goal to "wynn and incite the Natives of the Country to the knowledge and obedience of the onlie true God and Savior of Mankinde, and of the Christian fayth" was written in the Bay Colony charter.[18] During the Pequot War of 1637, in which settlers attacked a village in retaliation for the natives' attack on Wetherfield, Massachusetts, at least four hundred native men, women, and children were massacred. Survivors were enslaved in New England or shipped to the West Indies in exchange for African slaves, who were considered stronger than the Native Americans.[19]

Quakers and alleged witches, also religious outsiders in Puritan society, were tortured and executed for heresy. Lucky folks—like dissenter Roger Williams's—were banished. After his exile, Williams founded Rhode Island, where, as might be expected, he did not establish any religion.[20] Similarly, the mid-Atlantic colonies of Delaware, New Jersey, and Pennsylvania rejected models of establishment. Quaker William Penn sought freedom of religion and founded Pennsylvania in 1681 as a "holy experiment."[21] Penn's colony was notable for its relative toleration, though it did not extend far.

> George Fox established the Society of Friends, the proper name for the religion of the Quakers, in England in 1647. Reacting directly against the Reformed Calvinism in his country at the time, Fox taught that all Christians had an "inner light" and he rejected all outward signs and sacraments of communion with God.

The Anglican Church is the Church of England. It traces its formal beginnings to Henry VIII's 1534 Act of Supremacy, in which he declared himself its leader, though not much changed religiously in the country. With Queen Elizabeth's 1559 Acts of Supremacy and Uniformity and changes to the Book of Common Prayer, a new branch of Christianity was established. After the American Revolution, the Church of England became the Episcopal Church in the United States to differentiate it from the colonizer's religion and signal its organization under bishops (in Greek, "episcopos").

Citizens were required to believe in God and office holders to profess Jesus Christ as their savior, and violence broke out at times between Anglicans and Quakers, for instance.[22]

Maryland legally tolerated Catholicism at its founding by the convert Cecil Calvert in 1632. This arrangement would not last much beyond the first decade of settlement, however. From 1650 until 1658, revolts by Puritans escaping established and dominant Anglicanism in nearby Virginia caused considerable religious conflict and violence. Calvert was able to regain control and reestablish toleration—however shaky and temporary—by invoking the original colonial charter.[23] By the 1670s though, Catholic (as well as Protestant) clergy had largely left the colony because of the persecution and violence. After England's Glorious Revolution in 1688, when Protestants William and Mary ascended the throne, Catholicism was effectively banned. In 1692, Anglicanism was established in the colony.[24]

The first Jews in colonial America were Brazilians who arrived in New Amsterdam in the 1650s. The first permanent settlement, in the same colony, was established in the 1690s. Jewish communities took root thereafter in the growing urban centers of Philadelphia and Newport, Rhode Island as well as in Charleston, South Carolina and Savannah, Georgia.[25] Jews in America were not discriminated against to the systematic extent that Africans and Native Americans were, but they suffered periods of intense persecution and have been the targets of religious hatred and violence. The Christian charge of "deicide"—that Jews had killed the Christian messiah—which went unchecked by nearly all religious authorities for nineteen hundred years added profound theological weight to American anti-Semitism.[26]

THE GREAT AWAKENING

The period many scholars have termed—though not without dissent—the "Great Awakening" was centered in New England from about 1720 to 1760. Under the preaching of Jonathan Edwards, it resulted in a shift in attitudes towards clergy, worship, salvation, and believers' relationship with the divine. The era saw religious authority wrested from denominations and altered the way the laity saw themselves in relation to the church. Many of the ideas popularized at the time led colonists to view themselves as a distinct people with a distinctly scriptural role in providential history. Furthermore, the shift in consciousness to an **evangelical** and what would later become a uniquely American Protestant mindset fueled the desire to engage theology in the world and produced much of the eschatological mythology of the emerging nation.[27]

1.2 Evangelicals

The notion of evangelizing, or sharing the "good news" of Christianity, which is that Jesus has risen from the dead, dates to the biblical admonition to his followers. As a more formalized movement however, it dates to the seventeenth century Pietists who adopted a new, more rigorous style for Christian living. It almost immediately influenced a number of other Christian communities, especially those who became Methodists and Congregationalists in the United States.

British historian David Bebbington has elucidated the most widely used definition of the term "evangelical." In his schema, four components are necessary: conversionism, biblicism, activism, and crucicentrism.[28] "Conversionism" refers to the act commonly called being "born again." A conversion, modeled on the Biblical story of Saul who becomes Paul, is the moment when a Christian understands and personally accepts Jesus as his or her savior. "Biblicism" is the term Bebbington uses to identify the fervent emphasis on scripture, which evangelicals believe contains the model for Christian action. "Activism" is more or less synonymous with "evangelical"—to "evangelize" is to spread the Christian message, and central to Bebbington's definition is not just a desire to proselytize to others but the idea that it is one's primary responsibility as a Christian. A disproportionate focus on Jesus—a "crucicentrism"—is evident in evangelicals as well. Whereas some Christians emphasize the role of Mary, or God the father, or God the spirit, Jesus is front and center to evangelicals.

In the United States today, it has become a bit of a catchall for a variety of different Protestant Christian communities. Formal denominations like some Congregationalists, many branches of Baptists, Methodists, Lutherans, and Presbyterians are inheritors of the eighteenth-century Reformed churches' evangelicalism. Members of megachurches and other non- and post-denominational "Christians" would also likely self-identify as such. A small but growing number of younger Catholics might also. In addition, the 1980s formation of the Moral Majority under Jerry Falwell and others was a strategy to inspire southern evangelicals to engage in the political arena (and ironically, to vote against Jimmy Carter, a quintessential evangelical, and for Ronald Reagan). The Christian or Religious Right remains a pervasive force and powerful lobby in the United States.[29]

But that is not to say the Great Awakening had a massive or deep influence. It did not necessarily lead colonists to think of themselves as "Americans" nor did it directly spark the American Revolution, though scholars debate these points. The Awakening was a conservative transatlantic movement that significantly influenced the future of Protestant American Christianity.[30]

The era that is called the "Enlightenment" also had a distinct affect on the relationship between church and state during the colonial period, although it resulted not in religious fervor, but rationalism. Many prominent thinkers were influenced by European deists and applied those ideas to the situation in the colonies.[31] Some of these thinkers came to play crucial roles in the drafting of key political writings of the new nation. The great affect of the Enlightenment on the relationship between church and state then, is the influence it had on people, and by extension, the ideologies and writings that became foundational American documents.[32] In a sense, tensions between the rationalism of the Enlightenment and the religiosity of the Awakening are still being wrestled with today in the courts and public institutions of this country.

THE AMERICAN REVOLUTION

Religion had a profound effect on and was an integral part of the sentiments and ideologies of late eighteenth-century America and on the newly declared independent nation in the aftermath of the Revolution. Religious ideas permeated the political, philosophical, social, and cultural developments that led to and—as some scholars maintain—even necessitated the Revolution.[33]

Likewise, the Revolution had a profound effect on religion. The colonial Anglican church was twice shaken, of course: it lost ideologically and it lost clergy and property. Other Christian denominations also experienced significant tensions inside their community; some dissolved, others split, still others witnessed a great decline in membership.[34] All needed to figure out where they stood in a country that was beginning to tease church and state apart, or at least attempting to draw a line between them. Perhaps the single most important effect of the Revolution was the emerging understanding of the role religion would (or would not) play in the new republic. A large piece of this was the process of disestablishment.

DISESTABLISHMENT

In the wake of the Revolution, colonies became states and drafted constitutions in accordance with the new national one. Religions that had been supported by colonial governments and citizens began to be disestablished. This process was contentious and only partial, however. Churches and other religious institutions could still receive legal benefits— if not direct funding—for instance, and laws were enacted to control behavior and curb immoral activity and even blasphemy. In short, nearly every aspect of culture remained saturated with religious ideas.

Many aspects of the process of disestablishment were shaped by debates in Virginia. The question before the legislature and the public was whether or not multiple establishments for a number of Protestant denominations would be permitted or if the state would disestablish all religions. Thomas Jefferson, James Madison, Patrick Henry, and George Washington weighed in, and much of the First Amendment of the Constitution, as well as the language we use today to describe the church-state relationship emerged from this conversation.[35]

Disestablishment occurred differently in the mid–Atlantic. The question of multiple establishments arose in Maryland also, but unlike in Virginia, the state's first constitution allowed such an arrangement. By 1810 the legislature had amended that constitution and disestablished all religious communities.[36] Though Pennsylvania, New Jersey, and Delaware did not need to disestablish, per se, they reconsidered the relationship between religion and government and this was sometimes reflected in their state constitutions. Pennsylvania retained restrictions on who could hold office (only a Christian), and the 1776 State Constitution included not only a profession of faith in Jesus as the colonial charter had required, but an acknowledgement of the divinity of scriptures. It stated:

> And each member, before he takes his seat, shall make and subscribe the following declaration, viz: 'I do believe in one God, the creator and governor of the universe, the rewarder of the good and the punisher of the wicked. And I do acknowledge the Scriptures of the Old and New Testament to be given by Divine inspiration.' And no further or other religious test shall ever hereafter be required of any civil officer or magistrate in this State.[37]

New England was slowest of the former colonies to disestablish; Massachusetts for instance, did not do so until 1833. Importantly, as scholars have shown, this disestablishment was not to *permit* religious diversity, but rather, to *prevent* certain religious communities from receiving state support.[38] The older established Congregationalists did not want property holdings and church leadership determined by supporters of the upstart Unitarians, with whom they disagreed on the nature of Jesus' divinity, human goodness, and the individual's role in redemption.[39] The decreasing influence of the Federalist Party, which favored establishments, and increasing power of the Democratic-Republican Jeffersonians, who called for the separation of church and state, were also contributing factors.[40]

THE SECOND GREAT AWAKENING

What many scholars call the "Second Great Awakening" (though like the Great Awakening, there is disagreement among them) was an era of Protestant Christian religious changes from about 1800 to 1860 that led to what has been described as the "democratization" of American Christianity.[41] Popular religious movements and preachers, camp meetings and revivals, and an unprecedented increase in church membership were hallmarks of the period. New Christian denominations emerged: the Baptist and Methodist churches as well as "homegrown" American varieties of Christianity sprouted and in a number of cases, flourished.

Central to this era were attempts by evangelicals to gain spiritual control of a nation they thought was in need of saving. Believers mounted a campaign on at least two fronts: they raced to Christianize expanding U.S. territory and to combat the moral decay they observed in aspects of urban American life.[42] They believed the future of the nation rested on their success. As scholar Paul Boyer has noted, their political self-interests were evidenced by their frequently hostile and demeaning descriptions of those they believed they were helping, namely, non-Protestant Christians. The greatest influence they had was not on those whom they believed they were saving, but on the future shape of evangelicalism, then a rising tide of cultural, political, social, and religious power and capital.[43]

The religious revivals that swept the country in the early nineteenth century also championed the fusion of Protestant Christianity and nationalism and often sought to cleanse both from any foreign and non-Protestant influence. The organized nativism evident in cultural and educational organizations, labor, fraternal, and benevolent societies, political parties, and a vast media apparatus—to name a few institutions—began to emerge. Movements coalesced with explicitly religious motivations and theological principles, such as an emerging sense of what would later be termed "Manifest Destiny" (see sidebar 4.1). One scholar has recently called this confluence of ideas about nation and peoplehood and Christian dominance "evangelical nationalism."[44]

Another significant aspect of the Protestant religious revivals in the early nineteenth century was the increased focus on millennialism. The idea of America as chosen by God and as destined for greatness emerged in a complex biblical typology that shaped both the experience and interpretation of the nation's history.[45] Although it began with the notion of America as the "city on a hill," a New Eden or Jerusalem, the sentiments that stirred both nationalist and religious emotions exponentially increased in fervor when combined. Millennialism was the theological corollary to the geo-political ideology of expansionism. Ministers preached and Christians believed the millennium could be hastened with the expansion of the United States, which would eventually spread and dominate from "sea to shining sea." As scholar Ernest Tuveson claimed, "[T]he possibilities for territorial expansion … came into a kind of chemical combination with the general Protestant theology of the millennium, and with the already old idea of the destined greatness and messianic mission of 'Columbia.'"[46]

This evangelical fusion of ideologies and institutions battled all non-Christian belief with great intensity. Catholicism in particular, which combined foreign leadership with a way of being Christian that was fundamentally flawed in the eyes of most evangelical Protestants, was uniquely positioned to be the object of ire; it provided a ready target for polemicists and a rally-cry to their faithful. Lyman Beecher, one of the "front's" fiercest adversaries, stated in 1830 in a letter to his daughter Catharine:

> [M]y interest in the majestic West has been greatly excited and increased, and my efforts have not been without effect to create a love and a waking up both there and here. The moral destiny of our nation, and all our institutions and hopes, and the world's hopes, turns on the character of the West, and the competition now is for that of preoccupancy in the education of the rising generation, in which Catholics and infidels have got the start of us … If we gain the West, all is safe; if we lose it, all is lost.[47]

EXPANSIONISM

Religion played a significant role in the ideology of expansion as well as in the encounters and their consequences between religious individuals and institutions that resulted from that expansion.[48] The 1803 Louisiana Purchase, for instance, which doubled the size of the United States, added nearly one million Native Americans to the population, extended slavery and brought its victims to Louisiana and Arkansas, and incorporated a French and Spanish Catholic majority in the territory.[49] Those who sought an all-Protestant America were conscious of this, and it added much urgency to their mission.

Mexico was another battleground for expansionism and site of conflict where religion played a significant role; indeed, religious language permeates the legislation (both Mexican and American) as well as the polemics during debates over the annexation of Texas. The second article of the Plan of Iguala or the Three Guarantees, for example, which declared Mexico free from Spain, stated, "Its religion shall be the Catholic, which all its inhabitants profess." When Mexico's new constitution was drafted following Iturbide's defeat in 1823, Catholicism was again named as the established national religion. Title 1 stated:

> 1. The Mexican Nation is forever free and independent of the Spanish government, and every other power. 2. Its Territory consists of that, which was formerly called the viceroyalty of New Spain, that styled the captain generalship of Tucaton, that of the commandant generalship formerly called the Internal Provinces of East and West, and that of Lower and Upper California, with the lands annexed, and adjacent lands in both seas. By a constitutional law, a demarcation of the limits of the Federation will be made as soon as circumstances will permit. 3. The Religion of the Mexican Nation, is, and will be perpetually, the Roman Catholic Apostolic. The Nation will protect it by wise and just laws, and prohibit the exercise of any other whatever.[50]

The Imperial Colonization Law of 1823 and the General Colonization Law of 1824 were enacted to encourage immigration to Mexican states, Texas included, and decreed that allegiance to Mexico and Catholic Christianity be followed by those who immigrated. When the number of Protestant colonists from the United States outnumbered Mexicans in Texas in 1830, Mexico banned further immigration and passed the Law of Colonization, which further stressed Mexico's Catholicism. The Law also abolished slavery, more, perhaps, out of a desire to repel American citizens from immigrating than from abolitionist sentiments. Regardless, it was unsuccessful in attempts to end slavery, and further, it angered and alienated the diverse Texans.[51] With a population of about thirty thousand colonists, Texas declared its independence in 1836. Though the Mexican government refused, the United States recognized the declaration in January of 1837. In 1845, it annexed the territory.

In addition to legislative documents, other sources of the early nineteenth century reveal that religion was a primary concern for many. It motivated pioneers and explorers, railroad builders and robber barons to seek new lands and stake claims on the frontier, and it justified their actions while doing so. These ideas had potentially dangerous consequences for those already occupying the land. They also discouraged some Americans from including non-Protestants amongst those they considered part of the populace. In more violent manifestations, the elimination of all non-Protestant Christians from American soil became a central, even necessary component of both millennialism and Manifest Destiny. All those who would not conform or convert were at risk.

HISTORIOGRAPHY OF NATIVISM IN AMERICA

Before we proceed to the three episodes under investigation here, a brief overview of the historiography of nativism is in order. In this section, I will look at it in terms of general histories of the subject, as well as how nativism has been situated within the narratives of American religious history and anti-Catholicism.

Many scholars consider nativism a consequence of immigration and the ethnic diversification of American citizenry. Some are more concerned with the context of American life, and with the particular social fears that led (and lead) to its development. Some of these scholars con-

> Historiography is the study of how the past has been presented and shaped in narratives and scholarly treatises over time. As new interpretations emerge, and as the discipline of "history" changes, the stories we tell about the past do as well.

sider how political competition and a restructuring of organized parties played a role. Still others locate the roots of nativist bigotry in economic insecurity, the expansion of capitalism in America, and labor competition. A number of scholars have examined how nativism is located in the socialization of American citizenry and especially in the education system generally and school textbooks in particular. Others maintain transference of anxieties over changing gender roles, or racial anxiety produced bigotry against all others.[52] Many of the publications that fall into these categories, especially those that pertain to religion, anti-Catholicism, and the three episodes under investigation in this text will be examined in future chapters. In this section, I will look at the most important monographs and most recent scholarship on nativism.

Many general works on nativism do not consider religion to be a primary feature of or influence on the movement.[53] The New Social History movement of the 1950s was a watershed in the study of xenophobia in American history; however, it disrupted both consensus narratives and top-down intellectual histories in exchange for complicated marginal stories. Often, that meant members of outsider and minority religions were treated as worthy subjects for analysis.

John Higham's *Strangers in the Land* is indispensible reading and has remained the seminal analysis of the nativist movement since its publication in 1955. Higham defines nativism as "intense opposition to an internal minority on the ground of its foreign (un-American) connections" and presents the movement as a "product of a specific chain of events in eastern American cities in the late 1830s and early 1840s."[54] Nativism has three "stylized themes" in Higham's thought. The first of these is anti-Catholicism. Thinking of nativism and anti-Catholicism as synonymous however "does little justice to either." Hatred of Catholics alone does not lead to it; "anti-Catholicism has become truly nativistic, however, and has reached maximum intensity, only when the Church's adherents seemed dangerously foreign agents in the nation's life."[55] Further, "no popery" is inherently linked to sectionalism; it became an issue when "national unity strained to the breaking point."[56] Higham's other themes (of less importance here) are anti-radicalism and "racial nativism." The latter, unlike the other two, defined what America should be in Higham's interpretation. This is, to him, a more recent form and one that "affected nationalism long before it became a factor in American nativism." Expansionism also was embedded in this pervasively broad theme of an American "race," an identity and "spirit" rooted somehow in Anglo-Saxon blood.[57] As far as those on the receiving end of the vitriol and violence, the Irish bore the brunt of the nationalist fervor. Higham adds, "As the pillars of an alien faith, the Irish attracted a good measure of any anti-Catholic sentiment that might be in the air; an Irishmen's loyalty to his priest was too firm for anxious Protestants to rest easily."[58]

David Brion Davis outlined six continuous "clusters of ideas" that have shaped American identity through the country's history.[59] These themes lead some individuals to imagine a larger, counter-subversive power is at work and provide a context from which nativist movements emerge. Though he does not make this explicit, each "cluster" has religious dimensions. First, Davis claims, is the belief that a "hostile foreign power" exists and is gaining strength. Davis acknowledges that sometimes these foreign powers *do* exist, but stresses that "the point to be emphasized is that Americans have long been disposed to *search* for subversive enemies and to construct terrifying dangers from fragmentary and highly circumstantial evidence."[60] Second, many Americans have long maintained that Protestantism is the only means of "balancing individual liberty with public virtue" and the only way to steady a nation in chaotic times. Third, the idea that an elite, "hidden aristocracy" has been "lulling and duping the common man" and to which this populist commoner must react has run through American history. A fourth theme for Davis is American's anxiety over the control of public opinion by outside forces. In addition, at many points in history, the fear arises that Americans are not living up to the "priceless heritage won by the Founding Fathers." And lastly, Davis asserts, the popular belief in American exceptionalism, that it is their country's "mission to emancipate mankind" is common in U.S. history.[61]

David Bennett analyzes what he calls the "constellation of concerns, fears, and frustrations" that undergirded nativism and the Know Nothing movement writ large.[62] He takes a long view on such movements, and imagines nativism to be one particular manifestation of American exceptionalism, a tradition, he says "with a common vision of alien intruders in the promised land—people who could not be assimilated in the national community because of their religion or ethnicity" or "ideological commitments."[63] American exceptionalism and its manifestations are rooted in fear in two ways for Bennett: first, fear of those who believe their America is under threat, and second, fear that they instill in those who represent that threat, those they deem inassimilable.[64] Those fears cannot be attributed to economic factors, although labor and class issues, and poor national and international markets—such as the Panic of 1837—play a role. For Bennett, the real threat in the minds of nativists was that the American nation and Americans' way of life would be infected by these non-American others. Nativist political and religious groups emerged out of this fear to "cleanse and protect the land" from the threat, the "vermin in the garden" of their pastoral nostalgia, the "bestial presence" in their Eden.[65] Nativism at base for Bennett then is an ideology that incorporates the civil religion of America as well as the perception that the Catholic other can never be a member of that church. When nativism has emerged in the past, Bennett observes, it has been in the midst of "a complex of national and personal problems seemingly so intractable that displacement of anxiety and rage against the foreigner became the only available solution for many Americans."[66]

Similarly, Dale Knobel claims nativism has been an attempt to respond to complicated social issues, but he argues that the ideology contains enough ambiguity to provide answers for a multitude of questions and concerns. It constructed the American self relative to the other, and thus shaped personal and collective identities and narratives. It responded to the insecurity about what America was and would become on both a national and individual scale. And it connected the story about self as citizen to the narrative of American providentialism and to Americans' place in the world. And then, it provided folks with the ideology and the impetus to create local and national organizations to nurture those narratives and from which to exclude others.[67]

Tyler Anbinder's recent and significant *Nativism and Slavery* is a sustained examination of the Know Nothing movement in the North and its connection to the sectionalist crisis.[68] Central to his study is how the Know Nothings and anti-slavery position destroyed the second party system for a brief time, as well as illustrated the depth and pervasiveness of anti-Catholicism. In the end though, sectional positions on slavery also tore apart the Know Nothings and fundamentally altered the emerging Republican Party, which, after 1856, absorbed the anti-slavery nativists and became the "nation's dominant party."[69]

Like Anbinder, Peter Schrag considers race to be a fundamental factor driving nativist impulses. He divides outbursts of violence by region, seeing distinctions in the South, West, and Northeast contexts. He defines "pure nativism" as "... a principled belief in the incompatibility between the freedom of republican government and the despotic power of the Church."[70] Crucially, Schrag continuously reminds his reader of the connections between historical and current-day manifestations of nativism. His first chapter, "A City upon a Hill" is an excellent introduction to the broader themes of nativist religious tension in American history.

NATIVISM AND THE HISTORIOGRAPHY OF AMERICAN RELIGION

In this section, I will examine how the story of religious nativism is told relative to the broader narrative of religion in America, particularly in the nineteenth century. Scholarship in this area is vast. In American religious history, nativism is situated in scholarship on evangelical efforts (whether viewed as successful or not) to define and maintain an ideological grip on the growing, diversifying nation.

Traditional scholarship on religion in the early national period has emphasized the creation of an "evangelical united front" among Protestants as a bulwark against all others and an essentializing force around which those championing a Christian America could coalesce.[71] A bevy of other terms for this juggernaut abound in scholarship, and to it are added a few with slightly different emphases, such as Jon Butler's "Puritan Ur-text" and Mark Noll's "Puritan canopy," both of which describe the enduring influence of Puritan mythology and culture.[72]

Nineteenth-century scholarship viewed this emergence of Protestant unity in terms of God's providential role in American history.[73] More recent work has explained the development of a Protestant consensus as a reaction to disestablishment.[74] The anxieties that visited the "Protestant establishment" in the wake of the religious diversification have been a persistent theme.[75]

The consensus model has lost its hold on American religious history, and a more complex understanding of the challenges and anxieties that disestablishment and diversity posed now cast the specifically religious aspects of nativism in sharper relief.[76] Nathan Hatch for instance, urged scholars to think differently about the complexities of Christianity in the early republic.[77] A number of texts have appeared recently that suggest Protestant unity began to dissolve over the religious and racial divide of the Civil War, in particular Mark Noll's examination of the Civil War as a theological crisis, which, significantly, includes the claim that Catholic opinions are "unusually important" in such an understanding.[78]

Recent works have also incorporated ideas from gender studies and social history. Bruce Dorsey, for example, examines how nativists understood their position relative to immigrants as part of an evangelical benevolence strategy that was intimately connected to the gendered nature of nativism. On the one hand, nativists "defined their own activism as a broadly cast reform movement, one concerned not only with the limits of the citizenry, but also with the mission of a Protestant nation and culture."[79] On the other hand however, the immigrant Irish Catholics "recognized patterns of behavior that made America seem at once reassuring and hostile."[80] During the 1840s, Dorsey notes, three incredibly significant "shifts" occurred in both political and reform-minded individuals and groups that allowed for the development of nativism: first, the simultaneous disenfranchisement of blacks and suffrage for white men, as the requirement of property ownership was eliminated by most states and "popular political democracy … flourished"; second, the government took control of social services in the urban North that benevolent societies previously managed; and lastly, those benevolent societies broke from their tradition of infusing aid with morality and began to focus on direct legislative action.[81] Gender was integral to nativist tensions in a number of ways, Dorsey further maintains. Women took advantage of their growing political power "to advance a form of racial nationalism in an age of Anglo-Saxon expansion." Immigrant men imported ideas about gender and shaped notions of manhood to conform to and take advantage of "whiteness" and the privileges it conferred, a move that "provoked both prurient envy and political anxieties." Two factions of nativists emerged: the political and the religious. The political nativists' greatest fear was immigrant men's power in the public arena; but religious nativists were motivated by the ideology that nearly everything about Catholicism was inimical to Americanism, and linked it to the history of theological and religious difference.[82]

Other recent works that examine nativism in American religious history highlight Protestants and Catholics specifically, and some have tried to situate the Catholic narrative inside (or alongside) the Protestant.[83] Jenny Franchot examined the interaction and exchange between Protestants and Catholics; they had a symbiotic relationship she argued, each needing the other in order to shape and sustain its identity. The "otherness," the "foreign-ness" of Catholicism, for example, was both a projection of the Protestant imagination and integral to the construction of "Protestantism." Franchot primarily investigated the "encounter" between the two through an examination of anti-Catholic and nativist fiction, such as the fabricated tale of Maria Monk, the escaped nun. Through her analysis, Franchot supplied scholars with tools to analyze the religious communities side by side in terms of "the discourses of anti and pro-Catholicism" and how they "informed and at points ironically sustained each other."[84] Franchot's elucidation of "religious difference … as narrative crisis" is instructive for the study of nativism broadly as well as a particular analysis of violent incidents.[85]

Like Franchot, Elizabeth Fenton has examined anti-Catholic literature in the nineteenth century. Instead of understanding the nativist perspective as a unifying ideology for Protestants as Franchot did, she interprets it as emphasizing difference. The challenge of Catholicism to U.S. society and culture, Fenton posits, was its test of the limits of pluralism and accommodation of the religious other.[86]

Similarly, Philip Hamburger deconstructs what he calls the "myth" of the separation of church and state and claims it was due almost entirely to anti-Catholicism. It was shaped as Protestants "ever more emphatically defined themselves, their citizenship, their religion, and their liberty in terms of their individualism and independence." As the interpretation of the separation led to the enforcement of boundaries between them, Americans "found the most positive articulation of what their increasingly individualistic religious and civil identity implied for the Catholic Church and eventually other religious groups." Hamburger asserts the educational conflicts in the 1840s—specifically those in Philadelphia and New York— set the Protestant anti-Catholic strategy in motion.[87]

Tracy Fessenden also contends that anti-Catholicism was deeply implicated in the development of the relationship between and separation of church and state in American history, as we will see in this text. She also asserts that the process of secularization thoroughly "Protestantizes" American culture. It is an "ideology that has grown more entrenched and controlling even as its manifestations have often become less visibly religious."[88] It appears as though there is an absence of religion in American society and culture, because aspects of Protestantism have been subsumed, they have become fused American society and culture. "[P]articular forms of Protestantism" she further contends, "emerged as an 'unmarked category' in American religious and literary history," and "a particular strain of post-Protestant secularism, often blind to its own exclusions, became normative for understanding that history."[89]

ANTI-CATHOLIC NATIVISM

Nineteenth-century anti-Catholic conflicts have primarily been ana-lyzed as either watershed acts that consolidated Catholic energy and led to the creation of separate institutions or as key moments in the process of assimilation of Catholics into U.S. culture. In most scholarship, the key role anti-Catholicism played in the nativist movement is oversimplified or obscured, and economic, political, and ethnic hostility, although important factors, are treated as more influential than religious prejudice. Scholars of nativism routinely defer to other factors as equally or more central to nativism than religion, even when those involved claim they are acting on explicitly religious principles. In contrast, for example, most scholars of African-American history and race and racism in America now understand its development as occurring side-by-side with the biblically informed con-struction of "America."[90]

There are some significant exceptions, however. Robert Handy claims the anti-Catholic and anti-immigrant impulses in the nativist movement "wind together" and, like Dorsey, he has connected this to the rise of Protestant benevolent movements and voluntary societies.[91] Robert Swierenga, additionally, found that religion was the "key variable" in the behavior of voters from the founding of the United States up to "at least" the Great Depression.[92]

Ray Billington's *The Protestant Crusade 1800–1860* is the seminal work on anti-Catholic nativism, and its breadth and depth of sources is daunting. Billington considers the conflict to be essentially a religious one, and he situates convent and church burnings, riots, and other violence inside the Protestant strategy to retain civil religious dominance in the United States. He adopts an historical view of the discord between the communities; he sees it as a continuance of their troubled relationship in Europe, especially England, where anti-Catholicism "became a patriotic as well as religious concern."[93] The American people were "steeped in anti-papal prejudices" and they were "unable to resist the nativistic forces of their day," according to Billington.[94] Indeed, he goes so far as to assert that nativism was an attempt to complete, on American soil, the reform project begun by Martin Luther and John Calvin in the sixteenth century. Ordinary Protestants—with an "average American mind"—who were not well versed in Catholic doctrine or teachings or political or social positions, were led to believe Catholics were un-American.[95] The Bible was crucial in this regard. Billington asserted, "Leaders of the anti-Catholic movement were aware that their best means of appealing to the middle class was through the Bible. If Catholicism could be demonstrated as an enemy of the Gospel, it would become the religious duty of Protestants to destroy American Popery."[96] In his analysis of the Philadelphia riots, he adds the conflict between the Catholic hierarchy and parish trustees to this and asserts, like other scholars, that anti-Catholicism was fueled by the perception that it was undemocratic.

Randall Miller and others have documented the complicated nature of Catholic life in the antebellum South relative to nativism.[97] The Catholic trustee controversies of the late eighteenth and early nineteenth centuries examined in chapter 3 were interpreted as a fundamentally anti-American position to be sure, but Southerners in the antebellum period were primarily concerned with the preservation of their way of life (slavery included), and only secondarily anxious about the religiosity of those who defended it.[98] Southern Catholic support of slavery and sectionalism ensured a relatively more comfortable position in civic life for Catholics than their Northern co-religionists knew.[99] Some influential Creole Catholics even joined the Know Nothing movement against the Irish.[100] Ethnic tensions were more an inter-Catholic problem (especially in regards to trusteeism) than fuel for nativist suspicions, though in the upper South, cities had to contend with the same large numbers of immigrants as in the North.[101]

More recently, Catholic scholars Mark Massa and Philip Jenkins have analyzed the persistence of anti-Catholicism in America. Massa contends intolerance toward Catholics has two sides: an "irrational nativist bias," and a "pre-rational (and often deeply religious) pre-judgment about both Christianity and democracy."[102] Nativism, on the other hand, is an admixture of "sociological, economic, and historical fears about 'outsiders' that many citizen of the United States from the mid-seventeenth century to the mid-twentieth centuries shared." Because American civil religion served as the de facto faith, Massa contends, all non-reformed, non-Enlightenment non-Protestant religions were understood and categorized as "un-American" outsiders.[103] Jenkins is also shocked at how pervasive anti-Catholicism remains; it is "so ingrained" he notes, it has become "invisible." Catholics are given very little protection in the public square when it comes to preventing the insipid intolerance because Catholicism is seen as the problem. Little room is left in the collective conscience for empathy with the victims of discrimination.[104] The difference in Jenkins' interpretation is that he thinks contemporary manifestations of anti-Catholicism originate with "left/liberal" Americans—including Catholics—not the "nativist, xenophobic and right-wing" folks like those in the nineteenth-century.[105]

Massa and Jenkins adhere to the secularization theory albeit in different ways and claim—against Tracy Fessenden's assertions—American culture has become less religious and more secular, and that religion has been privatized. Catholicism, with its wide-ranging social prescriptions and the long-arm of parochial influence is way too visible in such a context. But the theory on which their conclusion relies has been seriously challenged.[106] Furthermore, even if the less-essentializing notion of the "privatization" of religious belief in America were to be taken at face value, we would still have to contend with the fact that, following Fessenden, what is called "secular" is a culture that is so saturated with Protestantism it does not look religious at all; it is so obvious, it is invisible. Catholicism stands out against *this,* not the absence of religion. Jenkins observes the corollary: anti-Catholicism is "so ingrained as to be invisible," but does not see that Protestantism is also embedded in U.S. society, culture, and political life.[107]

WHAT THIS TEXT IS ABOUT AND WHY IT MATTERS

Religious conflict has occurred many times in the past, but it is not as old as most of us assume, especially because the conditions under which it materializes are contingent on many factors. At the very least, people need to have contact with one another and realize that others believe something differently than they do. Further, they need to ascribe to exclusivist beliefs; they must contend that other religions or faiths are wrong and must be abolished. Religious difference does not necessitate conflict; a particular kind of religion does, one that is not universalist. Considered this way, religious conflict becomes a much more novel and recent development.

As we will see in this text, religion was central to the American project from its beginning. It is crucial to understand this in its own right, especially since many people wrongly believe religion no longer has an impact on U.S. history and current events, if it ever did. This most often betrays individuals' own desire for either more or less religious influence in civic life. It can also indicate allegiance to the notion that "modern" life in "advanced" countries will eradicate or has eradicated belief in or the need to believe in anything supernatural or transcendent, but a funny thing happened on the path to secularization: religion prevailed. It is vital to learn about religious conflict because it is devastating and destructive. It is sophomorically predictable. It is also a vibrant expression of the lived religiosity of many believers, and it keeps repeating itself with hardly any variation at all.

CONCLUSION

This introductory chapter has briefly sketched some aspects of American religious history and how it has been told to provide context for the anti-Catholic nativism explored in this text. The remainder will survey particular events in the second quarter of the nineteenth century that demonstrate how integral religion was to nativist outbreaks then. Taken together, the events are an ideal lens through which to unpack the explicitly religious foundation of nativism in American history. This study is confined to three decades and three cities. Chapter 2 will cover incidents in the 1830s in Massachusetts. Unrest in Philadelphia in the 1840s is explored in chapter 3. Chapter 4 examines the destruction of a stone that was to be added to the Washington Monument in the 1850s in the District of Columbia. Each chapter will also include a section that looks at how the incident has been described by scholars and historians. Following chapter 4, a selection of primary sources illustrates the crucial religious dimensions of nativism. Some of these documents have never been published. Those that have been are repositioned to foreground religion.

This story ends in 1856, just before the Civil War, as the United States was facing, arguably, its most fractured and tragic epoch. Beyond that, I leave the history in the hands of other capable scholars, many of whose works are featured in the bibliography and further reading section on the companion website.

CHAPTER 2

The Burning of the Charlestown Convent

In February of 2011 an event sponsored by a Muslim organization at a community center in Yorba Linda Southern California drew large and angry protests. Hundreds of people attended. Two Republican Congressmen and other local politicians addressed the crowd and, instead of allaying their anxieties, appealed to their basest religious stereotypes and amplified their rage. The gathered waved American flags and placards and chanted with increasing vitriol at the Muslim families:

> Go back home … Go back home … Go back home! … USA!
> USA! USA! USA! … Muhammad was a child molester!
> Muhammad was a pervert! … We don't want you here stupid
> terrorist! Go home, go home, go home, no shari'a! … Go home
> and beat your wife—she needs a good beating! … Go have sex
> with a nine year old and marry her.[1]

These angry outbursts were eerily reminiscent of events that took place in Charlestown, Massachusetts in 1836, where a Catholic convent was burned to the ground. Home to over fifty young students and fourteen nuns, the episode was the first large-scale anti-Catholic violence in the country.[2] Not only were Catholics there the target of local ire, but the rage was likewise directed at children. Moreover, a significant subtext to both conflicts was fear that the religious other was/is a sexual deviant who inflicts violence on women and children. The hateful language the protesters and politicians in Yorba Linda directed at Muslims is disturbing, but the scale of the barbarity in Charlestown, which included the desecration of dead nuns' bodies, illustrates how quickly rhetoric can descend to savagery, especially in the hands of a roused mob.

This chapter will examine the destruction in Charlestown and demonstrate that religion was the primary motivating factor for those who caused the violence. It will begin with some background on evangelical pursuits and the state of the Catholic community in and around Boston at the time to provide context. It will also sketch some of the broader national trends and prevailing ideologies that were a factor. It will conclude by examining the consequences of the destruction and how the narrative has been told.

EVANGELICAL BENEVOLENT SOCIETIES

As we saw in chapter 1, what scholars have called the Second Great Awakening was a widespread movement in the early nineteenth century, one that many American Protestants were caught up in and that paralleled trends and impulses in American society and culture more generally. It was also the single greatest force working actively against the inclusion of non-Protestant forms of religion in the national ethos. The religious revivals and increased fervor of the era were because of the conviction that America was a nation in need of Christianizing. "Christian," as defined by those who ascribed to this religious ideology, was of a very particular kind: evangelical Protestantism.

The proponents of evangelicalism used all the material and intellectual tools available to them to advance their cause. They built seminaries and churches and trained and sent missionaries everywhere they believed souls needed saving. They lobbied for constitutional and legislative change and ran political candidates on local and national levels. They founded printing houses to publish religious newspapers, schoolbooks, Bibles, and other reading material. They distributed and disseminated the material to schools and domestic and civic organizations. They started benevolent societies to help those suffering from discrimination, poverty, or addiction. Abolition and re-colonization organizations promoted different ways to address the "slave question." Suffrage groups and domestic societies likewise staked claims on what women's proper roles were and whether they should be assumed in public or relegated to the "separate sphere" of the home.

All of these complementary institutions in the "Evangelical United Front" were rooted in the assumption that non-evangelical Protestant Christianity was in some way deficient. They actively sought to eradicate non–Protestant Christian beliefs and to implement their version of evangelicalism continent-wide. Sometimes this intention was explicit, as when Lyman Beecher stated, "There is not a nation … in circumstances so favorable as our own for the free, unembarrassed applications of physical effort and pecuniary and moral power to evangelize the world."[3] At other times the message was more subtle, such as the American Tract Society's mission to "promote the interests of vital goodliness and good morals, by the distribution of such Tracts, as shall be calculated to receive the approbation of serious Christians of all denominations."[4] But either way, there was little room for religious pluralism, and anti–Catholicism spread as swiftly as the fires of revival.

Benevolent societies set to work in the early years of the nineteenth century. In northeastern cities in particular, where rapid industrialization and an increase of rurally skilled immigrants who could not benefit from its job opportunities, a lower class emerged in need of basic goods and services and in the eyes of the societies, of moral betterment. "Not far below the surface of 'voluntary' societies," education historians Elizabeth Hansot and David Tyack note, "lurked an impulse to coerce."[5] The American Sunday School Union, the primary publisher and distributor of Bibles and other religious reading materials, illustrated this inclination. Their mission was to ensure the continued hegemony of evangelical Protestantism in all aspects of American public life, an objective necessarily flanked by an equally resolute aim to abolish Catholicism from that same space. Either in common schools, where its materials were distributed, in its own Sunday schools, where often the only texts used were ASSU publications, or in community libraries, the Union had control over what was being published, distributed, and read by adults and children. It created its own market with its resources and influence and built what amounted to a monopoly.[6] From 1826 on, ASSU books were bound together, aggressively marketed, and sold to public schools.[7] By 1859, nearly two thirds of "public" libraries were in Sunday schools organized and controlled by the Union.

The American Tract Society, American Bible Society, and Society for the Propagation of the Gospel were similar to the ASSU; they were powerful, resourceful, national, and even international, and worked to ensure that Protestant evangelical Christianity spread as far and as wide as possible. They believed their success would usher in the kingdom of God on earth and hasten the millennium. That Jesus did not return to earth should in no way suggest they failed.[8] Scholars have noted that their publishing ventures inspired innovations in print culture and the development of mass media in the United States.[9]

A primary concern for these publishing organizations was printing the Bible. Some of their other publications however, like *The Protestant,* later the *Reformation Advocate,* and then the *Protestant Magazine,* existed solely to argue that Roman Catholicism was not a valid form of Christianity. These publications provided readers–from specialized theologians to children–with evidence of Catholicism's errors. It armed them with tools to debate against Rome and in support of reformed principles. Perhaps most crucially, the publications warned readers of the dangers Catholics and Catholicism posed to American society.[10]

These evangelical organizations did not operate without opposition however, and Catholics were not just a passive, discriminated-against minority. A Catholic press began to organize in the 1830s in opposition to the nativist Protestant newspapers and tract societies. They denounced the American Sunday School Union for instance, as an anti-Catholic and Presbyterian movement that purported to be an inclusive and pan-Christian organization. The *Cincinnati Telegraph*, along with the *United States Catholic Miscellany* in South Carolina, the first Catholic periodical in the country, reported on one of the Union's meetings in Philadelphia:

> If knowledge be power, and numbers professedly learned constitute knowledge, how enormous must be the power of this indefatigable sect ... We have been amongst the first to notice the dawn of those hopes of predominance, which now characterize the Presbyterians in our country, and which characterized them from the days of their birth. [W]e contemplate the scene with sorrow: it serves to conjure up all our reminiscences of the Scottish fiends who disgrace humanity, and to inspire us with a portion of dread for the future which may be, by the permission of God, at the hands of their fellow fanatics.[11]

In another article, the paper reminded its readers that some Americans had attempted to incite fear of Catholics in their fellow citizens, but the "ruse" had failed. The attempt to instigate anti-Catholicism could not, the paper continued, "turn the gaze of reflecting Christians from the continued, the unremitting struggles of Calvinism to attain civil and religious power."[12]

The Catholic press also began to criticize the financial dealings of the Protestant Bible societies and their agents as early as the 1830s. The *Kingston Patriot* was extremely suspicious of the wealth the "Biblicans," as they named them, were amassing. The paper listed their substantial earnings followed by the sarcastic, "How charitable! How benevolent!" They feared the "army" of Christians that Reformed Minister Ezra Stiles Ely claimed to have at his service would "*at the point of bayonet*" execute his strategy to unite church and state.[13]

GENDER NORMS & CAPTIVITY NARRATIVES

Many evangelicals at the beginning of the nineteenth century were deeply concerned with the proper role and place of women and men in society.

What is called the "cult of domesticity" or "true womanhood" arose to champion middle- and upper-class white Protestant women's role in domestic life, one that was at once perceived as central to the creation of a good Christian family and more broadly understood as necessary for the stability of the community and the republican nation. As men increasingly began to work on the outside, especially in cities in the Northeast, inside the home became the "separate sphere" for women's work.[14]

Alongside the growth of this notion in Protestant circles was the concomitant understanding that alternatives to it were at best inferior, and at worst aberrant. Since the cult sanctified domesticity as women's ultimate fulfillment of her duties as a Christian and American, nonconformity was increasingly perceived as unpatriotic and against God's wishes. Catholic women who chose not to have children or to cultivate Christian homes subverted their prescribed gender norms and challenged the ideologies that

2.1   Nuns and Sisters

"Women religious" in this sense, refers to a woman who has taken either simple or solemn vows of poverty, chastity, and obedience. Women who take solemn vows are "nuns" and are typically monastic. Those who take simple vows are "sisters" who are permitted to inherit property and who usually do work in the world.

All women religious belong to orders, of which there are over five hundred in the United States alone, and many of which have both nuns and sisters as members. They live a common life, and can usually be identified by distinctive dress. Some women's religious communities have what is called an "apostolate," or a specific mission and focus of their work, such as teaching or caring for the sick. Others are contemplative, meaning they spend much of their time in prayer and study. These are usually cloistered; they do not leave the convent except when absolutely necessary.

Since the post World War II era, Catholic Religious in America have declined sharply, though their numbers are growing rapidly in Asia, Africa, and Latin America.[15]

sustained those expectations. **Nuns and sisters** were a visible illustration of this subversion, and the convent functioned, in Jenny.

Franchot's words, as a "heretical alternative" to the cult.[16] Convent life, in other words, "inverted and subverted" norms for women at the time. Nuns were "captives in need of rescue … cultural deviants in need of control" according to this paradigm.[17]

Authors of women's manuals, magazines, and fiction regularly wrote on emerging evangelical ideas about womanhood as well as its ascription and subversion. "Proper" evangelical women and their foil, Catholic nuns and priests, began to appear as characters in captivity narratives, a genre that was popular in the eighteenth and nineteenth century. The narratives originated in seventeenth- and eighteenth-century France, Canada, and England, and purported to truthfully reveal what went on behind the cloistered walls of convents. The "exposés" were overwrought, wildly popular tales. Whether they criticized Catholicism directly or were more generally disparaging of a perceived anti-Enlightenment lifestyle or anti-individualism, they presented monastic life as deviant. The thinly veiled heuristic function was to teach women and men the dangers of the Catholic religion and vocational life to the non-Catholic woman, home, and nation. The narratives followed a prescribed pattern: a woman would leave all that she knew and join a convent, lured by a false impression of it or some other kind of coercion. Soon after, its horrors would be revealed to her, but she would be held there against her will. Either she would eventually escape and tell her story or she would die inside the convent and someone else would tell her story for her.[18]

These popular narratives shaped the public perception of Catholicism and convent life. Both Julia Beckwith Hart's Canadian story *St. Ursula's Convent: or, the Nun of Canada* (1824) and the British publication *The Nun* (1833) by Mary Martha Sherwood (nee Butts) detailed abuses that, along with a critique of Catholic doctrine, informed the plot at each turn. Both were written in English and widely read, and as Ray Billington notes, the Sherwood story in particular was popular in Boston.[19] Protestant minister George Bourne published the first American convent narrative, *Lorette,* in 1833 and again in 1834 in New York. He dedicated the story to Arthur Tappan, partner of Samuel Morse and like him, involved in anti-Catholic activities. In Lourette, two Catholic men, Diganu and Chritien, visited Canada and encountered Louise, a badly injured and delirious woman, wandering along a roadside. They took her in, helped her heal, and she eventually revealed to them the horrors she endured. The list of these horrors was typical of the genre: priests (Jesuits) murdering both their illicit children and the women who gave birth to them; rape; forced prostitution; and the use of alcohol for sedation. While Louise recovered, she received a Bible from an American visitor (Bourne?) and discovered its "truths." Thus, alongside the salacious anecdotes, the sub-plot of a Protestant conversion experience, an indictment of Catholic beliefs and practices, and growing support of evangelical positions (especially, of course, the centrality of scripture to "true" Christianity) unfolded through the characters' experiences.

The genre continued to grow in popularity and to shape the public's imagination in the early decades of the nineteenth century. In Charlestown, Massachusetts in 1832, a story circulated about a Catholic convert named Rebecca Reed, who had "escaped"—or, perhaps more accurately, walked out an unlocked gate and left—the Ursuline Convent. Reed had attended the school as a "charity student" (meaning her tuition was waived) but only remained there a few months. After her departure, she described abuse at the convent and claimed she had been held there against her will.

Though Reed's details were not written and published until 1835, a year after the convent was burned down, her story conformed to the convent captivity genre. It tapped in to the fears and misunderstandings of Catholic women's lives that existed at that time and were evidenced in the genre. As such, those who were familiar with such stories easily believed it. No longer relegated to evangelical bully pulpits, anti-Catholicism grew ever more atmospheric, and those who had not been prejudiced before joined the cause because of what Reed and others described. The public's suspicion of the Ursulines–and in some quarters, a push for action against them—spread.

LOCAL CONTEXT

Catholic convert John Thayer founded the Ursuline convent in Boston in 1820.[20] Thayer had apparently become quite impressed with Ursuline educational strategies through his travels. He convinced two Irish-born women, Mary and Catherine Ryan, daughters of friends of his, to go to Massachusetts and join the order.[21] The Reverend Charles Matignon also supported the cause, and Bishop Jean Lefebvre de Cheverus of Boston supplied the women with space for a convent and day school in the city.[22]

The first Ursulines in Boston were ethnically mixed: Irish, American, and Canadian. More young women from Ireland would eventually make the trip, as would those from the local area and surrounding states. Of the Americans, a number were converts, who as Jeanne Hamilton notes, had probably never encountered a nun. Students from the local region and as far away as Puerto Rico were in residence.[23]

The early years in Boston were transitional ones for the Ursulines. In 1823, newly appointed Bishop Benedict Joseph Fenwick took a "considerable interest" (one that lasted his lifetime) in the community and moved the women from their home to a more suitable, larger space with an outside recreational area.[24] Mount Benedict (as the bishop named it) was in Charlestown, part of the city of Boston today, but a separate municipality in the nineteenth century. With the move, the convent became a boarding school which no longer primarily served poor immigrant Catholic girls.[25]

The majority were Protestant Unitarians, between six and fourteen years old, from established families. Enrollment numbers varied through the early decade from about forty students to nearly seventy. The girls were instructed in more refined subjects than they would have learned in public schools at the time: the French language, dancing, and playing the harp for instance.[26]

There were a number of violent anti-Catholic events in Charlestown and Boston in the years and months leading up to the destruction of the convent. The Ursuline's dog was shot and their stable was burned to the ground. Nearby Catholic homes were stoned. The home and pub of Catholic Roger McGowan was torched. Newspapers and other forms of media too, published an increasing number of negative reports and articles about the women and girls. Stories circulated about the "elopement" of a young girl from the convent, for example.[27] In 1831, locals attempted to prevent Catholics from using their cemetery, and Bishop Fenwick's court case was on-going at the time the convent was burned. Additionally, some folks in Charlestown considered the Catholic "foreign" presence so near the battles of the American Revolution an insult.[28] Town leaders also became less inclined to religious tolerance after 1833, when the Workingman's Party seized power from members of aristocratic upper class parties.[29]

LYMAN BEECHER'S CRUSADE

Anti-Catholic Protestant minister Lyman Beecher delivered a sermon multiple times in Boston the day before the Ursuline convent was burned. Though he had been denouncing Catholicism from the pulpit for a number of years, this sermon was particularly timely, as many folks would have heard the rumors about the suspicious happenings at Mount Benedict. Beecher used the pulpit to incite fear and spread vitriol. His sermon was designed to be a wake-up call, a warning, about the Catholic threat to Christian America. He claimed the nation's success, its providential expansion, and the correct education of its children were irrevocably linked and all depended on ridding them of Catholic influence. Catholics and Catholicism posed an immediate and serious danger, not just to the current and next generation of Protestants, but to the future of America.

"Congregationalist," broadly defined, is a Christian church that looks only to the congregation for authority. When we speak of the Congregational Church, however, we typically are referring to Reformed Protestant churches that follow this structure, especially those that were formed by the Massachusetts Bay Colony in early America and their inheritors.

Beecher delivered his polemic at Bowdoin Street, Old South, and Park Street Hanover Churches, all **Congregationalist**, the latter of which he had led from 1826 to 1832. A number of local Boston papers published the text of the sermon on Monday for members of the public who were not Congregationalists or in attendance on Sunday. In it, Beecher argued:

> [T]he principles of this corrupt church are adverse to our free institutions, from the contempt and hostility which they feel toward all Protestants ... Roman Catholic Europe is pouring her population into the Valley in great abundance; and ... [I]f the subjects of the Pope increased beyond the increase of our own people, in the proportion which they had in the last ten years they would in thirty years more out number our native inhabitants ... Despotic princes in Europe would empty their coffers of treasure liberally, could they by means of the Romish church, subvert our free institutions and bring into disgrace all ideas of an effective government.[30]

The degree of influence the sermon had is very difficult to measure, but nearly all contemporary sources note that it was a primary reason for the burning of the convent the following day.[31] One writer, who assumed the name "Philemon Scank," wrote an epic and lengthy poem about the riot and anti-Catholicism (an excerpt is in the documents chapter here). Included in the rhyme, Scank claimed, "Beecher rav'd, and fir'd the bigot crowd." The subject of his raving was the "dire woes" that were spreading across the country with the papists, and "where nuns and priests their wicked lusts enjoy, and arts seductive on the youth employ." Scank also attributed to Beecher the idea that "Freedom must expire, unless these Sewers be given up to fire!!!"[32]

Bishop Fenwick directly accused Beecher of inciting the riots as well. He recorded in his diary how Beecher had given a number of lectures in Boston in the months before the violence, "the object of which," the bishop claimed, "was to vilify" Catholicism. Fenwick launched his own lecture series in response to the "foul aspersions" Beecher had preached against Catholics, and he noted that there was a significant amount of excitement among "all classes" of his flock over the series.[33]

Louisa Whitney, a student at Mount Benedict, also noted that in the months before the riot, Beecher had "been denouncing fiercely 'the Devil and the Pope of Rome' ... [and] exciting a strong feeling against Catholics and all their ways." She also demonstrated that in many ways, nineteenth-century youth were not much different from their twenty-first century cohorts. Whitney blamed Beecher for her enrollment in the convent, not for inciting the riot. She described how her Unitarian father was "violently opposed to Orthodoxy" and to spite Beecher, who abhorred Catholic schools, he sent Whitney to the Ursulines![34]

Beecher's *Autobiography* (which is actually a collection of reminiscences by his children along with selected correspondence) noted the controversy as well. Edward Beecher, Lyman's son, stated in an editorial remark that his father, "sounded an alarm in respect to the designs of Rome upon our country" in a series of lectures in Boston.[35] Both Lyman and Edward defended the elder minister against the accusations that he was responsible for the violence. Edward noted that Lyman had written that the destruction "is regarded with regret and abhorrence by Protestants and patriots" but that the violence had "no connection with any denomination of Christians." Edward also explained the elder Beecher had noted, "The sermon of mine to which the mob was ascribed was preached before my presence in the city of Boston was generally known, and on the very evening in which the riot took place, two or three miles distant from the scene, and not an individual of the mob, probably, heard the sermon or knew of its delivery." The deliberateness of both Beechers' explanations not only illustrates that many people were aware of the accusations, but also that the Beechers were on damage control in both the immediate and long term.[36]

The sermons and lectures from Sunday, August 9, 1834 and the months leading up to it were the beginning of Beecher's famous (or infamous) *Plea for the West*, an immediate sensation that now occupies a central place in the anti-Catholic nativist canon. But it was not only Catholics Beecher vilified. He was preoccupied with **Unitarians,** and their presence at the Ursuline convent caused him much concern as well.

> Unitarians, who focus on the oneness of the divine, are distinct from the majority of Christians, who are trinitarians and acknowledge the distinctiveness of each part ("person") of the Trinity. Unitarianism emerged in late eighteenth-century America as a movement within Boston Congregationalism, and was defined by a more optimistic view of humankind and human efforts at salvation.

The heated doctrinal debates between Congregationalists and the early Unitarians became a part of the conflict at the Ursuline convent, and Beecher was at the center of it.[37] Indeed, much of his early ministerial life was spent embroiled in the controversy over New England orthodoxy. Beecher was a central figure in the Connecticut and Massachusetts debates over antinomian and Arminian tendencies—questions about the degree of agency a human has over his or her salvation—in reformed churches. Beecher, Jedediah Morse, and Timothy Dwight (perhaps the only two men whose anti-Catholicism was greater than his own), championed what they called the "Presbyterianization" of Congregationalism: a return to orthodox Calvinism and away from the liberalizing optimism of the "Socinians."[38]

DESTRUCTION OF THE CONVENT

It is extremely difficult to uncover exactly what happened in Charlestown, Massachusetts in July and August of 1834. As we saw above, contemporaries blended fictional convent narratives (which were written to seem as truthful as possible) with rumors about the convent. The fiction supported the rumors, and the hearsay helped popularize the literature. Furthermore, it is unclear from extant sources whether anti-Catholics planned to burn the convent, and if so, when they made that decision, or if it was a spontaneous act, the catastrophic result of weeks (and even years) of tension.[39]

Regardless, we can cull together a rough timeline of the events of the very hot summer. The following religious women lived at Mount Benedict at the time: the Mother Superior, Sister Mary Edmund St. George (Mary Anne Ursula Moffat, a convert); Sister Mary John (Elizabeth Harrison, from Philadelphia); Foundresses Sister Mary Austin (Margaret Ryan), Sister Mary Joseph (Mary Ryan) and Sister Mary Angela (Catherine Molineaux); Sister Mary Benedict (Mary Barber, the daughter of an Episcopal minister); Sister Mary Claire (Rebecca De Costa, a lay sister from Boston); Sister Mary Ursula (Sarah Chase, a lay sister, who had left Virgil Barber's church like his daughter); Sister Bernard (Grace O'Boyle, a lay sister); Sister Mary Frances (Catherine Wiseman, another convert from Philadelphia); Sisters Mary Magdalene, Mary Austin (or Augustine) and Mary Joseph (siblings Margaret, Frances and Ellen O'Keefe).[40] More than fifty students were at the convent that summer as well.[41]

On July 28, 1834, Sister Mary John ran away from the convent. John had been at Mount Benedict where she taught music since 1822. The sister claimed later and others concurred that she was suffering from exhaustion. John went first to the Cutter's, influential Protestant neighbors, who were suspicious of Catholicism but were too refined to support violence or tension. After leaving them, John went to the home of the Cottings, the family of one of her music tutors, who were also somewhat anti-Catholic and questioned convent life. They aggressively interrogated John while in their care about why she had left Mount Benedict. The Cottings, like the Cutters, concluded that she was mentally stable and that she had left Mount Benedict because something had happened at the convent.[42]

Bishop Fenwick followed Sister Mary John in an attempt to convince her to return to Mount Benedict. Though at first she refused to see the bishop, her brother was able to convince her to speak to him, and they returned to the convent on July 29, 1834. After her return, she could not recall why she had left or much of what had taken place while she was gone.[43]

Sister Mary John's departure from and return to the convent, as told by the neighbors she had encountered during her leave, was an immediate sensation and subject of speculation and hearsay. Newspapers dubbed her "the Mysterious Lady."[44] Many locals believed she had been lured back to the convent, perhaps for a designated amount of time, and admonished one another to keep watch over the site. Some Charlestown residents were apparently under the impression that secret dungeons lay beneath the floors of Mount Benedict where disobedient nuns were held and tortured. They demanded an investigation into the incident, and threatened to destroy the convent if such an action were not taken. Rumors began to spread in Charlestown as well as in and around Boston that anti-Catholics were planning to attack Mount Benedict. According to scholar Nancy Schultz, although this rumor was widespread, most people did not believe "such violence was possible in a sophisticated American city" or "that the violence would be enacted against a defenseless community of women."[45]

Throughout the week following John's return, neighbors arrived at the convent and requested to see her. Mother Superior, already trying to manage a difficult situation was angered by this intrusion. In the words of one pupil, she "failed to appreciate the kind motives of these worthy Selectmen; she was furiously indignant at the abominable stories in circulation about her and her community, and when their committee were admitted to her presence, she overwhelmed them with a torrent of invectives, refused to allow them to examine her cellars, and if she had possessed the power, she would have scourged them from her gate."[46] At some point—again, the stories have widely variant details—the Mother Superior agreed to allow a group of selectmen to tour the convent. In return, the men would write the local papers to detail truthfully what they found to hopefully quell the rumors that women were being held captive.[47]

On Saturday August 9, 1834, Edward Cutter and his brother Fitch arrived at Mount Benedict. They were concerned about the safety of the girls and women, and with keeping the convent and their own property secure. They asked to see Sister Mary John, who spoke to the men and reassured them that she was not being held captive at the convent.[48] They left, apparently satisfied that no women were being held captive and that nothing dangerous or illegal was taking place.

But the Cutter's article denouncing the rumors did not appear in the paper. An unknown source claimed that when the men arrived at the offices of the *Post* they were informed they had missed the deadline for publication.[49]

Instead of calming words that would ease the tension between the locals and the nuns, posters were hung around Charlestown on Sunday morning, August 10th, that provocatively called for further inspection of the convent and even violence. One proclaimed:

> GO AHEAD! To arms!! To arms! Ye brave and free, the avenging
> sword shield us!! Leave not one stone upon another of that curst
> nunnery that prostitutes female virtue and liberty under the
> garb of holy religion. When Bonaparte opened the nunneries in
> Europe, he found crowds of infant skulls!![50]

John Runey and Samuel Poor had been elected by the Board of Selectmen to a committee to "take legal advice in relation to the confinement of a certain Female in the Nunnery" and they arranged for the entire board to tour the convent. On Monday, August 11, 1834 the selectmen searched the site for three hours, and they too found no signs of foul play. As they were leaving, a number of the boarders allegedly taunted one of the men from their balcony.[51] Within a few hours of this, according to some sources, other townsmen gathered and threatened to burn down the property. Some of them were drunk. Edward Cutter and John Runey allegedly tried to dispel those gathered.[52] At 7:30 in the evening the students went to bed as they always did.

By 9 pm the crowd of laborers and bricklayers in front of the sisters' residence had swelled to at least fifty men, led by John Buzzell. The mob broke through the gate and approached the convent chanting: "Down with the Pope! Down with the convent!"[53] One student reported that she heard them coming and woke her fellow boarders. They heard gunfire. The Mother Superior broke free from the nuns who were restraining her, ran outside, and confronted the mob. They wanted to see Sister Mary John but she could not be found.[54]

A short while later the mob started a bonfire on Alvah Kelly's neighboring land, and a much larger crowd gathered. As nativists often did, many of the men wore Native American—"Indian" in the vernacular of the time—disguises.[55] Of those assembled, about "two or three hundred" turned violent. They began to throw rocks at the windows of the convent. They broke down the door and entered.[56] By midnight, the crowd—"brutalized with drink"—numbered in the thousands, and perhaps a hundred men had entered the convent.[57] The girls and nuns watched as the mob went from room to room and lit each on fire. Newspaper accounts noted how since the large convent was on a hill, the blaze could be seen for miles.[58]

The Mother Superior was able to get all the girls out of the building and into the garden where they hid in the grass. Edward Cutter appeared

Figure 2.1. Burning of the Convent, in George P. Little, The Firemen's Own Book, engraving, Boston: Dillingham and Bragg, 1869.

and helped pull the girls over a wall in the rear of the property. They went first to his house, and later, as the mob was searching the area for the Mother Superior, Cutter took them to the home of Mr. and Mrs. Joseph Adams, other empathetic neighbors.[59]

The mob burned everything they could: Bibles, all the students' and sisters' belongings, schoolbooks, and pianos and other musical instruments. They burned the barn, library, and Bishop's lodge. They went into the convent tomb, opened the coffins of dead sisters, and burned the bodies. One source notes they "*took out the teeth* from the mouth of a female corpse (sic.) and *coolly put them into their pockets.*"[60] One man, Henry Creasy, stole consecrated Eucharist hosts.[61] Finally, they burned the convent to the ground.

The following morning, the girls and sisters were put into a stagecoach by another neighbor and driven out of Charlestown. In what can only be described as tragically surreal, the stage was departing at the precise time the rioters were dispersing from the fire and heading in the same direction as the women back to Boston. The following lengthy description by student Louisa Whitney offers a strong sense of the mood of the locals:

[T]he crowd was in a mood of high good-humor, and its heart
may have warmed to our disreputable appearance, so like its
own. At any rate, the idea of acting as our escort to the city
seemed to seize upon it as a good joke. So we slowly rode the
gantlet between a double file of amiable ruffians, who saluted us
with jeers, yells, shrill whistling, and cat-calling, roars of laughter,
rough jokes, and questions … Many mock-respectful low bows
were bestowed on us, and much wild waving of arms and hands
by way of salute. We scarcely understood any of the questions
put to us in such rough, vulgar utterance as the crowd made use
of, but we did not feel afraid of them; they were evidently good-
natured and meant us no harm. 'Saved yer diamonds?' shouted
one young man to Penelope, who was resting her basket on the
edge of the stage window. The lovely, fearless girl shook her
head, and displayed one of her stockings with a smile; the crowd
applauded vehemently. 'I've got something of yours, I guess!'
bawled out another, holding up his clenched fist to the carriage,
which probably contained some valuable which he had stolen.
'We've spoiled your prison for you,' cried a third. 'You won't
never have to go back no more.' Indeed the general sentiment
of the mob seemed to be that they had done us a great favor
in destroying the Convent, for which we ought to be grateful to
them.[62]

Minor rioting continued around Boston through Friday night, as
rumors—fueled by perhaps by the Mother Superior—spread that Irish
"laborers" were "descending" to protect Catholic sites.[63]

IMMEDIATE AFTERMATH

The damage to the Ursuline convent at Mount Benedict was tremendous.
As the Mother Superior reported, "Nothing was saved—and in the loss was
also comprehended money, to a very large amount, in gold, silver, and bank
bills, the sum of which cannot be exactly ascertained, as all the papers and
account books were destroyed." She also listed all of the music instruments
and the books, clothing, and other personal property that belonged to the
pupils at the convent.[64]

Bishop Fenwick called Catholics together at the Franklin Street Church
on Tuesday after the riot had ended. He assured them Protestant Bostonians
deeply regretted the incident and civil authorities would not permit such
a horrible act to happen again. He pleaded with them to avoid retaliation,

and alluded to the Bible by asking Catholics to "turn the other cheek" and "Love your enemies, do good to those that hate; and pray for them that persecute and calumniate you." Speaking even more directly about current events—and betraying a certain trust that the system would defend the Catholic cause, he said, "There are those around you who will see that justice is done you." He also asked those gathered to tell others what he had said.[65] Many still expected Catholics to riot however.

The day after the riots, Boston Mayor Theodore Lyman called Protestants to an afternoon meeting at Faneuil Hall where he not only denounced the burning of Mount Benedict but clarified the facts surrounding Sister Mary Joseph's departure from and return to the convent. The gathered persons listened to remarks by local politicians and passed a number of resolutions that were reprinted in many papers. They called the attack on the convent a "baseless and cowardly act," and pledged, as the "Protestant citizens of Boston" to "unite" with their "Catholic brethren" and to protect them and their property from further damage. Attendees at a similar meeting in Charlestown resolved to put up a reward for the capture of the perpetrators.[66]

In Charlestown and Boston, mobs roamed the streets in the days following the destruction of the convent. Indeed, the night after its destruction, a crowd threatened the Franklin Street Catholic Church and another near the convent ruins. A mob gathered again at the site, lit a bonfire, burned surrounding property and trees, and destroyed the garden.[67] Though one source claimed only the presence of the militia prevented further damage, another noted "there was no force, civil or military, to restrain the violence."[68] On August 13, two nights after the riot, rumors again spread that Catholics were arming themselves in preparation to retaliate, and the *Recorder* noted "more agitation and alarm in the city than at any previous time," although no violence ensued.[69] On the Friday after the riots, Protestants burned Catholic homes and a barn near the former convent. The drawbridge between the city and Boston was lifted in an effort to prevent further Bostonians' entry.[70]

THE TRIAL

In the immediate aftermath of the burning of the convent, public meetings were held to ascertain what had happened. The indictments and later trials of the perpetrators are crucial to observe how punishment was or was not meted out, and to ascertain public perceptions. An intensely complicated set of conflicts and motivations emerges from the trial transcripts and other extant published and unpublished sources however. These reveal—at the very least—the intersections between religion and nativism, and related class and gender issues.

The men found responsible were indicted on eighteen criminal counts of burglary and arson. John Buzzell, William Mason, Sergeant Blaisdell, Alvah Kelly, and Ephraim G. Holwell of Charlestown; Prescott P. Pond, Benjamin Wilbur, Aaron Hadley (the younger), Nathaniel Budd (the younger), and Thomas Dillon of Boston; and Marvin Marcy (the younger), and Isaac Parker of Cambridge were tried. They were all working-class men, although as historian Wilfred Bisson notes, some were community leaders and local-scale politicians.[71] Buzzell, Blaisdell, and Kelley were brickmakers; Marcy and Wilbur were mariners; Pond and Parker were cordwains; Budd was a baker; Mason a gardener; Holwell a rope maker, Hadley a carpenter; and Dillon a painter. The indictment claimed the men:

> … with force and arms … feloniously, willfully and maliciously did set fire to, and the same dwelling-house, then and there, by the kindling of such fire did feloniously, willfully and maliciously burn and consume, against the peace of said Commonwealth, and contrary to the form of the Statute in such case made and provided.[72]

The trial began on December 2, 1834. In the selection of the jury, anti-Catholicism was not permitted to be a reason for rejecting a person. Neither was a juror's admittance that they were pleased the convent had been burned.[73] Clearly, an impartial jury would not be found.

Many of the details of the convent burning and the events that led up to it came to light at the trial. Alvah Kelley and Edward Cutter allegedly planned the destruction. John Buzzell was one of the main organizers; he worked for Kelly and had assaulted an Irish immigrant who worked at the convent weeks before the men burned it. Prescott Pond, noted anti-Catholic and brother-in-law of Rebecca Reed, belonged to one of the fire companies that stood idle and watched the convent burn. Other companies did the same.[74]

Only one out of the twelve men tried was found guilty of burning the convent. Marvin Marcy, who was sixteen at the time of the riot and believed to be innocent, was sentenced to life in prison. Bishop Fenwick and Mother Superior later joined Protestants in a successful campaign for his release.[75]

RENUNCIATIONS

Formal renunciations of the violence came from many quarters. Non-Catholics such as Protestant clergy and civic groups expressed revulsion at such a crime. Their statements however, frequently contained anti-Catholic invectives, as they referenced the freedom of all to practice their religion. A "friend of religious toleration" began his description with the statement, "It is too late to inquire as to the expediency of tolerating the Catholic Religion in a protestant country, if the United States, as a nation, may be called such. It is here, and it is here by constitutional right, entitled to protection."[76]

Caleb Stetson, a Unitarian minister at the First Church of Medford, stressed the duty of citizens to abide by the law. The public might not want convent schools, but how, he asked, "can any Christian, can any good citizen, can any man of common humanity hesitate to declare his deep abhorrence of such deeds of darkness and sin?" He urged the public to consider the future, and warned, "[T]he spoiler may exult in his victory today, but what is his protection against a mightier spoiler tomorrow?"[77] Stetson defended Lyman Beecher as well, who he mentioned was "accused of exciting the multitude to acts of outrage, by his discourses against the doctrines and practices of the church of Rome."[78] To this, Stetson claimed that all religious communities seeking freedom of worship should submit to public critique.

In the wake of the convent burning, citizens in Charlestown, Boston, and across the country feared religious violence had become a permanent aspect of American life. A Protestant correspondence in the *New York Transcript* made explicit reference to the religious nature of the convent burning, and was adamantly against what he or she called a "religious war" in the United States. The writer claimed that Catholics' right to worship "is guaranteed by the constitution and laws of the land." The writer maintained he or she would "not willingly war" with a Catholic, although the Catholic was the antagonist, "opposed to [the Protestant] creed or opinions." "A very good American citizen," the writer intoned, had a responsibility "to frown down the fanaticism and intolerance of the day." This renunciation of the violence, sadly, was infused with anti-Catholicism. From the writer's perspective, intolerance and opposition to Protestantism was the reason Catholics were not "good American citizens."[79]

LASTING IMPACT

The Ursulines moved to a new site in Roxbury after the destruction of their home, where a Committee of Vigilance and Protection was established to safeguard them. The committee resolved to prevent any plans for riots, to assume nightly patrols of the nun's property, and "hold themselves ready at a moment's warning to repair to any place of riot and repress with energy the lawless attacks of a lawless mob."[80] Mother Superior, the committee noted in their minutes, supplied a fire and nightly refreshments. Nevertheless, rumors of attacks remained common, and in May of 1835, the Ursulines left Roxbury and moved to Canada. Though a few sisters tried to return in the later years of the decade, their attempt to found another school was unsuccessful. In 1840, the Boston Ursuline community was permanently dissolved.[81]

Anti-Catholic outbursts continued in and around Boston however. For the first anniversary of the riots, anti-Catholics held a celebration and shot an effigy of Bishop Fenwick.[82] In 1838, Caroline Gilman penned a description of the condition of the ruins during her 1836 travels. Her words revealed the empathy and sadness many people felt over such a violent conflict. Though the following quote is extensive, Gilman provided a valuable textual illustration of the convent ruins. She also established that defacement of the property continued:

> These blackened walls tell a story of deep and awful pathos. I walked on the broken terrace, where the sisters and their young pupils used to sit, while the traveler on the road below paused a moment at the sight of their graceful forms as their dresses fluttered in the wind; I passed the wall over which the frightened creatures leaped at midnight by the light of their burning home; and I saw the rifled tomb, which the mob left empty, as it is now! On the few walls that are still standing, one may see mottoes and words indicative of the feelings of the portion of the community who destroyed them. It will hardly be believed that a couplet like the following is one of the least vulgar and blasphemous there: 'The Priests go to hell/While the Yankees ring the bell.' … I scarcely know whether to wish the whole ruin leveled and obliterated, to avoid the accusation it seems to speak to the mind of a stranger, or to let it stand as a solemn warning to the descendants of those Pilgrims who sought on this very soil 'Freedom to worship God.'[83]

RELIGION IN THE URSULINE CONVENT BURNING

Anti-Catholicism was atmospheric in 1830s Massachusetts and, in this context, fiction was fact, education was propaganda, and difference was deformity. It was both a motivation for the destruction of the convent and a justification—in the aftermath—for its burning. This section of chapter 2 will tease apart a number of explicitly religious factors that surfaced to explore the extent to which religion was a primary reason the convent was burned. These interrelated factors include: historical and popular anti-Catholicism, religious competition, and the perception of Catholic sexual deviance.

ANTI-CATHOLICISM

Anti-Catholic sentiment in Boston and Charlestown was transported with the pilgrims and Puritans. It was also home-grown, a consequence of the particulars of its time. With the exception of Lyman Beecher, perhaps no other writer in the country spoke out more vociferously against the Catholic threat generally and Catholic education specifically than Theodore Dwight, Timothy's brother. His title *Open Convents or Nunneries and Popish Seminaries Dangerous to the Morals and Degrading to the Character of a Republican Community* sums up his perspective fairly well. Published in 1836, the polemic provided a laundry list of reasons why convents and seminaries were so dangerous. It also included forwards by William C. Brownlee and Samuel Morse, exemplary of the most vitriolic anti-Catholicism in print.

Dwight summarized both Reed's publication and a much more salacious convent captivity narrative by Maria Monk that detailed sexual trysts and indiscretions, and worse, rape and murder at the convent where she was allegedly held. Dwight went to painstaking lengths and used explicit detail to show that Monk's narrative was true. And he explicitly connected the stories to the Ursuline convent. He asserted, "In all instances where the inside of these institutions is unfolded to the view of the world," what becomes clear, Dwight maintained, was that "the most severe, unfeeling, and unrelenting, is the head of a Convent." He insisted that the condition of Catholic clergy "is the most abject and the most degrading ... of all forms of human slavery."[84] He warned that although the Inquisition "might not" be established in the United States, what American should eventually expect

> ... that nuns will be suspended by their feet, with their heads downward, sentenced to degrading penances and the most

2.2 Nunnery Committees

During the height of nativist political power and anti-Catholic paranoia over convents, Nunnery Committees were established in a few states. In Massachusetts, for instance, legislators founded the "Joint Special Committee on the Inspection of Nunneries and Convents." The purpose of the committee was to evaluate the education at convents, and more urgently, to ascertain if women were being held prisoner or if nuns were stockpiling "arms and instruments of war."[85]

The Nunnery Committees that were dispatched to investigate a Roxbury and a Lowell, Massachusetts boarding school were a pathetic lot, and their behavior and actions while visiting the schools became a full-blown scandal. *The Boston Daily Advertiser* disclosed that the men had spent considerable money on wine, cigars and a prostitute, and that they had propositioned the nuns and frightened the young girls at the schools.[86]

barbarous imprisonments, until their constitutions are destroyed and their lives sacrificed; that infants, the fruits of licentious intercourse between the priests and the nuns will be strangled, and the contumacious females suffocated for resisting the licentious attacks upon inmates of the school or cloister.[87]

Upon scrutiny, Maria Monk's narrative was found not only to be false, but to have been written under the direction of a number of Protestant men. Theodore Dwight was one of them. Ministers J.J. Slocum and Arthur Tappan were responsible as well, and, after the case went to court, it was revealed that Slocum wrote most of the narrative. Writer George Bourne, whose own captivity narrative was discussed above, also had a considerable hand in the fiction; the similarities between his and Monk's narrative are striking.[88] Dwight's and Tappan's polemics and histrionics led to the forming of the so-called **"Nunnery Committees"** by the state legislature.

Fear that students were being held against their will and abused by the nuns and members of the clergy were given justification by captivity narratives and were greatly assisted by the polemics that attempted to show they were true. In the immediate aftermath of the convent burning, narratives of Mount Benedict, including Reed's *Six Month in a Convent*, became wildly popular, and the historical events were confused and often blurred with the fictions. As Jenny Franchot points out, anti-Catholic narratives and polemics were referenced as factual evidence in the trial transcripts, and perpetrators and witnesses offered fictional events and rumors as justification for why the riots happened.[89]

Rebecca Reed's narrative was one of the primary fictions used. Reed described daily life at Mount Benedict in great detail to warn of the "errors of Romanism" and the "snares" and "delusions" from which she had just escaped.[90] She claimed strict adherence to rules and complete submission to the nuns was demanded, as was nuns' complete submission to the bishop. Superstitious medieval rituals like licking the floor, moreover, were taking place. The young Protestant women were forced to conform to Catholic doctrine and read Catholic history in her account. Physical and emotional abuse was used to control the students, and although it was much less pronounced than in other narratives, some sexual abuse was alluded to (Mother Superior and Bishop Fenwick would "caress" the girls).[91] The nuns would not permit students to repeat what was happening and censored their letters home.

Throughout the published narrative (which was released in 1835) Reed's intent appears to have been to influence those who might send their daughters to Mount Benedict. This is reinforced in the introductory remarks by the publications committee, who likewise focus on the danger of Protestant girls being educated by Catholics. Those same "preliminary suggestions" in the introduction attempt to disassociate Reed from the rioters who burned the convent by shifting blame to those who send their children there. The committee stated, "[I]f Protestant parents will resolve to educate their daughters at Protestant schools, and patronize no more Nunneries, then no more Nunneries will be established in this country, and there will be none for reckless mobs to destroy."[92]

RELIGIOUS COMPETITION

As noted in the introduction, in 1833 Congregationalism was disestablished in the state of Massachusetts, which meant, among other things, that the state would no longer exclusively support the church. The denomination would have to finance its ministers, properties, taxes, and schools. Every religious community from that time forward would, in theory, be afforded the same freedoms and assistance and subject to the same restraints. It also meant that religious communities had to compete with one another for adherents.

In the aftermath of the burning of Mount Benedict, numerous letter writers and editors of magazines debated how much specifically Catholic instruction was taking place at the convent. Regardless of the anti-proselytizing policy the nuns adhered to, folks were under the impression that Catholicism was being taught to the girls, and for many in Charlestown, it was unacceptable for any children to be learning about the Catholic church or performing any of its rituals or practices. This led to questions and disagreements about Catholic religious practice and theology in general. The debates reveal the misunderstandings and tensions that surrounded the convent's operation as well as those that were evident more broadly in the relationship between Catholics and non-Catholics in the Charlestown and Boston in the middle of the 1830s.

One of the most heated discussions was over Bible reading. Over the course of about six months following the convent destruction, numerous people were called on to address this issue: Bishop Fenwick, the Mother Superior, parents of students, editors of local papers, etc. At first the concern was over what students were doing at the school: were they reading the Bible or not, and if so, which translation, and when and how they were reading were questioned. The editor of the *Boston Recorder* asked, for example, "Did the pupils, while there, use Catholic forms of worship? In what ceremonies, or forms of worship, not in general use among Protestants, did they bear a part? If in any, was it *required* of them? If not, how were they induced to do it?"[93] The paper promised to publish the answers to these questions.

The Protestant Samuel Williams, whose four daughters had attended the convent, came forward and responded to the editors' inquiries. He explained that students were required to have an English translation of the New Testament; they could read from it whenever they chose during the week, but they were required to do so on Sundays. Williams explained that Protestant students had separate daily prayers from Catholic students, and they could bring their own prayer books with them to the school. On Sundays, all children were required to attend Catholic Mass, in Latin, but Protestants were required to bring their prayer books or Protestant Bible translation with them to it. Williams concluded by addressing a number of false rumors about required religious practice at Mount Benedict. He claimed non-Catholic children were not participating in "other ceremonies, or forms of worship, not in general use among Protestants." They had never been "*required* [emphasis Williams'] to cross themselves at any time, or on any occasion" or to read the Catholic translation of the Bible.[94]

Over time, the concern of the interested parties shifted from a question of what was being done at the Ursuline convent to what Catholics were taught more generally. The destruction of the convent was one manifestation of

> The frequently misunderstood Catholic doctrine of papal infallibility was only formally defined as dogma at the First Vatican Council in 1870 and is very rarely invoked. (Strict interpreters claim it has only been invoked twice.) In order for it to be applicable, the Pope must be speaking on behalf of all Catholics on formal matters of faith, and *ex cathedra*, or "from the chair," literally, his seat as the Bishop of Rome.

a larger theologically conflict: scripture and who had the power to read, interpret, and control access to it. For example, during the trial of those accused of burning the convent, Bishop Fenwick was called on to explain and defend the Catholic position on the Bible. He testified that Catholics are not encouraged to read translations other than their authorized versions and further, that they do not hold the Protestant version correct.[95]

"X," an anonymous letter-writer to the editor of the *Boston Recorder* presented theological challenges to Catholicism in a ten point, five-column article in response to Bishop Fenwick's comments at John Buzzell's trial. Among his criticisms, X claimed that in the Catholic Church, priests are given the authority that should belong to "Christ himself," and that they use that authority to "introduce rules and ordinances." **Papal infallibility** is unquestioned and Catholics worship Mary. They are not permitted to read the Bible, and they believe, X claimed, that a *"real sacrifice for sins"* [emphasis his or hers] took place at mass. The "Doctrine of Purgatory," X contended, was "on even more slender grounds," as was the doctrine of indulgences. One of his final claims was that in the place of a "doctrine of 'repentance,'" Catholic theologians "substitute … *doing penance*" [X's emphasis].[96]

Many of X's positions should sound familiar. The doctrinal contentions he or she engaged in had been taking place, as we have seen, among and between members of the Protestant clergy. In the aftermath of the burning of the convent, however, those issues became topics in the popular press and the public square for the first time. Debate about the differences between Protestants and Catholics—and the outsider status of the latter—was moving into the mainstream American conversation. Though X appears to be a well-informed critic (who even mentions particular theological schools), many will emerge whose arguments are rooted in ignorance, misinformation or deception, and even delusions.

PERCEIVED CATHOLIC SEXUAL DEVIANCE

Catholic clerical practices also came under attack throughout the conflict in Charlestown. Protestantism had no comparable tradition of celibacy, monastic, cloistered, or communal living; these practices were in fact, devalued in the evangelical understanding of family, community, and nation. As discussed above, the convent was a space where Protestant gender constructions were subverted and transgressed.[97] The destruction of the convent where these acts that were believed to be transgressive were taking place was a symbol of support for the Protestant cult of domesticity. It was mob justice for the defiance of evangelical gender and familial ideals. The convent's burning threw into sharp relief the public's fear and anxiety toward those outside of the constructed and imposed gender norms. As one frenzied opponent to celibate clergy wrote to the editor of the *Boston Recorder*:

> [M]any, *very many*, of the most respectable and influential of our citizens, have a deep conviction *that Convents have been, are now, and while continued, ever will be, highly injurious to the great interests of the community.* They do not believe that a company of *unmarried women* can be placed, for life, under the sole control of a company of *unmarried men*; be excluded from the society of others, except so far as their directors are pleased to permit; and everything which may be said or done, be hidden from inspection and kept an inviolable secret, without great mischief accruing to the persons themselves and to the public [emphasis writer's].[98]

The arrangement of the convent was "anti-Christian" and "anti-republican," the writer added.[99]

The characterization of Mount Benedict's Mother Superior in the press and trial transcripts and in the recollection of rioters and students also illustrates how the celibate nuns were conceptualized. Contemporary sources illustrate the extent of difference that was perceived between Catholic religious and non-Catholic women. In doing so, they also show the degree to which Protestant ideas about gender functioned as normative in early nineteenth-century Charlestown and in American culture more broadly. A writer in *The Recorder* reported Mother Superior's "characteristics of mind and heart" were attributable to her vows. Because of them, he noted, she "bound herself never to exercise" the "affections" of her "female character." She had willingly given up the opportunity to experience the love a woman feels for a man or for her child. She had "intentional[ly] and irrevocably" become "a being of no sex." The writer equates celibacy with having no sex at all. In this interpretation, women only have one means through which to express their "character"—either they conform to their ascribed gender role and its expression, or they have no sexuality at all. Because of this, the writer claimed, the Mother Superior "must become somewhat different from ordinary women."[100] She was an aberration.

In these descriptions, it is evident how Catholicism and Catholics functioned as a trope, as a way for Protestants to define themselves relative to the other. In casting Catholics as different, and in categorizing and describing that otherness, as well as clearly demarcating between the two, the *Protestant* self is shaped and defined. As Jenny Franchot stated, "[T]he Catholic body marked the boundaries of a normative Protestant self intent on a purity that would signal the attainment of perfection."[101] Furthermore, because the Protestant self was American, the Roman Catholic other was not; because the Roman Catholic other was not American, the Protestant self was. Creating the Protestant American self meant rejecting the Catholic non-American other.[102]

URSULINE CONVENT BURNING HISTORIOGRAPHY

Scholarship—as well as literature—on the burning of the Ursuline convent in Charlestown is by far the most voluminous of the episodes of religious nativist violence under examination here. I will examine the major publications chronologically in this section.

As we have seen, fictionalized accounts proliferated in the years following the convent burning.[103] A number of popular, secondary sources were also published in the aftermath of the incident that described the events.[104]

In the 1950s and 60s the rise of social history brought the immigrant experience into interpretations of American (primarily urban) life, and drawing on this, the first scholarly analyses were historical and sociological.[105] Eminent University of Pennsylvania scholar E. Digby Baltzell attributed the conflict to what he called the "liberal" and the "fundamentalist" varieties of Boston Protestantism. He claimed the "rigid" Congregationalism in common schools drove elite Unitarians and Boston Brahmins to send their daughters to Mount Benedict. "Quite naturally," he continues, "the fundamentalists saw an evil conspiracy between the Unitarians and the papists."[106] Baltzell's most famous "fundamentalist" was Lyman Beecher. Though Baltzell admitted Beecher "preached violent and anti-Catholic sermons" the day before the convent was destroyed, he did not attribute direct blame to the minster. For Baltzell, both incidents were indicative of the spirit of the times.[107]

In a different vein and anticipating more recent analyses, Joseph Mannard examined how Protestant women interpreted Catholic convents as a "menace" but also as a "model" as they crafted their evangelical educational strategies.[108] He also makes the important historiographical note that convent burnings and more generally, popular attitudes towards convents provide historians with the opportunity to examine "rank-and-file nativists."[109] In his work on a convent riot in Baltimore, he discovers that the economy there was stronger than in many other parts of the country and that factory wages were actually on the rise. By showing this, Mannard calls into serious question the many interpretations of nativist violence as a lower class pursuit, but he does not situate religious belief as central factor in the conflict or catastrophe.

More recently, scholars in gender studies, cultural studies, and literary criticism have added sophisticated examinations, and historians have incorporated new data and re-interpreted old findings.[110] In Jenny Franchot's highly sophisticated analysis, she examined how the narrative of the convent burning was constructed, and how that construction was deeply shaped by the ideologies, imaginations, and fictions of anti-Catholicism. She suggested a hermeneutic or typology developed whereby nineteenth-century persons "read" themselves into the narratives. Writing on the convent burning is "marked by divided and divisive political agendas and philosophical affiliations." These tensions, according to Franchot, have stood in the way of any "coherent generic identity" to be able to form and thus, no one "meaning" of the destruction has emerged or been able to claim status over any other. Because of this, fictional and polemical writing (novels and novellas on the destruction, escaped nun tales, wild anti-Catholic conspiracies) "represent themselves as factually responsible history." Likewise, factual writing (autobiographies, personal confessions, the trial transcripts, etc.) was "frankly saturated with references to various anti-Catholic fictions … all variously pointed to as evidence explaining, if not justifying, the behavior of the rioters."[111]

Historian Daniel A. Cohen has penned three varied articles on the riots. One examines convent life at the time more broadly than others have, and another revises interpretations of Rebecca Reed, who he locates inside the "contested class and gender images embedded in public discourse" rather than dismissing her as dishonest and troubled as she had been depicted previously. In the process, he gives her agency in a time of "profound social transition." He also directly challenges representations of Reed and the Ursulines as "polar opposites" in previous scholarship, such as Billington's. Throughout, he explores the construction of religious identities in the public imagination. Importantly, like Mannard, he also found evidence that all economic tiers were represented among participants of the Charleston convent riot, whereas previous interpreters of the incident (and other nativist violence) blamed lower-class folk.[112]

Jeanne Hamilton also examines how religious identities are constructed but with the complications of ethnicity and gender and class added to the already complex process. She attributes the destruction of the Ursuline convent to local "resentment" of the nuns because they represented the Irish, Catholics, and as discussed above, a "contradiction" of normative gender roles. She also posits that the conflict splintered Protestant denominations along class lines.[113]

In an even richer explication of the ways religion complications gender identities and vice versa, Tracy Fessenden has claimed that whatever convent narratives "are able to say about 'the female self' or about women in

general, as well as the degree to which they are able to homogenize Protestant and Catholic (and other) women" is inextricably tied to a strategy of
distinguishing "Protestant and Catholic spaces, subjectivities, and histories." In order to make the distinction between them, that strategy needed
to explicitly "gender" Catholicism as female. Although Protestant women
"resisted this homogenization of 'woman,'" Fessenden maintains, they also
used that negative gender distinction to "serve their own interests." Fessenden also takes historians to task for neglecting the Catholic role in what
has been called the "feminization" of religion.[114]

At least three scholarly works go beyond analyzing the construction of
gender in terms of the female and examine how the burning of the convent
sheds light on the construction of masculinities, how normative male gender roles were upheld, and how their transgression was met with violence
in the early nineteenth-century. These masculinities, furthermore, were
viewed through an explicitly Protestant perspective that considered aspects
of Catholic masculine sexuality abnormal. As Bruce Dorsey has asserted,
"[T]he celibate priest and the independent nun raised the spectre of a different gender and sexual order."[115] He claims also that nativists used very
particular images of Catholic men, both clergy and laymen, in order to
"generat[e] rival masculinities that destabilized prevailing ideas about gender."[116] We will see this at work, for instance, in the song written by Know
Nothings in chapter 4.

David Bennett contends the "verbal violence" convent narratives
described was directly connected to the physical destruction of Mount
Benedict. The narratives also illustrated gender anxieties that were consequences of the changing economic and occupational spheres. Bennett
surmises that the repression of sex because of these changes in work and
religious regulations led to a fascination with captivity narratives. Fictions
like Monk's *Awful Disclosures* were explicitly about sex, and by defending
Protestant women and their moral authority, nativists were also defending
the "American way." "The gross [sexual] deviance" portrayed in the convent narratives, Bennett surmises, "served to unite militant Protestants and
recruit others to their cause" and unified Americans to "meet the threat
posed by the enemy within."[117]

Similarly, Marie Pagliarini contrasts the "wicked Catholic priest" with
the "pure American woman" in her analysis of gender in the literature
of nineteenth-century anti-Catholicism. She found that this was illustrated most clearly in Protestant depictions (whether fiction or polemics) of
priestly celibacy, the confessional, and the convent. The literature reveals to
her the "values, fears, and ambiguities" in the imagination of the Protestant
producer and consumer of such material.[118]

CHAPTER 3

The Philadelphia Bible Riots

In July of 2010, Pastor Terry Jones of the Dove World Outreach Center, a nondenominational church in Gainesville, Florida announced he would host a Qur'an burning on the anniversary of the September 11, 2001 attacks on American sites. In a televised interview Jones explained:

> … I believe it's Islam's mission to dominate the world, to replace local governments, to replace the constitution of the United States with Shari'a law. I believe that's very obvious, as you look around the world you see the fruits of Islam. You look at the trouble that England is having, that Germany is having, Holland, you see countries that are dominated by Islam, even countries like Saudi Arabia, you see there are no individual freedoms and rights.[1]

Under an intense amount of media scrutiny and admonitions from many quarters, Jones rescinded his threat. A year later though, he put the Qur'an "on trial," and after declaring the scriptures guilty of a number of crimes, burned the Muslim holy book. In April of 2012, he again held a public ceremony—"Stand Up America Now: Worldwide Burning of Korans" Day—at which other ministers from his church spoke and he prayed. Jones declared:

> Today, we are calling for a United States-wide, a worldwide, peaceful revolution. We must take our freedoms back. We must no longer allow us to be silenced, and our freedom of speech, our first amendment, our second amendment rights to be taken from us. It is time to stand up. Today, we will, as an act of protest, as an act of standing up, as an act of saying 'You can push us no

longer, we will no longer be silent, we will no longer sit down, we will no longer be at ease, and we will no longer appease Islam, Shari'a, and the Muslim community.' We will today, all across this globe, burn the unholy, ungodly, perverted book of Islam, and the unholy, evil, so-called prophet Muhammed.[2]

With that, Jones lit the Qur'an with a blow-torch to the sounds of laughter. Other voices in the background of a video of the event chant, "God save America ... Amen ... God save Europe, and God save the Muslim communities from their evil." Those gathered then recited the Pledge of Allegiance.

Jones and others like him believe the Qur'an is "anti-American" and by extension, so are those who use it. They misunderstand or do not know what is in the Qur'an, nor do they know how it functions in the lives of practicing Muslims. What's more, they seem to be unaware that different Muslim communities and individuals interpret and use scriptures differently. To Jones, the Qur'an is simply wrong and must be burned.

Many of the nineteenth-century Protestants in this chapter feared and hated Catholics for not using their Bible as the ultimate moral and social authority. They were then, as some are now, unable or unwilling to imagine that other religious communities do not define or conceive of sacred texts in the same way they do. "Sola scriptura," or "the Bible alone," the famous rallying cry of sixteenth-century reformers Martin Luther and John Calvin, has no meaning outside of the Protestant congregations that developed from and define themselves according to Luther's and Calvin's ideas.[3]

Although many Americans were outraged—horrified even—at the events in Charlestown in 1836, religious nativism and the violence that resulted was in its infancy. Eight years later, three hundred miles to the south, on another brutally hot summer night, the most violent conflict in urban American history began. Over the course of the summer, in two separate conflicts which each lasted a number of days, every Catholic church in Philadelphia was threatened with attack. Two were burned to the ground and one was badly damaged. Two libraries, two rectories, a schoolhouse, and multiple blocks of homes were also torched. About thirty people were killed and hundreds injured. The Philadelphia Bible Riots caused at least a quarter of a million dollars worth of damage, an astronomical amount for the time.[4]

This chapter will examine the riots, especially those that occurred from May 5th to 9th, 1844, as a local manifestation of a growing national conflict and the end-result of a volatile mix in which bigotry was conspicuous and disputes were resolved through bloodshed.[5] The riots happened because of at least three specifically religious factors: first, distinctive ways the Bible was understood, translated, and functioned in different Christian communities; second, the transnational and historical animosity between Protestants and Catholics; and third, the evangelical imperative to Christianize—according to their definition of Christian—the American nation. I begin here with the national and transnational context, and then turn to the local setting to see how this conflict unfolded. Then I will examine how different Christians understood and employed scripture differently. Lastly, I will explore how the riots have been examined and understood by scholars.

NATIONAL AND TRANSNATIONAL BACKGROUND

Tensions between Protestants and Catholics in Philadelphia grew steadily in the nineteenth century and drew energy from both transnational events and local religious affairs. Catholic emancipation, passed in Great Britain in 1829, worried many. Now that Catholics had the same rights as other British citizens, anti-Catholic concerns about papal influence surfaced (again). The history of conflict between England and Rome and Catholic monarchs in Europe made this anxiety understandable.[6]

In Rome, Pope Gregory XVI was well aware of events taking place in his U.S. mission.[7] He was angered by **trusteeism** and other challenges to episcopal authority in the United States, but he reserved an entire encyclical for the condemnation of Protestant Bible societies.[8]

In *Inter Praecipuas*, issued (coincidentally) on May 8, 1844, the day of the Bible Riots, he wrote, "Among the special schemes with which non-Catholics plot against the adherents of Catholic truth to turn their minds away from the faith, the biblical societies are now prominent." He berated them for disseminating scriptures, "without discrimination among both Catholics and infidels." The translators, Gregory claimed, through "ignorance or deception," were reproducing erroneous texts. He condemned the Christian League of New York by name, plus "other societies of the same kind," and claimed their mission was sparked by an "insane desire for indifference concerning religion among Romans and Italians." The Pope wrote that it was not just Bibles that were problematic to Catholics, but "other evil books and pamphlets."[9]

Pope Gregory was correct; Protestant Bible societies had intensified their efforts to "Christianize" Catholics and anti-Catholicism was gaining momentum in many places in the United States. As we observed in the last chapter, benevolent societies were convinced America should be a nation of Christian believers and made it clear that non-evangelicals were

3.1 Trusteeism

The trustee controversy caused tension in the Catholic Church in Philadelphia and elsewhere from the colonial period through the late nineteenth century. Trustees were responsible for the administration of a parish—such as priests' wages and even appointments in some cases, church finances, property management, funeral arrangements, and sometimes funeral services. Some parishes did not have trustees, but for those that did there was no standard composition; they varied by state law and other factors. Some parishes had all clergy or all non-clergy, some had a mix of both. In most parishes, there were few disputes among board members or between them and the hierarchy. In others, struggles over power and authority and money erupted. In Philadelphia, conflicts arose at both Holy Trinity and Saint Mary's Churches.

Historians who analyze the trustee issue have varied opinions about its causes and impact, although the authority question is always at the fore. Some scholars (particularly an older generation of Catholic historians) betrayed their own desires for the church—i.e., whether it should "Americanize" or remain thoroughly Roman—in their outlook on the trustee issue. Some scholars argue that it was primarily caused by factors and influences external to the Catholic Church; others contend that both internal and external influences were at work in the developing trustee ideology. Patrick Carey maintains that in terms of the developing governing structures of the church, Protestant forms were of less influence on Catholics than has been previously suggested. He argues, along with Dale Light, that the effect of Republicanism on all churches contributed to the animosity between the lay and clergy in Catholicism. Carey and more recently Rodger Van Allen remind us that the trustee troubles were neither as serious or pervasive as the hierarchy contended.[10]

unregenerate. They printed and distributed Bibles, textbooks, primers, children's magazines, and other instructional reading material that was explicitly anti-Catholic. In Philadelphia, for example, the American Sunday School Union published an issue of their *Youth's Penny Gazette* that included the assertion, "[A] large portion of the false and foolish constructions which are put upon the Scriptures, to make them speak what 'wicked men and seducers' want to prove, may be traced to the followers of the Pope."[11]

Anti-Catholicism was growing in other cities as well. In New York City in the early 1840s, the Reverends John Hughes and John Powers petitioned for funding for Catholics. They reasoned that the inherent Protestantism in public schools was not just counter to Catholic teaching, but disparaged Catholicism. The private philanthropic Public School Society however, persuaded the Common Council of the city against such financing. As the issue became public, the notion that Catholics had a disdain for scriptures—especially Protestant versions—spread.[12]

Tensions were not restricted to urban America. A Catholic priest publicly burned a number of copies of the King James Bible in 1842 in rural Champlain, New York. The scriptures he burned had been distributed to Catholics by Protestant Bible societies. Newspapers and anti-Catholic writers sensationalized the story. Anti-Catholic John Dowling published one prominent narrative of the incident in Philadelphia with an introduction by like-minded Protestant minister William Brownlee. Their piece amounted to a polemic proving an "atrocious act of Popish intolerance" had taken place.[13]

PHILADELPHIA CONTEXT

Catholic visibility increased dramatically in the first decades of the nineteenth century, and nowhere was this more evident than in Philadelphia. The diocese, which encompassed all of Pennsylvania, south Jersey and Delaware, was created in 1808 and marked Catholic expansion (both literally and symbolically) across the former colonies. Growth in the Catholic population proceeded apace with anti-Catholics' fear, and justified paranoia about the size and strength of the Catholic community.[14]

In Philadelphia, institutions devoted to the maintenance of Protestant hegemony, noted here in chapters one and two, continued to grow in the late 1830s and 1840s. Indeed, many pan-Protestant benevolent organizations were founded in and called the city home. Political parties provided voters with candidates and platforms that assuaged and even fed their fears. Publishing societies produced a steady stream and variety of anti-Catholic materials: newspapers for working men; ladies magazines for elite women; tracts for street distribution; textbooks for common (or public) schools, and children's libraries, to name a few. The American, Baptist, Pennsylvania, and Philadelphia Bible societies were located in the city also.

One of the most virulently anti-Catholic groups in American history was also founded in Philadelphia. The American Protestant Association began in 1837 in the lecture room of Trinity Episcopal Church, where prominent Protestant ministers gathered to rebuke the claims of Catholics to rights of citizenship in the United States. One hundred and five clergymen, who represented no less than nine different Christian denominations, signed the Association's Constitution. The document outlined their alarm over Catholic challenges to the "right" of all Protestant children to use the King James Bible in school. The ministers appealed to "… the duty of every Protestant man in the country, to arouse from his slumbers at the danger which threatens our institutions."[15] Some members even suggested Catholics were the anti-Christ, using as "proof" the fact that priests were celibate and that Catholics abstained from meat on Fridays, two things they claimed were "foretold" in prophecy on the anti-Christ. The Association's 1843 Annual Report pronounced they would "stand ready on any suitable occasion which may be given," to protect the King James Version of the Bible.[16]

Bishop Francis Patrick Kenrick had arrived in Philadelphia from Bardstown, Kentucky in July of 1830, just as this anti-Catholicism was gaining strength. He came first to serve as Bishop Conwell's coadjutor, or assistant, but within a year he assumed full responsibilities for the aging cleric.[17] Kenrick was tasked by Rome with solving the trustee controversy, reconciling the divergent factions of Philadelphia Catholics, and improving relations with the Vatican. In addition, he was called on to manage a rapidly growing constituency and to undertake capital projects to meet their needs. He needed to accomplish all this in the context of increasing animosity towards Catholics. Notably, he achieved many of these ends, although not without both private and public conflict.[17]

Kenrick's infrastructural accomplishments were particularly noteworthy. At the time of his appointment, there were four Catholic churches in Philadelphia; by the end of his episcopacy, there were eleven, plus a planned cathedral and two colleges. He erected confessionals in every parish and founded the diocesan seminary, Saint Charles of Borromeo.[18] He built forty of the seventy parishes that were functioning in 1838 in the diocese.[20] By 1840, there were ninety-one Catholic churches in Pennsylvania alone.[21] The growth was so rapid that in 1843 the Vatican approved Kenrick's request for the Philadelphia diocese to be divided from Pittsburgh.[22] Church building continued to increase rapidly.

The visibility of individual Catholics—at least clerics—increased under Kenrick's leadership as well. In 1832 he held a diocesan synod at Saint Mary's Church attended by thirty priests.[23] He added fifteen priests to the diocesan ranks in the year 1838 alone.[24] In 1842, Conwell died and Kenrick became Philadelphia's third bishop. He held another synod that year for a much larger diocese that was attended by fifty-five priests.[25] The sizable gathering—particularly the spectacle of a synod—attracted much attention from both Catholics and presumably, those who would have preferred to see Catholicism disappear.

The Catholic community was not only growing, it was also diversifying, and Kenrick oversaw the establishment of different churches for distinct populations. He claimed his greatest triumph was Saint John the Evangelist Church, at Thirteenth and Chestnut Streets in the burgeoning western edge of the city while he was still Conwell's co-adjutor. Kenrick planned for the church to serve as his cathedral when he became bishop, and for it to be an enormous, highly visible architectural contribution to downtown Philadelphia.[26] Its intended parishioners were wealthy, elite Catholics, some of whom were members of a "pan-American" community with ties to France's Caribbean exploits.[27]

The Reverend John Hughes, an outspoken advocate for religious toleration of Catholics and a tireless apologist for the church, became Saint John's founding pastor. Hughes did not just want to build a symbol of growing Catholic presence and strength though, as was apparently Kenrick's desire. Hughes wanted the church to impress and even intimidate other Christians. As construction was nearing completion, he mused it would:

> [S]hame the Quaker Meeting; make all the Bishops of all the churches jealous; cause those who gave nothing towards its erection to murmur at its costliness, and those who did contribute, to be proud of their own doing. Whilst it will make every Protestant wish it were his; it will expose the godly Presbyterian to the danger of squinting in his efforts to look the other way as he passes. As a religious edifice it will add to the pride of the city. There are crowds who go to see it every day, and the leading Protestants and infidels proclaim it is the only building in the place that is entitled to be called a *church*.[28]

Saint John the Evangelist was dedicated on April 8, 1832, with a lavish ceremony which the *Catholic Telegraph* of Cincinnati reported was "performed with edifying accuracy" that "corresponded with the elegance of th[e] beautiful edifice."[29] Bishop Kenrick celebrated a high mass and New York's Vicar General the Very Reverend Dr. John Power delivered the sermon. Catholic triumphalism, and even arrogance, was carved in stone in the center of Philadelphia. Protestants took notice.

BIBLE USE IN SCHOOLS

Bishop Kenrick's battle for Catholic students' rights began almost immediately on his arrival. In 1834, the Commonwealth of Pennsylvania passed the Free School Act and made the King James Bible a compulsory textbook.[30] The Philadelphia School Board clarified the commonwealth's injunction, and specified that the Bible must be free of "note or comment," which evidenced the fundamentally different approach of Catholics and Protestant to the Bible. To Protestant school board members, the stipulation that it would be read without comment meant it was not being read as a sectarian exercise. To Catholics, it meant their Douay-Rheims version, which had extensive notes and comments, could not be used.

Kenrick, already angered by the common schools' use of a text called *Conversations on the Bible,* which encouraged all students to read the King James, began a letter-writing campaign in the *Catholic Herald* under the pseudonym "Sentinel." He declared *Conversations* would "place the Protestant Bible in the hands of Catholic children." He discussed how in common schools in Ireland no Protestant Bibles were permitted, a point that would have resonated with his majority Irish flock. He claimed, "all the influence and power of the British government could not succeed" in forcing Irish Catholics to read Protestant scriptures. He challenged Catholic clergy to "dissemble" the "insidious attempt to taint the very source from which the rising generation is to drink," and dared Philadelphians to "exclaim against this violence offered to the conscience of Catholics."[31] Kenrick's letter was endorsed by an editorial piece that ran with it in the *Herald.*

Kenrick tried to persuade Protestant denominations to support the Catholic cause with an appeal to the religious liberty of all. On April 12, 1838, he wrote another letter to the *Herald* in which he focused on the sectarianism of the King James Bible and of common schools in general. He called on **Baptists** and members of denominations that did not use the King James for support. He did not want to keep religion out of schools, he claimed, but he feared it was impossible to prevent individual teachers from sectarian proselytizing. Because of this, he demanded legislation that would deny the use of any religious literature whatsoever in order to "secure ... against the stratagems of fanatics" and to preserve religious liberty.[32] "The effort to bias the tender minds of children is so constant" he wrote, "it is vain to talk of religious liberty" in the U.S.[33]

Like the Puritans, "Baptist" churches emerged from the Reformed movement in early seventeenth-century England. There are a number of Baptist movements, many of them overlapping in theology with Puritans and Congregationalists, though to different degrees on different issues. Central for Baptist communities was (and is) the practice of "believer's baptism," or baptizing only those who are already members of the faith community.

School children continued to read the King James Bible. In April of 1841, a Catholic schoolteacher and "respectable lady" in the Southwark ward of the city was fired for refusing to read it to her students. Kenrick was enraged. He admonished Catholics for their inaction and begged them to challenge the injustice. Again, he argued for religious liberty, both freedom *from* Protestantism and freedom *for* Catholicism. The editor of the *Herald* picked up on his references to religious liberty and called for an "immediate expression" against the "sectarian coercion" and a meeting to demand "protection, and an extension ... of [Catholics'] ... legitimate rights."[34]

Not all Catholics supported Kenrick. "Truth" was the first to respond in the *Herald*, and although sympathetic to Kenrick's position, he claimed that the woman in question intentionally violated her duties. She had not been coerced to be a teacher, and she knew the responsibility that went along with it, so Truth maintained she was correctly fired for her violation. Truth also mentioned she was wrong to deny Protestants the very thing Catholic parents wanted: that *their* children be taught from *their* Bible. Nevertheless, Truth encouraged Catholics to "strike at the root of the principle and not at the branches."[35] Sentinel replied that according to this reasoning, Catholics would have to "forego the office of teachers" which would infringe on their freedom of conscience. A third Catholic, "Liber," accused the public schools of being exactly the same as Sunday-morning services in a Protestant church. The writer compared the school master to the parson, anti-Catholic texts to the sermon or the "lecture against Popery," as Liber called it, and the school house to the meeting house. He claimed anti-Catholicism was "in constant fermentation" and called for committees and watchdog groups to monitor and report any use of anti-Catholic materials to the state legislature. Liber added this was not just to satisfy the needs of Catholics, but because Protestants could not objectively recognize the sectarian nature of the schools.[36] In June of 1841, an anonymous Catholic expressed a similar opinion. The writer viewed the introduction of Protestant texts as the work of **Presbyterian** "fanatics." He claimed the "main spring" of Presbyterianism was its "hatred of what it vulgarly and insolently terms Popery."[37]

In November of 1841, Kenrick pushed his argument regarding Catholic religious liberty to its logical end. He proclaimed: "THE READING OF THE PROTESTANT VERSION OF THE BIBLE IS UNLAWFUL AND NO CATHOLIC PARENT CAN PERMIT HIS CHILDREN TO USE IT AS A SCHOOLBOOK OR OTHERWISE." To his legal points he added the Catholic

A "Presbyterian" church is governed by a group of regional or national elders or presbyters, as distinct from congregation or episcopal organization. The Presbyterian church emerged historically from the teachings of the Reformers, especially John Knox. In the United States today, some branches, like the Orthodox Presbyterian Church, are quite socially conservative; others, like the Presbyterian Church, USA, are socially progressive and squarely in the "mainline" of liberal Protestant traditions.

belief that the Protestant Bible was a "mutilated work" since it excluded the apocrypha. He also claimed that reading the Bible was also considered an act of worship. Reading it as a schoolbook profaned what was sacred because it familiarized students with it. Kenrick argued that if a student used a Bible alongside other secular texts and workbooks, the Bible would lose its religious value.[38]

A month later in 1841, "Justitia" penned a letter to the Whig *North American and Daily Advertiser* (whose slogan—"impartial but not neutral" — was revealing). Justitia quoted at length from his or her Catholic counterpart and warned Protestants of the intentions of the Pope "… and his minions against the free institutions of our country." Justitia claimed Catholics were foreigners who "dare trample on our Bible" and "have the impudence to tell us that no rule of faith, or no Bible shall be tolerated, but the *ipse dixit* of their master—a poor miserable tool of a bunch of cardinals." The writer noted that the Commonwealth of Pennsylvania had established free schools at great cost, and Catholics should be grateful for the education. Justitia concluded:

> It is time now that the question should be asked, discussed and settled, whether a Priest or a Bishop, who has taken the oath of allegiance to the Pope, as his spiritual and temporal master, can become a citizen of the United States, and whether if he does take the oath of allegiance to our Government, he does not commit perjury.[39]

Sentinel responded to Justitia almost immediately and added an historical appeal. He described how Catholics were among the founders of the United States and Philadelphia, and reiterated that they should not be subjected to Protestantism and the King James Bible in public schools. Sentinel referenced members of other religious groups—"the Infidel, the Jew, the professor of Christianity in every possible variety"—whose liberties were also in jeopardy. Kenrick also claimed a distinction between public and private expressions of faith: Protestants should not, he claimed, make their private creed public, and therefore secular schooling should not contain religious instruction. The use of the King James disregarded the religious freedom of millions of Americans, and the effort to "identify" it with education in the United States,

> [O]nly marks more distinctly the sectarian character which it is attempted to give it and should awaken those friends of liberty's conscience who, since the defeat of the Sunday School Union

plan, have slumbered, as if all were secure, because an aspiring sect had ceased to operate so openly.[40]

Liber, who was still incensed by "Presbyterian fanatics" (as mentioned above), again wrote the *Herald* and called for direct action against the school board's legislation. It did no good, he claimed, to discuss how "a junte of vainglorious philanthropists" who control public schooling have no regard for Catholic principles or religious freedom for Catholics. Catholics must take control of their children's education. Priests must announce from the pulpit that "the wolf is among them;" they must "forthwith gather together" for "self-preservation." The editor of the *Herald* agreed, but as a gradualist, stipulated that until Catholics were able to build all their own schools, they needed to "keep before the public eye the grievances and injustices against which Catholics are struggling."[41]

Kenrick's original appeal was for Catholic students to be excused from reading the King James Bible and other Protestant religious exercises. In the early 1840s though, he claimed Catholic children should be able to read from the Douay translation. On November 14, 1842, following the dismissal of a second Catholic teacher who refused to read the King James, Kenrick approached the School Board of Philadelphia with the request (included here in the documents section) that Catholic children be either excused from reading the King James altogether or be allowed to use the Douay in the classroom. Further, he requested that the religious exercises that opened and ended the school day be confined, for Catholics, to the "household of faith," that is, other Catholics. He insisted that books Catholics considered slanderous—such as those that ridiculed the pope—not be used. And lastly, he appealed for equal rights for his flock. He did not, as anti-Catholics would later attest, request the removal of the Bible from schools.[42]

The Philadelphia School Board ruled in January of 1843 that Catholic children whose parents were "conscientiously opposed" to their children reading the King James Bible could read a different version, provided it was "without note or comment." This immediately disqualified the Douay-Rheims and ensured the freedom to read their own biblical translation did not extend to Catholics.[43]

The ruling caused more tension than it dispelled. Some Protestants were furious when Bishop Kenrick's letter to the school board became public. They considered his request an outrage, an insult, and a direct violation of fundamental American religious values. Congregational minister Walter Colton penned one of the more vitriolic arguments against Kenrick's (included here in the document section). His response illustrated both the range and depth of anti-Catholicism as well as how intimately the Protestant idea of America was implicated in that bias.

THE MAY RIOTS

The mood in Philadelphia in **1844** was tense. Anti-Catholics were becoming anxious and even paranoid that core American values were under assault. Labor strife was on the rise, economic inequality was increasing, and immigrants were competing with native-born workers in certain parts of the city. The use of religious texts in public institutions was being challenged. Some Protestants imagined their very way of life threatened. Unwilling to relinquish it, their anger turned to rage.

3.2 1844

In addition to the Philadelphia Bible Riots (and the Methodist church schism we will examine in chapter 4), a number of events occurred in 1844 that stand out in American religious history. The most horrifying was the murder of Joseph Smith, the founder of the Church of Jesus Christ of Latter-day Saints. The "Mormons" had emerged from the "burned over district," a region of upstate New York in which it is said, the fires of religious revival spread so rapidly in the early and mid-nineteenth century it was as if the land itself was ablaze. That the Mormons had their genesis in such a quintessentially "American" Protestant movement, yet were violently persecuted as outsiders (or a "cult," the codeword for non-normative religion in America) is one of the tragic ironies of American history. In many respects, nothing is more American and Protestant than Joseph Smith's church, but the prophecies and visions of God, Jesus, and angels Smith claimed to receive were subject to nearly immediate challenge and rebuke. Violence against his followers began with a series of attacks and tarring and feathering, and in 1831, the Saints left New York and settled in Kirtland, Ohio. By 1838 many in the church had gone as far as Missouri to attempt to outrun persecution. In 1840, the community of ten thousand settled in Nauvoo, Illinois. Here, in 1844, violence again found them: Joseph Smith and his brother Hyrum were killed by a mob while imprisoned.[44]

Also in 1844, not far from where Joseph Smith grew up, thousands of people suffered what is called the "Great Disappointment." William Miller, a convert to evangelicalism and an itinerant preacher, used the biblical Book of Daniel and Book of Revelation to determine a date for Jesus' return. When the first date and then a second passed without incident, Miller returned to his Bible and recalculated his equations; October 22 was confirmed. Thousands of "Millerites," expecting to be taken up to heaven by Jesus, sold their belongings, quit their jobs, and said goodbye to their families and friends. October 22 came and went. After this Great Disappointment, some folks abandoned Miller, others worked on his formulas and arrived at new dates; still others reinterpreted the event, and claimed that although Jesus did not return to earth, *something* happened. One follower, Ellen Gould, had a vision in which it was revealed to her that on the

22nd, Jesus had entered the inner sanctuary of his heavenly kingdom. Before he could return to earth, his faithful needed to reform. First, Gould's faithful moved their Sabbath to Saturday. In an effort to improve their health and physical condition—an incredibly noteworthy innovation—they moved to southern California, founded sanitariums, eschewed meat, and encouraged the consumption of fresh fruits and grains. The "Sabbatarians," and then "Adventists" grew rapidly, and today they are known as the Seventh-Day Adventists. In a fascinating intersection between American culture and religion, the Adventist emphasis on health led them to encourage followers to eat grains for breakfast, and one of their members, the physician John Kellogg, developed breakfast cereal.[45]

On Friday afternoon, May 3, 1844, members of the American Republican Association met on the corner of Second and Master Streets in Kensington, a working-class, Irish Catholic neighborhood in the northeast section of Philadelphia, "for the purpose of expressing their political opinions." The men were driven from the site so they gathered elsewhere, aired their grievances about the "flagrant violation" of their right to assemble, and planned to meet again the following Monday on the same corner. They publicized the rally, acknowledging that their "mistake" on Friday had been not "assembling in force, to beat off the foreign rabble."[46] They invited all Philadelphians to "visit with their indignation and reproach this outbreak of a vindictive anti-Republican spirit, manifested by a portion of the alien population."[47]

The reports of events over the next few days vary considerable from source to source (as we observed in regards to the Ursuline convent burning), but a general sketch of what happened can be reconstructed from a number of sources. On Monday afternoon, May 6th, a large crowd gathered on Second and Master Streets. Anti-Catholic Lewis Levin, an Anglican convert from Judaism, climbed onto a makeshift stand to pontificate. When rain began to fall, those assembled took cover inside Nannygoat Market, the heart of the Kensington Catholic community. A scuffle ensued and rocks and bricks were thrown. Rumors circulated that Irish were armed with guns and the scene became chaotic. Some people retreated, some stood their ground, and some attacked the convent of the Sisters of Charity at St. Michael's at Second and Phoenix Streets.

Protestants raided Catholic houses; the Catholics inside returned volleys. Shots were fired, although it has never been determined whether the first shot came from outside the market or from the crowd itself. Most sources agree an eighteen-year-old Protestant named George Shiffler (sometimes cited as Schiffler) was the first to be killed, and he immediately became a symbol for the rioters.[48] Figure 3.1 shows how Shiffler was portrayed as an American patriot and a religious martyr.

Figure 3.1 J.L Magee, *Death of George Schiffler, in Kensington,* lithograph, c. 1845.
Courtesy of the Library Company of Philadelphia.

One source described the scene and the other mortalities and injuries in great detail:

> Henry Temper, in the employ of Mr. Lee, barber on the Frankford Road, while engaged on the side of the Native Americans, received a shot in his side, which glanced off the hip bone and only produced a flesh wound. He received several small shots in the legs. He was attended by Dr. Bethel, who considers his case in no way dangerous. Thomas Ford was struck in the forehead with a spent ball, which did him but slight injury. Another, named Lawrence Cox, had his hip seriously injured, in what way we did not learn. Patrick Fisher, late constable of the ward, was shot in the face, but not dangerously wounded ... A young man named Nathan Ramsey, blind maker, in Third Street above Brown, received a shot through the breast bone, perforating his lungs, and he was carried from the ground to an apothecary store in Second Street, above the junction of Germantown Road. Here he was visited by his wife and mother, who appeared almost distracted. The young man is mortally wounded. Another young man, named John W. Wright, son of Archibald Wright, salt merchant, residing in Fourth Street near Tamany, was shot through the head and killed instantly. He was not participating in the riot, but was in conversation with a friend, about sixty yards below the Seminary when he fell. He was carried to the same place where Mr. Ramsey lay, and his father had his remains removed.[49]

Fires were started and rumors spread that St. Michael's Church was going to be attacked, but they proved unfounded for the time. Eventually Kensington turned quiet for the night.

The Native American Party called a meeting on Tuesday, May 7th, at the State House in downtown Philadelphia. They elected leaders and officers, called speakers, denounced the Catholics' reaction, and took up a collection for the family of Shiffler and other injured Protestants. Some in the crowd, which numbered between two and three thousand, grew agitated and wanted to return to Kensington and enact revenge.[50] They carried an American flag proclaiming it was the one that had been "trampled on" after Shiffler was killed. The mob burned the Hibernian Hose Company and again charged Catholic homes, burning many. According to the *Public Ledger*, at least eight men were killed, over fourteen wounded, and as many as thirty buildings burned on Tuesday. Sheriff Morton McMichael called out the military brigade under the direction of General Cadwalader. The riots ceased for the evening.[51]

Wednesday, May 8th, was the most destructive day of the riots; as the violence spread out of Kensington and into the city proper. Overnight, a nativist had painted Saint Michael's with the words, "POPE PROPERTY."[52] As day broke, nativists searched Catholic homes for weapons. The militia was powerless against the force and number of the mob, and was distracted away from their watch on Saint Michael's Church by the posse lighting homes on fire. At some time in the afternoon, with no soldiers to stop them, the nativists burned Saint Michael's Church, library, and rectory to the ground. Revered Donohue's books, papers, and furniture were destroyed, and the altar-piece and vestments were stolen.[53] The cemetery was desecrated. Then, the Sisters of Charity convent home and an additional five homes surrounding the church were burned. High Clark, a school controller who had been directly involved in the conflict over the King James Bible, watched his home and valuable library on Fourth and Master Streets go up in flames. Whole blocks were looted, including the homes of prominent Catholics.[54]

The rioters marched south after dark. A large crowd was already gathered at Saint Augustine's Church on Fourth and Arch Streets closer to the center of downtown. Mayor John M. Scott attempted to calm the crowd with a call to "all good citizens" to "preserve the public peace." He was hit by a rock. In a half-hour's time, the church and rectory, along with one of the most valuable libraries in the country at the time were burned to the ground. Other homes nearby were destroyed as well.[55]

Primary source descriptions of these events are highly romanticized. A few mention how as the outside walls of Saint Augustine's succumbed, an inside wall did not burn. The wall was illustrated with a large eye and inscribed: "the Lord seeth." Elizabeth West, a young non-Catholic woman who lived close to Saint Augustine's, described:

> [O]ur city is a scene of rioting never was there such a time here before—the military are out and everything is in disorder and excitement.—Stace stopped in to say he thought St. Augustine church would be burned tonight and his words were too true. At 10 o'clock the flames were winding round the steeple.—it was most awful but grand. I never saw such a splendid sight: tho' I felt as if it were mockery to look at it—our city is all excitement and it is said the Governor is here but such is not the case. —we went to bed at 11 at which time the parson's house was burning.[56]

An anonymously written pamphlet, "The Full Particulars of the Late Riots," described the scene at St. Augustine's similarly, referencing how "dense masses of smoke curled out from every window." It claimed the church burning was "the most beautiful yet terrifying appearance we ever witnessed before of the kind." The writer noted in great detail how "the flames reached the belfry, and burst out from the upper windows in broad sheets" and "the whole steeple was soon wrapt in the devouring element and presented a terrific aspect, the clock struck ten while the fire was raging in its utmost fury."[57]

Pennsylvania Governor George Porter declared martial law on May 10th. A number of arrests were made and coroner's inquests held.[58] The same day, the funeral for George Shiffler took place. Anti-Catholics marched through the streets, again proclaiming him their martyr and carrying the flag they declared was tattered by Catholics. West recorded, "... the excitement still prevails—phrenzy has taken hold of men's minds."[59]

INTERIM

On Saturday, May 11th, the *Public Ledger* reported that the "excitement" was "subsiding" and that a large number of Catholics were camping outside the city out of fear and for their own protection. The streets of Kensington and the city proper were cleared and under the control of the military. The *Ledger* tallied the property damage and emotively described the desolate situation in Kensington in a manner that suggested they had become sympathetic to those who were attacked. The report stated:

> Ruin lifted its wan and haggard head through the blackened and yawning walls on every side, while the emblem of mourning and death hung from the muffled knocker and partly closed shutter. It was a heart-sickening sight, the like of which we hope we may never again look upon in this or any other city; and next to this, the humiliating display of the American bunting as a mean of protecting the property of any class or sect of citizens from the prejudice and destructive propensities of another.[60]

Songs and poems were published almost immediately after the riots that mythologized those killed and attacked Catholics, the pope, and the hierarchy, such as "Verses Composed on the Slaughter of Native Americans." This song and others like it pit the freedom loving, American Protestant "Bible defenders" against the murderous, foreign "Popish banditti." Note the symbols and illustrations on the broadside too, especially the depiction

Figure 3.2 "Verses Composed on the Slaughter of Native Americans," broadside, Philadelphia: 1844. Courtesy of the Library of Congress.

of the "open Bible," accessible to all. Also included were a bald eagle, a grieving widow, and "Columbia," the personification of the goddess Liberty. Through images and songs such as these, national symbols were linked to Protestantism and represented its struggle against Catholicism.

Bishop Kenrick suspended all Catholic masses for Sunday May 12, 1844, out of fear of further violence and property damage. In his public letter to his flock he referenced the "constitutional right to worship God," but begged Catholics to be patient. God was testing them, he intoned. He reminded them of the Catholic **doctrine of good works** and likened their suffering to that of Jesus on the cross.[61]

Although Catholic Mass had already been suspended for Sunday the *Ledger* reported this was "needless," as the unrest seemed to have ended. Major General Patterson, the leader of the troops called out to quiet the riots, issued a command on Sunday from the Headquarters of the First Division. He cited religious liberty of all to "worship their Maker in their own way, unmolested and unawed," and reminded Philadelphians that he had not ordered any churches closed. He adamantly defended his decisions during the riots, and claimed that he had assembled enough troops to "protect *all* religious denominations of citizens; at *all* places within his command [emphasis his]."[62] Members of the Society of Friends also apparently urged Bishop Kenrick to retract his decree cancelling mass, fearing Philadelphia would become known as a "church-burning city."[63]

> The Catholic belief that good works merit salvation is usually held up against the principle—famously espoused by Martin Luther—of "faith alone," the reformed understanding that salvation cannot be achieved through any human action, but only through God's saving grace. The dichotomy can be exaggerated though. Catholics believe faith is a central component of Christian life, and Reformed churches hold that good works emerge from faith, although they do not determine one's salvation.

All told, the May riots led to the death of at least twenty-four people and property damage reaching upwards of a quarter of a million dollars.[64] Many Philadelphians were horrified by the events and fervently hoped calm would prevail in the city. A few even worked actively to that end. Some prominent Catholics sent a letter to the directors of the public schools asking them to help stop discrimination against Catholics. They requested a statement affirming that Catholics did not ask for the removal of the Bible from schools. The letter was received by George Wharton, former member of an ecumenical group called the Philadelphia Association of Young Men for the Celebration of the Fourth of July. He replied:

> Gentlemen:
> In answer to the request contained in your note, that I would
> state whether as far as Roman Catholics are concerned,
> they have asked for the exclusion of the Bible from the Public

> Schools,' I reply, that to my knowledge, as a Director of the
> Public Schools of the City of Philadelphia, and a Controller
> of those of both City and County, (which office I have held for
> several years) no such request has ever been made, nor do I
> know of any efforts on their part with the alleged object view.[65]

The Grand Jury convened in the aftermath of the May riots was made of up nativist sympathizers, at least two active members of nativist political parties, and the father of a Protestant man who was wounded during the rioting. Not surprisingly, they disagreed with Wharton's assessment and determined Catholics attempted to "exclude the Bible from our Public Schools." The nativists had gathered, in their estimation, to hold a "peaceful exercise" to strategize how to prevent the Bible's exclusion. The jury found Catholics guilty of inciting the riots as well as causing most of the property damage. It claimed they were a "band of lawless irresponsible men, some of who had resided in our country only for a short time."[66]

Prominent Catholics William Stokes, Archibald Randall, and others penned a pamphlet entitled, "Address of the Catholic Lay Citizens of the City and County of Philadelphia, to their Fellow-citizens ..." in response. They discussed the charges leveled against them. They denied that Catholics had rushed Nannygoat Market, as was contended, and said they were "credibly informed" to that end. They claimed Catholics had remained in their homes until it was no longer possible for them to stay, and that they had not wished to fight. The citizens denounced the "shedding [of] human blood ... by whomsoever perpetrated ... in whatever way it occurred."[67]

THE JULY RIOTS

Independence Day celebrations had always been extravagant events in Philadelphia. In 1844, anti-Catholic nativist agitators were eager to use July 4th as an opportunity to remind their fellow citizens that Catholics were foreigners who did not—and could not ever—belong in the United States, and the parades and pageantry were even more audacious than usual.[68] Floats and banners commemorated Shiffler's death and the Kensington riots. As we observed above in illustrations to songs and poems, "open Bibles" in the hands of representations of George Washington and Columbia were numerous.[69] One notably more aggressive banner depicted an open Bible in the claw of an American eagle.[70] Historian Susan Davis has described how "liberty and the eagle ... joined the ballot, the Bible, and flag in repetitive reworkings of ideas about purity and threat, insult and danger."[71] The images were exploited by anti-Catholics to excite the crowds and to assert in no uncertain terms that the Bible was the symbol of their movement and their country.

Catholics anticipated this histrionic display and were fearful that their churches would be attacked again. They also allegedly attacked the Native American Party's tent in Fisher's Woods in South Philadelphia. Then, with the approval of Pennsylvania Governor David Porter, they began stockpiling weapons nearby at St. Philip de Neri Church between Third and Queen Streets. Someone witnessed the weapons being brought in to the church, and an angry crowd gathered outside and demanded they be removed. As in the May riots, Lewis Levin was present and addressed the crowd. The militia was called and fired on the crowd to clear it, but nativist Charles Naylor threw himself in front of their weapons. He was arrested and held in the basement of St. Philip's.[72]

The following day, Saturday, July 6, 1844, the crowd charged the church and pulled Naylor out. They barraged the church with a battering ram and stones until a wall had been breached and occupied it. A standoff ensued between the anti-Catholics and the militia. By morning, Governor Porter had assembled over five thousand troops from surrounding cities and counties. After two days, they restored order, but not before thirteen more Philadelphians were dead and an additional fifty had been wounded.[73]

By July 8th, the 1844 riots had ended. Philadelphia was, at long last, quiet. The scars of religious bigotry would remain however.

IMMEDIATE AFTERMATH

After the July riots, Bishop Kenrick raised no further objections to the religious nature of common schools. Indeed, he recorded in his diary in the early part of 1845, "Things are quiet and going along smoothly now."[74]

The political aftermath of the riots was neither quiet nor smooth. Anti-Catholic political party memberships increased in Philadelphia and nationally. The parties organized fraternal organizations, hose and firemen's societies, clubs, insurance programs and reading rooms. For a few years the political parties associated with nativism seemed poised to take control of the entire country. In the elections of 1844, nativist party members won seats in Congress, the Pennsylvania Senate, and county offices. Lewis Levin, leader of the riots, served three times as Congressman on the nativist ticket. They were as successful in the outlying areas as they were in the city proper.[75] Indeed, by 1845, the movement was "in full control" of Philadelphia county.[76]

LONG-TERM IMPACT

The Bible Riots left Catholics, Protestants, and the city of Philadelphia altered in significant ways, but they also had repercussions on larger scales. As we will see, anti-Catholic violence spread to other places. But such large-scale religious violence had serious implications in places where no actual rioting took place, as well as in the national and presumably, global imagination. A country that spent much time and energy etching its commitment to religious freedom in the collective consciousness (and a good bit of stone as well) could not ignore such a profound contradiction between the ideal and the reality.

Catholic strategies varied in the aftermath of the riots. Many folks advocated for segregated Catholic institutions to parallel Protestant-dominated (though allegedly "secular") ones. The plan to retreat into separate Catholic spaces was not universal though, and tension increased between those occupying different positions on a spectrum between assimilation and separatism, complicated further by the many ways to live out each approach. Catholics constructed their identities (individual and collective, consciously or not) under circumstances conditioned by countless factors, from the highly complicated to the trivial. Some people wrestled with how to express their faith and demonstrate to non-Catholics that they could be "true" Americans at the same time. Some, fearing persecution and violence from the non-Catholic majority (and cognizant of the political successes of anti-Catholic parties) withdrew from American society in a more fundamental way. Two agrarian communities in Pennsylvania were founded, for instance, to exist separately from the wider society.[77] Ideally, the utopias allowed Catholics to maintain their faith without persecution as they also sought to recreate an environment similar to immigrants' homeland.

The riots caused significant structural changes to Catholic life in Philadelphia; one scholar has called the situation nothing less than a "reformation."[78] Parents and clergy knew they needed alternatives to educating their children in Protestant theology, scriptural interpretation, and daily doses of anti-Catholicism. They sought to construct a separate and comprehensive Catholic school system to stand alongside the common and public schools that preached Protestantism. Bishop Kenrick is widely credited with establishing this system, how much of this growth can be attributed directly to him is unclear. Although nothing like the organized network that exists today, perhaps it is best to say Kenrick consolidated and organized the process.[79] His administration was instrumental in bringing religious orders to Philadelphia as well as founding homegrown ones though, and these orders were responsible for much of the education of the city's youth. The Sisters of Charity, the Ladies of the Sacred Heart, the Sisters of St. Joseph, the

School Sisters of Notre Dame, the Visitation Sisters, Sisters of the Good Shepherd, and the LaSallian French Christian Brothers joined the Jesuits and Augustinians under Kenrick's watch.[80]

Protestants of all denominations were significantly affected by the riots as well. Disagreements over various social, political, and economic issues came to the fore in the aftermath of the Bible Riots, to say nothing of theological divisions. Some individual Protestants developed more explicit ties to anti-Catholic organizations, and once aligned with them, created powerful political coalitions and supported successful candidates for local and national offices. The degree to which this was sectarian politics, however, and thus, a potential violation of principles to which evangelicals adhered, was often a major source of tension, so the number and variety of Protestant religious communities continued to multiply. Some Protestants disagreed with what they interpreted as too much entanglement between church and state; some advocated for greater political participation, for example.

As part of the larger impulse to reform society, evangelical Protestants continued their benevolent pursuits. Some worked in para-philanthropic and educational realms, inter-religious societies like the temperance movement, and suffrage organizations. The cause of universal education and the common school system also motivated many. Some of these various movements merged into the juggernaut of benevolent evangelical cultural organizations in early national Philadelphia.

The riots also moved the city of Philadelphia to undertake massive consolidation plan. Civil services were integrated, so citizens would receive fire or police protection from unaffiliated municipal servants and not sectarian and partisan local groups. One late nineteenth-century cartographer wrote the "serious riots in 1844 called general attention to the insufficiency of the police system and the dissatisfaction led to an appeal to the Legislature for consolidation."[81] This did not stop fire companies from brawling amongst themselves and against each other sometimes, but it did help to ensure that neighborhood lines could be crossed by citywide law enforcement. The consolidation planners also created distinct neighborhood boundaries in the immediate aftermath of the riots, although the project was not completed until 1854. Often this exaggerated physical divisions between the Protestant and Catholic communities.

RELIGION IN THE PHILADELPHIA BIBLE RIOTS

The primary cause of the Philadelphia Bible Riots was religious tension between Protestants and Catholics, and a number of issues were closely related in this conflict. The use and function of the Bible, its interpretation, and who had the authority to teach that interpretation were central. The symbolic importance of scriptures for different communities was likewise integral. Lastly, factors relating to religious liberty emerged for one of the first times in American history in the years and months leading up to the riots. In many ways these questions remain.

BIBLE USE AND INTERPRETATION

The Bible was at the center of the centuries-long hostility between Protestants and Catholics, although scholars have downplayed its significance in the riots as "merely" symbolic or as a part of a pattern of conflict. But scripture and its use—symbolically and literally—was a fundamental feature of the historical conflict between Protestants and Catholics. The Catholic hierarchy's authority to translate and endorse their translation of scripture goes to the heart of doctrinal battles between the communities. The issue came to the fore—again—in the dispute over the use of the Bible in the Philadelphia public schools. The question was two-fold: first, would the Bible be used by schoolchildren, and second, would those children who used a version of the Bible other than the King James be allowed to use their translation? This later point was a question of translation and also pitted the authority of the Catholic hierarchy against the authority of the public school system and state legislature.

The Bible is a fundamental part of Christian practice and beliefs, but it functions differently in Catholic religious life than it does in many Protestant communities. Reading the Bible is always considered a religious act in Catholic theology, for example, and at the time of the riots, Catholics were only permitted to worship with other Catholics. The Catholic church has also taught that the power to interpret the Bible is with the hierarchy, but this was challenged at least as early as the reform movements of the fourteenth century. One Catholic response to the challenges was the Council of Trent, which commenced in 1545, and reaffirmed the church's position that the "unbroken succession" of the hierarchy had the authority to interpret and translate the truths contained "in written books and in unwritten traditions."[82]

The spirit of the European movements to reform the church, both from within and from without, and the hostility they generated was transplanted to American soil.[83] Most Protestants in the United States used the Geneva or the King James Bible. When mid-nineteenth-century American Catholics used the Bible however, it was the Rheims-Douay translation, which by that time had added admonitions against the proliferation of biblical translations and Catholic contact with unauthorized versions.[84] In 1757 for instance, the

Congregation of Propaganda added a 1564 declaration by Pope Pius IV that stated that Catholic Bibles *must* have comments in order to be authorized; in essence, this made it impossible for Catholics to use any Protestant versions (which as per the reformer's *sola scriptura* leitmotif, had no comments).[85] At the First Provincial Council of Baltimore in 1829, U.S. bishops warned against other translations and declared that bishops should make the Douay "as free as possible from error." At the Second Provincial Council in 1840, they declared that only translations approved by "a responsible and authorized member of the tribunal of the Church," were considered the word of God. Anyone who—like the reformers—asserted an individual right to translate the Bible outside of the tribunal or encouraged other translations the bishops claimed, "despise[d]" the church, "usurp[ed] her commission," and denied the authority of the tribunal founded by Jesus.[86]

Protestant and Catholic Bibles had and have some very specific differences. Catholic Bibles had interpretive notes, which as we have seen, became a part of the controversy over public school Bible-reading. The number of books in each translation differed also. The Douay Bible contained the Apocrypha, literally "additional books" that were in the Septuagint but not part of the Protestant canon. Terminology differed also: the Douay Bible used religious language like "Sabbath" and "heaven" whereas Protestant versions favored the more secular "day of rest" and "sky."[87] Although these differences might seem trivial, they could suggest distinctive and possibly contradictory understandings of key ideas to religious believers.

BIBLE AS SYMBOL

An additional religious cause of the Philadelphia Bible Riots was the symbolic importance of the Christian Scriptures in different communities. As we have seen so far, the Bible was (and is) an icon through which Christian men and women understood themselves, their place in the community, nation, and world. The worldview of many nineteenth-century Christians—Protestants especially—was charged with Biblical meaning.

As important as the literal differences in Bible translations were members of varied Christian communities had also learned how to think and intuit their world through their particular Bible. They *knew* their translation was the correct one, and the power of different translations to represent and to reflect the Christian moral Universe cannot be overestimated. In the nineteenth century, loyalty to a particular translation of scripture and the religious authority that authorized and interpreted it grew in intensity. As in our own time, and many others, this multi-scaled religious dissent turned violent.

This symbolic understanding of the Bible illustrates how the Philadelphia Bible Riots were also about religious freedom and liberty in the United States. Both the establishment and the free exercise clauses of the First Amendment to the Constitution were cited by Protestants, Catholics, and others to support their arguments. Catholics and their allies desired freedom from Protestantism in public institutions, and they also desired to freely practice their beliefs. It is crucial to keep in mind that many of the questions we are familiar with today—Bible reading or prayer in public schools, nativity scenes on civic property—were emerging for the first time in episodes such as this. The non-Protestant community had grown large and powerful enough to force a public conversation about if and how common institutions—and thus civic life in general—could accommodate the religious other.

As we read above, Bishop Kenrick, and others (Catholics and non-Catholics) understood the use of the King James Bible to be a sectarian exercise, and thus, criticized it as a violation of the religious liberty of all who did not use the translation in their religious worship.

ADDITIONAL EVIDENCE

Understanding the central role the Bible and religion played in the riots is crucial, but there are other forms of evidence that make clear the conflict in Philadelphia was about religion. First and foremost, we know that all nine Catholic churches in Philadelphia were attacked. The parishes served Catholics of different ethnicities and classes, who lived in different neighborhoods, and had different occupations.[88] On Thursday, May 9th, the Philadelphia *Public Ledger* reported on threats to Catholic churches. The editors' claimed:

> Fears are entertained that attempts will be made to fire other Catholic churches, and the military have been strongly posted in the vicinity of them ... All the avenues leading to St. Mary's and St. Joseph's Churches, in Fourth, near Prune and in Willing's Alley, have been guarded by troops ... A slight demonstration was manifested by a collection of persons at the corner of Market and Thirteenth streets, but it was promptly met and checked by the strong military forces established at Thirteenth Street for the protection of St. John's church between Market and Chestnut.[89]

Individual Catholics, moreover, were attacked: clergy and non-clergy, immigrant and U.S.-born, poor and well off. A number of anonymous

Catholic sources mentioned attacks against individual Catholics, including priests and nuns (many of whom removed their clerical clothing), and recorded that each church was either under protection or was attacked. One writer in the *Records of the American Catholic Historical Society,* claimed: "Meetings and incendiary speeches were held daily and nightly near [St. Michael's] and a spirit of intense hatred engendered against priests, sisters and Catholics of every nationality."[90] Sister M. Gonzaga, who lived at Saint Joseph's Asylum on Thirteenth Street, provided an additional example of the religious nature of the riots. In a letter to her mother, dated May 9, 1844, she wrote that the sacred vessels had been removed from a number of churches (including Holy Trinity, an exclusively German community) for fear of damage or harm to them. She also noted that the asylum was being protected, and that the rioters had "sworn vengeance against all the churches and their institutions." She continued, "The truth is, it is nothing but a party of Protestants leagued against the Catholics under the name of Native Americans and the Irish. It is believed to be actually more religion than politics which is the cause of the riot."[91]

In addition, nativist tension in Philadelphia and elsewhere was not primarily over immigrants and immigration. Indeed, anti-Catholic Germans founded chapters of the American Protestant Association.[92] Nor was the fighting primarily about ethnicity. Had it been, Irish would have fought on the side of other Irish, regardless of whether they were Protestant or Catholic; they did not.[93] Religious perspectives divided the mobs and the conflict writ large. The "Full Particulars" pamphlet stated: "Out of the windows of nearly every Native American and Protestant Irishman in the district hung the American and tri-colored flags. This was regarded as sufficient protection from the mob."[94] The writers of "The Truth Unveiled" concurred with the "Full Particulars" writer. At the opening of that pamphlet, the writer highlighted the religious aspects of the riots. He or she hypothetically inquired:

> [H]ow is it, that hordes of Irish Protestants have attended their meetings, and have been welcomed with joy by these saviours of their country! In a word, if 'Native Americanism' be not sectarian, how comes it THAT TWO CATHOLIC CHURCHES, ONE CATHOLIC SEMINARY, TWO CATHOLIC PARSONAGES, AND A CATHOLIC THEOLOGICAL LIBRARY, WHICH CANNOT BE REPLACED IN THE WORLD, HAVE BEEN BURNT?[95]

Furthermore, the rioters and riot leaders belonged to different Christian denominations and religious backgrounds, some that displayed more anti-Catholic tendencies, like Congregationalists, and others, like Unitarians, who by and large did not. John Perry was a Unitarian minister, for example, as was John Gihon, who was also vice president of the Native American Party.[96] Lewis Levin, who, as mentioned above, had converted from Judaism to Episcopalianism, was secretary of the Native American Party and editor of the anti-Catholic *Daily Sun*.[97] Among the riot participants, Walter Colton, who had attacked Kenrick after his request to the school board, was a Congregationalist minister, Charles Stillwell a Swedish Lutheran, and William Wright a Methodist. The two latter men were both killed in the riots.[98]

PHILADELPHIA BIBLE RIOTS HISTORIOGRAPHY

I have argued here that the Philadelphia Bible Riots, like other instances of nativist violence in this text, cannot be adequately understood as an ethnic or immigrant clash or as an economic or labor conflict, nor can they be accessed by an analysis of tensions around American institutional development or public schooling.[99] Scholars have not sufficiently dealt with the religious aspects of the riots, nor has the Bible been taken seriously as the primary and fundamental reason for the conflict that led to them.[100]

Surprisingly, there is only one monograph exclusively on the Bible riots.[101] In *The Philadelphia Riots of 1844,* Michael Feldberg presents them as indicative of Jacksonian era politics. In response to Billington's work, he attempts "… to place the struggle … in a wider context, viewing it as an ethnic, rather than simply a religious, conflict."[102] He concludes the economic downturn, combined with cultural differences between Protestant natives and Irish Catholic immigrants led to the destruction of class loyalties. Although Feldberg takes religion seriously and admits the Bible had "extraordinary symbolic relevance," it did not have importance beyond the "wider war" or as one of many "patterns of conflict" to him.[103] He asks what it was about the Irish in particular that angered native-born Protestants so intensely and why this conflict turned so violent in the face of many other possible conflicts.[104] Feldberg posits:

> Almost every one of the new groups and subcommunities that emerged in the Jacksonian era was organized according to some strict principle of exclusives, and by the 1840s ethnicity and religion became the dominating criteria. [T]he networks of institutions that permitted the city to function were restricted in membership wherever possible to those who shared a common form of worship or a similar view on the benefits or evils of rum or the accident of birth on American soil.[105]

Combined with his sketch of the city's inability to contain even minimal antagonisms from becoming the kind of full-scale violence that had resulted in the burning of Pennsylvania Hall just a decade previous, the riots appear almost inevitable in Feldberg's account.

Ethnicity has often been cited as the primary reason for the riots. Because they began in an Irish Catholic neighborhood and the two churches burned were predominantly Irish, scholars have viewed them as the culmination of conflict between native-born Protestants and *Irish* Catholics that had been increasing through the early decades of the nineteenth century. The literature then, has highlighted that they were part of a larger pattern of ethnic discrimination and bigotry toward immigrants but a deeper analysis does not bear out this contention. Although a small number of Irish were making their way to America's cities in the early nineteenth century, the enormous needy masses, so well referenced in various popular media and scholarly literature, did not begin to arrive until 1849 and 1850. So, as historian Gary Nash questions, if the riots were primarily based on ethnicity, wouldn't violence in Philadelphia have dramatically *escalated* in 1850 and after, when tens of thousands more Irish came to Philadelphia?[106] Even more crucially, Michael Carroll and Kirby Miller have revealed that most pre-famine Irish immigrants were Protestant, and were neither uneducated nor destitute.[107] In other words, although the Catholic community was predominantly Irish, *the Irish community was minority Catholic*. If Catholics were being attacked and Catholic churches burned, they would have most likely been Irish.

David Montgomery acknowledges the strife between members of different Christian churches, but examines the riots in the context of neighborhood labor conflicts. He asserts evangelicals were responsible for divisions and animosities between Protestants and Catholics of the same class, and that these animosities led to the violence. He claims that when the Trades' Union dismantled, there was no longer an institution able to unite the various members of the working class such as "the Catholic weaver, the Methodist shoemaker, and the Presbyterian ship carpenter as members of a common working class."[108] He concludes, "By their very nature, evangelical demands fragmented the working class as a political force in antebellum Philadelphia and thereby created for historians the illusion of a society lacking in class conflict."[109]

Education historians Vincent P. Lannie and Bernard Diethorn attribute the riots to the "storm of controversy" surrounding Kenrick's request that Catholic children be excused from the reading of the King James Bible.[110] They understand the riots as an early test case for twentieth-century legal battles over religion and schooling. They claim conflict was "inevitable" because both Protestants and Catholics believed God was on their side and wonder why there was not *more* violence.[111] They conclude: "[N]ot only fear of Catholic hostility to the Bible and American institutions but also the dismay that public education would lose its Protestant character caused many Protestants to stand firm in their opposition to Catholic demands."[112] In this analysis, it is not so much religious belief per se that drove historical actors, but fear of a loss of control over institutions, especially ones that were responsibility for inculcating the young with the national moral "character."

Religion scholar Tracy Fessenden picks up on the legal issues Lannie and Diethorn cite and that Phillip Hamburger (discussed in chapter 1) also analyzes. She posits that the "metaphor of separation" between church and state emerged in the context of Catholic-Protestant struggles and situates the Bible Riots as a key episode in this developing understanding.[113] Fessenden's constitutional argument complicates the riots considerably, although it obscures religion somewhat in that she interprets Catholic arguments as a "political critique."[114] She establishes a strong link between separationism and Catholic-Protestant conflict, and thus, provides a stepping-stone into the view that nativism—and the policies, laws, and constitutional interpretations that result from its strength—requires a religious analysis.[115] Her argument, moreover, helps directly connect today's virulent nativism with its nineteenth-century manifestations.

The Philadelphia Bible Riots illuminated underlying hostilities and necessitated the construction of pragmatic strategies for members of all religious groups. They showed that, for a time at least, disestablishment led to denominational entrenchment. Although in the early years of the nineteenth century, cooperation between and amongst members of different religious communities was evident, it was perhaps not very wide, deep, or enduring. The tension between them, especially as it manifested in the struggle to define America, continued in cities to the south, and became a central factor in the construction of one of the nation's iconic pillars: the Washington Monument.

CHAPTER 4

Destruction of the "Pope's Stone"

In 2009, controversy erupted over proposed plans for the building of Park 51, an Islamic cultural center to be located in lower Manhattan. Opponents immediately began to call the site the "Ground Zero Mosque," though it was neither a mosque nor at the location of the former Twin Towers. The 9/11 Families for a Safe and Strong America argued:

> Imam Rauf embraces Shariah, a sociopolitical system of jurisprudence based upon the Koran which supersedes man-made law and which rejects the Constitutional doctrine of the separation of church and state. Islamic countries that embrace Shariah and political Islam are known for brutal policies that discriminate against women, gays, and religious minorities. Shariah law is entirely incompatible with the Equal Protection clause of the 14th Amendment and would violate 1st Amendment protections of speech, assembly and the free exercise of religion. We feel that the attempt to use our loved ones' deaths and the painful legacy of 9/11 still felt by New Yorkers to engage in a campaign to reverse America's core doctrine of religious freedom—and to do so under the guise of interfaith understanding—is a gross insult to the memory of those who were killed on that terrible day.[1]

Their arguments bear an uncanny resemblance to those maintained by nineteenth-century opponents to a Catholic contribution to the planned Washington National Monument. One detractor declared:

> [K]eep the foreign influence, especially of avowed deadly enemies to human rights, and above all, the Roman Power, from

desecrating that pure pillar, so sacredly dedicated to the memory of the good and great Washington! The friend of human rights, and the foe to despotism and tyranny! Fellow countrymen, in the name of all that you hold dear in this world, let its high-towering column not be blemished by a foreign, despotic, and tyrannical hypocrite's hand, or a hypocrite's gift![2]

In both instances, the foreign other was deemed incompatible with American values. Also in both instances, the objecting party believed their symbol would be tarnished by the inclusion of the other, and called on Americans to help prevent it. And in each case, a particular site, a location, was imbued with meaning, and came to represent all that Americans allegedly hold dear. National sacred space was created and the fear of its infection by forces deemed "un-American" and thus, evil, was potent.

Horrified as many Philadelphians and Americans were at the anti-Catholic violence in 1844, the nativist movement and religious bigotry continued to spread. For the remainder of the 1840s, various nativist groups and political parties found mediums and audiences for their message among the voting public. When it became public that the Vatican would send a marble stone to be included in the planned Washington Monument, anti-Catholic organizations and individuals were outraged. In the nation's capital in 1854, the "Pope's Stone," as it was called, was destroyed by one such nativist group.

This chapter will unpack this nasty incident. Although no lives were lost, and the property damage was minimal in comparison to the violence in Boston and Philadelphia, the symbolic meaning of the act of vandalism was profound. The District of Columbia and the monument to the first U.S. president represented fundamental aspects of American identity. This chapter will begin with a brief sketch of the political climate in the 1850s and the broader national movements and ideologies that emerged to see how they supported this American myth-making. Then, we will look at the history of Washington, DC, an intentionally planned symbolic geography that carved those foundational myths and historical narratives in the late eighteenth-century landscape. We will observe how dominant—white, Protestant, Anglo, male—individuals and groups determined not just the story, but the act of creating and telling it, and how those with power denied representation—both symbolically and literally—to others. Most importantly, we will understand how religion shaped the entire project and process. The chapter will conclude by looking at how the "Pope's Stone" incident has been examined in the literature (however sparse) and how some current scholarship could help us interpret the meaning and significance of the event.

THE ADVENT OF SECTIONALISM AND POLITICAL NATIVISM

In the early decades of the nineteenth century, a number of issues arose that directly related to the question of who was an American; some answers threatened to tear the country apart. Two movements in particular saw significant growth in the years following the Philadelphia riots: sectionalism and politically active nativism. The former originated, developed and matured in full force as the southern confederacy. The latter originated in the North, although nativism had (and has) significant southern manifestations. Aside from these differences however, both movements had fundamental similarities. Both were varieties of nationalism. Both contained racist and xenophobic elements. Both had religious undercurrents and a deep distrust (at best) of non–Protestants. And both led to violence on exceptional scales. Further, the country was embarking on an era of unprecedented expansion that we have come to call **"Manifest Destiny,"** a strategy for territorial confiscation that was commodified and sanctified. This desire to seek one's fortunes across the continent and stake claim to land as far and wide as possible has become so normative, so central to American history, and so ingrained in the American psyche, it is nearly synonymous with the adjective "American."[3]

As we have seen, the annexation of Texas, and the purchase of Florida and corresponding Indian removals there led some to define American identity by ethnicity, race, and religion. Even more than the divisiveness of those events, the growing rift between sections of the country, especially over the institution of slavery, threatened national unity and led to the development of distinct regional cultures and perspectives. In particular, the question of Missouri's status on slavery upon entry to the union cut to the core of ideas about what America was, or should be, how to maintain or achieve that ideal, and who should be included in the project. Both abolitionists and supporters of the slave system believed God was on their side, and both used their Bible as proof.

Christian denominations were torn into northern and southern branches. Methodists and Baptists—communities that together accounted for over half of all U.S. Christians in antebellum America—split in 1844 and '45, respectively.[4] Presbyterian churches splintered into New School and Old School factions in 1857 and 1861. As scholars have recognized, white, southern Christians did not only accept slavery, they encouraged it and participated in the economy of human bondage.[5] Christian Smith notes, "Slavery was clearly part of the southern vision for an orderly and virtuous Christian America with limited central government ... part of a Christian society purer than the aggressive and economically and socially oppressive North."[6]

4.1 Manifest Destiny

Journalist John O'Sullivan introduced the expression "Manifest Destiny" into the American lexicon in 1845. The phrase rapidly came to capture and reflect the growing sense—among white, male, elite, Anglo-Saxon Protestants, that is— that America had a divine imperative, a mission, a messianic calling to settle and "civilize" lands and peoples on the North American continent, and eventually, the world. The West, the frontier, was paradise, the biblical garden, reserved for God's chosen people. Undergirding this was an Americanized millennialism: the idea that as inheritors of God's covenant, Christian Americans were at the fore-front of history, and the triumph of their culture and religion over all others would be demonstrated in territorial conquest. This victory, in turn, would make evident the superiority of Christian culture and herald in the second coming of Jesus to his kingdom on earth.

The ideology of manifest destiny was much older and more widespread than this nineteenth-century American manifestation. Indeed, it had been in existence for four hundred years before it was applied by U.S. expansionists and was, some have suggested, the perspective that would begin the process of "globalization." This so-called Doctrine of Discovery, as we saw in chapter 1, was a set of fif-teenth- and sixteenth-century Vatican pronouncements that divided the world between Christians, or the "civilized," and "heathens," primitive non-Christians who were unfit for God's eternal salvation. These declarations were applied by all "Western" colonizers to divide the globe and find theological justification for the slaughter, enslavement, relocation, forced conversions, and annihilation of the culture of hundreds of millions of people.

In the United States, evangelicals like Lyman Beecher and Samuel Morse appropriated the Catholic doctrine, and politicians like James Polk popularized it as an easy way of "subduing" huge populations and "securing" the land for Amer-ican economic interests. In this way of thinking, American racial supremacy— whether formally codified in policy or as an ideological notion—was a calling, a "burden," and an obligation that justified the destruction.[7]

To be clear: sectionalism and the southern secession movement— though part of complicated historical processes—were because of support for chattel slavery. The proslavery position—and *proslavery Christianity*—is inseparable then, from the production of Confederate nationalism. That is not to say northern supporters of slavery did not also look to Christianity and their Bible for its justification; they did. Nor is it that there were no southerners who believed slavery was morally reprehensible; there were. The distinctive aspects of southern sectionalism and secession though, were the direct result of support for African American enslavement.

Religion was fundamental to those regional identities. In a recent text on religious and racial "dilemmas" from 1835–1860, W. Jason Wallace describes a country lacking a coherent identity, where political convictions varied, culturally unifying symbols were largely absent, and where "geography determined one's commitment to a political economy of slavery or free labor."[8] This "sectionalism" was the result of the championing of northern and southern regional identities each of which, according to Wallace, "self-consciously exploited the vices of the other."[9] The forms Protestant Christianity took varied considerably, from positions on the millennium, to understandings of Calvinism, to biblical interpretation. Importantly, Wallace demonstrates that northern evangelical opposition to American slavery and to Catholicism was rooted in the same impulse to resist tyranny.[10] The Civil War, then, was a religious schism, a theological catastrophe from which the American nation remains unhealed.[11]

Political nativism, like sectionalism, grew considerably in power and influence after the Philadelphia Bible Riots of 1844. National and international events created a fertile climate for its spread. Formal, organized nativist political parties began to emerge in the 1840s—especially in Philadelphia and New York—from what had previously been fraternal organizations. In 1845 in Philadelphia, the Order of United American Mechanics and their offshoot, the Patriotic Daughters of America were founded. Harriet Probasco, editor of the anti-Catholic nativist newspaper, *The American Woman* (included here in the documents section), organized the latter. On July 4th of that year, also in Philadelphia, delegates established the Native American Party which soon became the American Republicans.[12]

The Native American/American Republican Party composed their first declaration in Philadelphia, a city that, following the riots, came to be thought of as a battleground for nativists. The party's demands included: only native-born citizens should be allowed to run for or hold public office; the Bible should be taught in public schools; and there should be a twenty-one-year waiting period for naturalization. All of this, to their way of thinking, was for the protection of the country. They claimed 110,000 members.[13]

A number of explicitly anti-Catholic groups were also established in the mid and late 1840s. In 1848, the American Protestant Society and Christian Alliance joined forces. A year later, that organization merged with the Christian Union, and Foreign Evangelical Society to found the American and Foreign Christian Union.[14]

Despite the proliferation and success of activist nativist groups, they began to wane as 1850 approached. Nativist fraternal orders, Dale Knobel maintains, kept the "spirit" of nativism alive when political parties floundered after disappointing election campaigns. This was especially evident, as we shall see, in Baltimore.[15]

Recall however, that nativism was—and is—cyclical. In the early 1850s, a new crop of nativist parties known collectively as "Know Nothings" succeeded the American Republican/Native American Party. This name, used by both members of the groups and their detractors, referred to their relatively secretive nature and the response members would give when questioned about their nativist activity: "I know nothing," they would say.

In the late 1840s and early 1850s Irish immigrants fleeing the **potato famine** began to arrive in the United States in astonishing numbers. Many settled in East Coast cities such as Boston, New York, and Philadelphia. As the newcomers took a toll on public social services, perception of them grew increasingly negative. Crime rose. And, of course, worse still, they faced significant anti-Catholic bigotry. Nativists claimed American-born workers were being displaced, though this was not the case. In actuality, the immigrants then as now, "augmented the labor supply and helped to stimulate industrial expansion and demand.... they took the worst paying jobs and helped raise the relative social and economic status of many natives."[16]

> In Ireland in the 1840s and 1850s the terrible blight that struck potato crops all over Europe was particularly devastating, as centuries of British colonization and "planting" patterns had resulted in the dominance of the potato, especially for subsistence farmers. Up to a million and a half people died in the Great Famine, and as many as one million more fled Ireland as a result.

Yet the negative perception of the Irish Catholic immigrants not only prevailed, but increased. When coupled with growing American exceptionalism, as well as the notion of manifest destiny and expansion, an impenetrable wall was created between those persons considered American and those not. Historian David Bennett, who as we saw in chapter 1, has written one of the seminal texts on nativist movements, has stated, "[T]he millennial role of 'true Americans' would be as protectors of the promised land in the climactic battle against alien, destructive forces." This dualist view, a politicization of millennialism, perceives good versus evil as the primary theme of American history. In this narrative the foreigner plays the role of the evil other. The "new aliens," Bennett posits, have always been perceived as "vermin in the garden," and as a "bestial presence."[17]

In 1852 the nativist fraternal organization the Order of United Americans merged with Philadelphia's Native American Party and formed the American Union Party in Trenton, New Jersey. Two years later they took over the Order of the Star Spangled Banner, which had been founded in New York in 1850, and at this point, their popularity skyrocketed. In 1855, the Order of the Star Spangled Banner became the American Party.[18]

In the election that same year, nativists and Know Nothings were not only popular, they were victorious. Northern cities along the East Coast elected politicians who promised to safeguard American institutions—including religious ones—from the imagined foreign threat. Decisive victories in Massachusetts and fifty some local elections nation-wide, as well as the election of nativist Robert Conrad for mayor of Philadelphia, illustrated the power the party held. Millard Fillmore's defeat as presidential candidate was disheartening to the movement, but he attracted some support regardless of the loss.[19]

A number of prominent Catholics did not help dispel the anxieties of others. The Reverend John Hughes who, as we have seen took a bold stance against Catholic discrimination, announced his intent to convert all Protestants. In 1848 he published, "The Decline of Protestantism and its Causes," a widely-circulated sermon that alludes to Beecher's "Plea for the West." In it, he claimed:

> Protestantism pretends to have discovered great secrets. Protestantism startles our eastern borders occasionally on the intention of the Pope with regard to the valley of the Mississippi, and dreams that it has made a wonderful discovery. Not at all. Everybody should know it. Everybody should know that we have for our mission to convert the world, including the inhabitants of the United States, the people of the cities, and the people of the country, the officers of the navy and the marines, commanders of the army, the Legislatures, the Senate, the Cabinet, the President, and all! We have received from God what Protestantism never received viz., not only a commission but a command to go and teach all nations. There is no secret about this. The object we hope to accomplish in time is to convert all pagan nations, and all Protestant nations even England, with her proud parliament and imperial sovereign ... There is no secrecy in all this.[20]

"Dagger John" Hughes, as he was later known, was not the only Catholic to respond to anti-Catholicism. The Catholic population had grown considerably by the middle of the nineteenth century, and a number of questions and controversies arose inside the church that necessitated both negotiation and Vatican oversight. Archbishop Gaetano Bedini, Apostolic Nuncio to Brazil, arrived in America in June of 1852 to investigate, among other things, the conflicts between German- and Irish-American Catholics.

It is not difficult to imagine how this visitation would be received by anti-Catholics at the time, given the growing anxiety (and even fear and paranoia) many Protestants displayed toward their co-religionists. Indeed, a number of scholars link Bedini's trip to a shift in the relationship between Protestants and Catholics.[21] David Endres claims it was unprecedented in the annals of nativist conflicts. It placed, he asserts, the "polarizing strength of anti-Catholicism and xenophobia" into sharp relief. The presence of a Vatican representative—and all of the ceremonial pomp that attended such a visit—on American soil "acted as a catalyst widening the chasm between the perception of accepted political ideals and an imported 'foreign' theology."[22] It was too much for many anti-Catholics to bear. Wild rumors circulated about Bedini's past and his intentions in the United States. Some folks, drawing on the reservoir of anti-Catholic misconceptions, claimed he was in the country to sell indulgences.[23] He was burned in effigy multiple times in Cincinnati, and in February of 1854 was forced to sneak out of the country.[24]

During Bedini's visit and continuing after his departure, anti-Catholicism sharply increased yet again.[25] New pornographic convent tales were published.[26] Riots broke out again in Charlestown, Massachusetts in 1853 following the alleged kidnapping of Hannah Corcoran, a young Catholic who had converted to Baptist Protestantism and who claimed to have been drugged and held against her will by priests.[27]

Although New York and Philadelphia were the centers of nativist political organizing in the 1850s, there was a significant anti-Catholic and anti-immigrant sentiment in the capital city of Washington. A number of factors contributed to this and played a role in its growth: the presence of elected nativist politicians; the self-conscious display of nationalism; proximity to the American myth-making apparatus; and a more politically active public. Anxiety towards and fear of Catholics rose exponentially.

By the early 1850s, nativist media, moreover, was a strong genre in its own right. Although many periodicals were short-lived, the histrionics of editors and contributors were effectual. Political parties capitalized on the resentment and anger toward newcomers and non-native Americans and fed the media frenzy. An advertisement for the newspaper "American Patriot," typifies the more bigoted illustrations.

On the cover-page illustration "Americans" hold banners bearing nativist slogans such as: "Beware of Foreign Influence" (from George Washington's Farewell Address), and "None But Americans Shall Rule America." Two quotes directly reference religion and signal nativist anxieties. One states, "The Bible The Cornerstone of Liberty," and another, "Education, Morality, and Religion." Revolutionary War battles are named on other banners, a reminder of the American overthrow of tyranny. Crass stereotypes stand in for and depict Catholics: priests, a drunken woman with several children, troublemakers, criminals, hobos. A ship bearing the papal coat of arms has landed on the U.S. shore, and

Figure 4.1   "American Citizens We Appeal to You in all Calmness: Is It Not Time to Pause?" American Patriot, Boston: J.E. Farwell & Co., 1852. Courtesy of the Library of Congress.

the presumably Catholic folks embarking hold signs that read: "We Are Bound to Carry Out the Pious Intentions of His Holiness the Pope," and "Americans Shant Rule Us!!" From behind the ship a basilisk—the deadly mythological serpent—emerges from St. Peter's Basilica in Rome and crosses the Atlantic. A large hand strangles the monster. The title banner reads, "Already the enemies of our dearest institutions, like the foreign spies in the Trojan horse of old, are within our gates. They are disgorging themselves upon us, at the rate of Hundreds of Thousands Every Year! They aim at nothing short of conquest and supremacy over us." The text states the American Patriot supports "protection of American Mechanics Against Foreign Pauper Labor, Foreigners having a residence in the country of 21 years before voting, Our present Free School System, and Carrying out the laws of the State, as regards sending back Foreign Paupers and Criminals." It is clear the editor(s) and illustrator(s) understood themselves as under assault from and as victims of the Vatican's influence. They believed their money was being stolen, their morals and privacy compromised, their freedom of speech and religion challenged. The paper was fighting "Papal Aggression & Roman Catholicism, Foreigners holding office, Raising Foreign Military Companies in the United States, Nunneries and Jesuits," and was against "being taxed for the support of Foreign paupers millions of dollars yearly To secret Foreign Orders in the U.S."[28]

HISTORY OF WASHINGTON, DC AND
THE WASHINGTON NATIONAL MONUMENT

The plan to commemorate George Washington originated in the same spirit that led to the creation of the District of Columbia in 1790. The Residence Act established the Federal District, which would become the capital of the United States of America.[29] The blueprint included commemorative space—a "complex patriotic landscape" —from its origins.[30] Pierre Charles L'Enfant was commissioned by George Washington in 1791 to design a city that would serve both practical, administrative considerations and manifest the "symbolic power to carry the Constitution into effect."[31] L'Enfant envisioned a 400-foot wide "Grand Avenue" stretching from the current National Mall site with boulevards diagonally connecting the multiple circular and square nodes. The most important buildings L'Enfant positioned on a higher plane in his proposed capital.[32]

Thomas Jefferson had a significant influence on the city's layout as well; he championed a grid design that was less grandiose and more "pragmatic" than L'Enfant's.[33] The "rigorous checkerboard" grid had a central axis with an east-west orientation and was bookended by the Capitol and the planned President's House.[34] Although one scholar argues that Jefferson's was "as unlike L'Enfant's plan as can be imagined," L'Enfant incorporated a good deal of Jefferson's plan, as those who have visited DC will recognize.[35] His "Grand Avenue" became Pennsylvania Avenue. The Mall, in L'Enfant's thinking, would be the site of cultural—not political—institutions and buildings. In 1792, L'Enfant was fired and Andrew Ellicott took over the project.[36]

George Washington died in 1799. Plans to memorialize him with an equestrian statue had been discussed since immediately following the American Revolution, but it was only after his death that the movement took on urgency. Congress drafted a resolution which formally called for the statue as well as what would become the Washington Monument to be "carried into immediate execution." The equestrian statue was to be located at the Capitol. The "marble monument" to Washington would "commemorate his services," and "express regrets of the American People for their irreparable loss." One hundred thousand dollars was designated for both pieces, and the president was given oversight of the commissions. The resolution passed in 1790, and that same year, the government officially relocated from Philadelphia to the District of Columbia.[37]

Monuments to Washington began to proliferate in the early decades of the nineteenth century. The first—another equestrian statue—was erected in Baltimore in 1829. Artist Horatio Greenbough also depicted the first president atop a horse in his Union Square sculpture, and he designed a statue of Washington seated in a Jupiter pose, pointing at the sky, in DC.[38]

In 1832, a group of prominent citizens founded the Washington National Monument Society. Officers included John Marshall, Chief Justice of the Supreme Court, Judge William Cranch, Washington's mayor John P. Van Ness, and elite citizens William W. Seaton, Samuel H. Smith, and George Watterston.[39] According to one scholar, the society "envisaged a monument that would ... become the tallest structure in the world. Their Washington National Monument was meant to be the ultimate act of monumental aggrandizement, outshining the capital and dashing the building's claim to the commemorative center."[40] It would be paid for with private contributions.

In 1838, Congress passed "House Resolution 473" to authorize the building of the monument. Oversight of the Society's operation was given to the president, and the land "between seventh street West and the Potomac" was designated. "Care" of the monument as it was being built and after its completion was given to the Commissioner of Public Buildings, and whatever "regulations for its preservation and security" might be necessary in the future would be determined by Congress.[41]

Robert Mills entered the design contest held to drum up excitement for the monument. In addition to his commemorative monument to Washington for the city of Baltimore, the architect had a number of high-profile plans and commissions in Washington through the 1830s and 40s. He redesigned the canal that ran through the National Mall to re-center the Capital building. He submitted proposals for the National or Smithsonian Institute and botanical gardens, and even sketched a design for the entire Mall and landscape.[42]

Mills' 600-foot tall obelisk plan for the Washington Monument bested a number of high-profile submissions.[43] Mills' monument, critics have noted, was a manifestation of the contradictory impulses and ideologies in American society at the time, a "conflation of many sources."[44] The contradictions between American values and American actions was apparent, and at times, profound. Although slavery was questioned in some quarters, for instance, the presence of slaves in the nation's capital as well as the ways the slave trade had "insinuate[d] itself" in the DC and Mall landscape gave the lie to republican ideals.[45]

THE WASHINGTON NATIONAL MONUMENT'S CONSTRUCTION

Construction on the Washington Monument began after Congressional approval was granted in 1848. The cornerstone was laid in an elaborate July 4th ceremony that year. Speaker of the House, the Whig Robert C. Winthrop, was chosen to orate. He praised Pope Pius IX for "... having led the way in the great honor of this day ... the regeneration of Italy."[46] The Reverend Mr. John McJilton of the Protestant Episcopal Church offered a prayer. Masonic Grand Master Benjamin B. Frank also gave an address.[47]

In 1850, President Milliard Fillmore and other Washington elites commissioned horticulturist Andrew Jackson Downing to devise a cohesive plan for the Mall, including the Monument's central place in it. The design he produced "promised a deliberately different experience of time and place," according to art historian Kurt Savage. As opposed to the uniformity of previous designs, Downing's was "meandering, variegated, revelatory."[48]

Money for the project was tight from the start. In 1851 the Board of Managers of the Monument Society proposed a non-partisan publication, *The Monument*, in which they would disseminate important news, literature, scientific information, Congressional proceedings, etc, and from which a portion of subscription costs would be donated to the monument. Still, by 1852, contributions had dwindled. George Watterston, Secretary of the Society, penned a widely reprinted and impassioned appeal on behalf of the Board of Managers. He claimed an inability to complete the monument would "reflect lasting discredit on the gratitude and patriotism of its citizens." Furthermore, Watterston feared it would "prove to the world that republics are too apt to be forgetful of what is due to themselves and to the memory of those who, under Providence, have made them great, prosperous, and happy." Honoring the memory of Washington, he argued, was honoring themselves. He appealed to Americans' pride and competitiveness to contribute as Norwegians had when they raised funds for a statue for Charles XII in two days. He claimed that if "each white inhabitant" of the "twenty-five million of souls enjoying freedom, independence, and prosperity" gave three cents, the monument could be completed. This request was specifically directed at the states, whose "duty" Watterston claimed it was, to finish the "imperishable memorial of their veneration and gratitude."[49]

The press eagerly reported on the Washington Monument from the start, and circulated Watterston's appeal as they also noted the financial hardships. The *Barre Patriot* in Massachusetts reported, "The Washington Monument is languishing for want of means."[50] Another paper claimed the Monument had "not a pocketful of rocks."[51]

Nativists had adopted George Washington from the start and used his image and their interpretation of his politics to their own ends. His memory was frequently invoked to prove a point. "Beware of foreign influence," from his Farewell Address, was one of their slogans.[52] Because of this intimate association with him, nativist parties believed they had a vested interest in his commemoration. As noted above though, the Washington

National Monument Society solicited donations from all over the world for the monument.

In January of 1852, the American public learned that **Pope Pius IX** intended to contribute a stone to the Washington Monument, although the conveyance of this information is difficult to trace with absolute certainty.[53] The editor of the *Maryland Examiner* allegedly located a copy of a December 1851 letter from Colonel Anthony Kimmell of Maryland to his son that claimed the pope had "ordered two blocks of handsome marble."[54]

That same month, Lewis Cass, Jr., the American ambassador in Rome, wrote to Society Secretary Watterston to inform him of the pope's intention. Cass explained, "The block was taken from the ruins of the ancient Temple of Peace, adjoining the palace of the Caesars, and is to receive the inscription 'Rome to America.'"[55] The Massachusetts *Barre Gazette* reported that a "Gen. Cass" received a letter from his son—"Mr. Cass," the "Charge at Rome"—who was informed directly by the pope that

> Pope Pius IX (1846–1878) remains the longest reigning pontiff in history. He oversaw the centralization of papal power, encouraged the church's "Romanization," and summoned the First Vatican Council in 1869, even though the dissolution of the Papal States resulted in his loss of temporal sovereignty. He also defined the dogmas of the Immaculate Conception (1854) and of papal infallibility (1870).

he would be donating the stone. The *Gazette* added, "It may be considered a voice from the ruins of once Imperial Rome that Peace alone can save the Republican Empire in America from the sad fate of the ancient, but now fallen Mistress of the World."[56] Watterston replied to Cass on behalf of the Society and offered their "sincere gratification." He assured Cass that the stone would be both "interesting" and "acceptable" and that it would be placed "in a conspicuous position" in the monument.[57]

Rapidly thereafter, protests against such an inclusion were launched, primarily in cities where the nativist movement already had a foothold like Baltimore, DC, and Philadelphia and where "organs of the party kept up a continual fusillade."[58] Nativists held a meeting in Southwark, Philadelphia at which "violent addresses" were offered and resolutions passed.[59] A Philadelphia paper claimed those gathered were against any "despots of the old world, among the worst of whom they classed Pope Pius" contributing to the monument. William Prichett presided, and George G. West and a Rev. Mr. Owens addressed the crowd.[60] On March 9th an even larger gathering was held and with Dr. A. R. Shaw presiding, the group appointed three vice presidents, one from each ward in Southwark. A Protestant minister spoke about the papal "design against American freedom" and then West, a lawyer, proposed three resolutions that passed unanimously. The first was against the Monument Committee's acceptance of the stone. The second declared those gathered would prepare a "protest block" to be placed "on top of the objectionable stone." The third resolution stated that the objections to the gift from the pope should not be perceived as a "mass of hostility" towards the Catholic Church, and that its adherents were free to worship in the United States.[61]

Baltimore native John Weishampel published the source most aggressively hostile toward the stone. In it, Weishampel claimed responsibility for the large demonstrations and called on all "friends of free institutions" to "wake ... up to action ... before it be too late to avert the desecration of the Monument, by placing the Pope's block or any other Foreign material in its sacred walls." Weishampel had a lengthy list of objections to the "Pope's Stone" and hoped the Washington National Monument Society would concur and reject it. His first argument was semantic: the inscription "Rome to America" was inappropriate, he claimed, because the monument was being erected for a national figure, yet the inscription was foreign. Other objections ranged from the trivial to the overwrought. The Washington Monument was being designed, Weishampel believed, "to stand to the end of time for the admiration of the people of all nations under the sun" as the "rainbow token of salvation from foreign bondage." The stone however, was "condescending" and "hypocritical" because it appeared to be a token of friendship. The monument should be about George Washington, and the liberty and human rights he triumphed, and thus, "no despots ought to be allowed" to contribute "under any pretence whatsoever."

Like the Southwark meeting attendees, Weishampel adamantly claimed that his objections were not against the Catholic church—twice he mentioned that all Christian churches should contribute on their own or ecumenically—but rather, that he opposed the "Politico-Religious policy" of the Roman Catholic church. "We as a people believe that God raised up our Washington to lead us out of bondage," he stated, and the despotism of the pope was at odds with this. After taking over America, the papacy would, he maintained, "burn our Bibles, bind our consciences, make slaves of us, and put us to the stake, the rack, or the dungeon, for attempting to exercise the free minds with which a gracious Creator has gifted us." Lastly, Weishampel took aim at the influence the stone would have on both Protestants and Catholics. It would be a "mortification to nearly every American Protestant who looks upon it." It would cause Catholics to "look through it *at the Pope* and not at Washington," Weishampel feared. All that visitors—especially "foreign papist[s]"—would remember from DC was the generosity of the pope. Although Weishampel suspected the protesters might not be able to prevent the inclusion of the stone, he suggested they provide a "protest block" to be placed next to it. Such a block would demonstrate Protestant awareness of "the hypocrisy and schemes of that designing, crafty, subtle, far-seeing and far-reaching Power, which is ever grasping after the whole World, to sway its iron sceptre, with blood-stained hands, over the millions of its inhabitants."[62]

Weishampel ended his address with a call for a large gathering to take place, presumably in Philadelphia on April 12, 1852, although there is no evidence it did. Protests were arranged in other cities though. On June 25, 1852, George Stewart, the president of a group opposed to the stone, reported in a letter to the Monument Society that a "large preliminary meeting … of respectable citizens of West Baltimore City (without distinction of party or sect)" was held. The popular Weishampel spoke to the crowd, and much of what Stewart reported is similar enough to his pamphlet to suggest he had a stump speech prepared for these gatherings. The group drafted resolutions, claiming that nothing from a monarch should be within the "sacred walls" of the Washington Monument. They noted that the government of Switzerland's offering likewise should not be accepted, and that they "seriously object[ed] to any other country donating materials."[63] The pope and George Washington had "not one principle in common," and the pope was an "intolerant foe." Furthermore, the pope was "activated by a selfish motive to take advantage of this monument to present to the eyes of his subjects here." The resolutions urged every "true-hearted American" to withhold money from the monument fund. They concluded, "Resolved, that the warning voice of Washington to 'Beware of Foreign Influence' is applicable in these cases of intermeddling in our domestic affairs … We call upon American freemen to aid us in preserving our national tribute from desecration by the hypocritical contributions of any and all aristocratic and despotic powers."[64]

Petitions and additional letters were also submitted to the Monument Society. Private citizen Maury Babbitt submitted at least one hundred and ten petitions signed by residents of New Jersey, the majority of them from Newark.[65] Babbitt reported that they had held a meeting there, at which they appointed a committee to circulate the petitions which were signed by a "large majority of the most intelligent and influential men of this city, without distinction of political or religious faith, and except in very few instances, without hesitation."[66] The language of this petition is also strikingly similar to Weishampel's. Its crafters (and presumably, signers) took issue with the fact that "… the inscription 'Rome to America' engraved upon it, *bears a significance beyond its natural meaning*; that the contribution is an artful stratagem, calculated to divert the attention of the American people for the present from his animosity to republican institutions by an outward profession of regard; that this gift of a despot, if placed within those walls, can never be looked upon by true Americans, but with feelings of mortification and disgust …"[67]

As Weishampel had suspected, the protesters failed in their attempts to convince the Washington Monument Society to reject the stone, and in October of 1853, a number of newspapers noted it had been received.[68] In his 1885 history of the Monument, James Griffith reported that DC's Catholics were planning a "fitting reception" for the stone, but that they cancelled it because of the protests. They did turn out by the thousands to follow the truck that delivered the marble though.[69]

DESTRUCTION OF THE "POPE'S STONE"

On March 6 of 1854, the stone from Rome was destroyed.

At a meeting early in the evening, one group of DC Know Nothings passed a resolution "to destroy the stone at all hazards."[70] About nine men under the direction of someone named either "Nailor" or "Sailor" were chosen for the job. Two wore blackface; others dressed in Native American costume.[71] At a fever pitch, they rallied around their common enemy and charged to the future Washington Monument grounds. They broke onto the construction site where the stone from Rome was being stored with others that had yet to be added to the monument. Although some sources reported there were two guards—"one named Hilton and another Capt. Stuart"— most sources only discuss Stuart.[72] The mob tied him in his "watch-box" and placed paper over the windows so he could not see out. When he asked what was happening and if he was going to be harmed, he was told to keep quiet. A source that claimed to be one of the men who destroyed the stone (and whose detail would seem to corroborate this claim) described:

> With some skids, bars and blocks which we found on the grounds we rolled it from where it was lying in an old shed at the foot of the monument down the hill to a scow that was moored in the canal basin, now known as Babcock's Lake. After some little trouble we got it safely on board and started out of the basin into the river and down the Washington channel until within about fifteen yards of the Long bridge draw. While on the way down we broke off part of the slats and clipped a piece off one corner of the stone about the size of two bricks, with a sledge hammer, each taking a small piece. When we got near the bridge a confederate gave us a signal that all was OK by swinging a red lantern from the bridge. We then eased the stone

over the side of the scow and away it went with a splash to the bottom of the [Potomac] river. We then went back in the scow to the monument, relieved the man who was standing guard over the watchman, cut the rope around the watchbox quietly, and scattered in different directions for our homes.[73]

Another source claimed Stuart escaped by burning through the rope with a poker heated in his fire. Once free, he apparently realized his dog had been poisoned and the stone had been "broken into a thousand fragments."[74] He also discovered the other watchman, Hilton, was missing.[75]

Most newspaper articles agree with the above account that the stone was thrown in the Potomac River. A few mentioned that it was broken up into small pieces first.[76] Curiously, some sources attributed a degree of responsibility for the destruction to one of the guards, who, it was claimed, had a weapon on him that he did not use, which led at least one source to speculate the vandalism was an inside job.[77] Regardless, Stuart was fired for negligence after the vandalism was investigated. The Board of Managers of the Monument Society offered a five hundred dollar reward if those responsible were discovered, arrested, and convicted. Although a Grand Jury was convened in June of 1855 to investigate, the persons responsible were never found.[78]

A few nativist papers added additional anti-Catholic spin to the story. The *New York Observer and Chronicle* doubted the reports that the Know Nothing Party was responsible. It claimed, "It was not probably a native American who did it, but a foreigner politically enraged against the despot of the seven hills and his minions."[79] The Massachusetts *Barre Patriot* suggested Catholics did not want the monument to be built. It published "A Catholic Prayer for the Washington Monument," which allegedly illustrated this Catholic position and stated, "We sincerely hope the monument will never be completed. Let it remain for some years and then be sold to some Barnum for utilitarian ends or purpose of quackery. But let it not lift its head to Heaven, for ages, in mockery of the mighty dead, and to the everlasting shame of the living."[80]

Whether the Know Nothing movement and nativism gained members and momentum from the destruction of the "Pope's Stone" or if the act of vandalism was ultimately damaging to the cause is difficult to say. Frederick Harvey, definitive historian of the monument's construction, claimed the violence severely damaged the movement's image and recruitment. Fundraising efforts by the Society, which had always been a challenge, were also impeded according to him.[81] In the elections of November of 1854 however, the nativist John Towers won the mayoral seat in Washington, DC, and a number of other nativists were elected to national and local positions.

In December of 1854, construction halted as the Monument Society ran out of money after building 150 feet.[82] Two months later, the Know Nothings gained control of the Society. While members were presenting an appeal to Congress for funds, a group of dissident nativist members held a meeting that had only been announced in a few Know Nothing newspapers. They elected a new board from among their own, and received 755 of the 765 votes.[83] Vespasian Ellis, editor of the well-known nativist paper the *American Organ* (which had announced the meeting) was elected vice president with J.M. McCalla, another prominent Know Nothing, as treasurer.[84] The *Pittsfield Sun* reported that the "scheme" to overthrow the society was "doubtless concocted" at a meeting in Cincinnati.[85]

The original Board of Managers of the society refused to acknowledge the unsanctioned meeting or the Know Nothing board. The new board, in turn, refused to acknowledge the original board.[86] A considerable amount of confusion as to who was responsible for their records and what future election procedures would be ensued.[87] For all intents and purposes, two separate Washington National Monument Societies existed. Congress withdrew the funding it had appropriated for the monument because of the turmoil.

AFTERMATH OF THE DESTRUCTION

The Know Nothing Party held control of the Washington National Monument Society for three years, during which the monument grew just four more feet.[88] What's more, builders had previously rejected the stones—condemned them as "unfit for use," Harvey claimed—that were added during this time. The Army Corp of Engineers later removed them.[89]

The Know Nothings relinquished control of the Society in 1858 and a year later, Congress formally incorporated the Washington National Monument Society to prevent a repeat of the affair.[90] The charter for incorporation became the Society's constitution; by-laws were drafted and offices and committees named.[91]

From 1855 until 1876, when Congress revived interest, the Washington Monument stood dormant. One contemporary recalled, "The unfinished shaft, looking like a great broken tooth, stood in an utterly unimproved field, a monument to the fecklessness of popular ideas and ideals."[92] Many interpreters of this time consider the deep religious and cultural divisions in the republic during the Civil War years to be the primary reason. There was no singular national narrative or vision to which all Americans ascribed and aspired during this time. But that is not to say the Society did not try to revive interest and proceed with construction. Solicitation of national banks was undertaken in 1867 as a means to jump-start the stalled construction. The appointed committee drafted letters for the appeal, in which they stated the Society believed the country was ready to resume working towards the monument's completion, that the "obstacles" of the past were no longer a factor. They cited the work that had already been done at the site, and that 174 of the 343 feet were completed. Curiously, considering the conflict that had surrounded it, their list of "distant nations of the Old World" that had sent contributions to the monument included Rome.[93]

Congress tried to assist the process as well. In 1869, they passed another act for completion of the monument. Neither the Society's strategies nor the government's interventions were effective however. The Washington National Monument—or rather, the portion of it that was constructed—atrophied.

Anti-Catholic nativist violence continued to spread. In the District of Columbia, especially, "Know Nothingism" was the "rising star" as one journalist reported.[94] Support for the movement was widespread, enthusiastic, and became an aspect of popular culture. In "The Famous New Anti-Know Nothing Ditty," which was performed to "immense applause" at the circus in DC, a nativist supporter lampoons Catholics and especially the pope. The usual litany of anti-Catholic invectives were displayed: Catholics are not allowed to read the Bible, the pope is the tyrannical anti-Christ trying to take over America, etc. But the song is also quite vulgar for its time, and many of the themes of Catholic sexual deviance mentioned in chapter 2, as well as sexual immorality in general are on display. Implications of priests breaking their vow of celibacy with wives and daughters of Know Nothing members were a means of ridiculing priests as well as challenging nativist men to protect their daughters and sexually satisfy their wives. In another part of the song, the Catholic priest is the feminized or asexual foil to the rugged masculinity of the Know Nothing. Still another verse employs a double-entendre to suggest the relationship between Pope Pius and certain politicians goes beyond the ceremonial.

In the aftermath of the destruction of the stone, violence was not contained to the District of Columbia. Newark, New Jersey, where much nativist activity had taken place, was the site of a number of attacks on Catholics and Catholic property, the most significant of which was the attack on St. Mary's Church. In September of 1854, Irish Protestants and members of the American Protestant Association destroyed the German Catholic church, killed Catholic Thomas McCarthy, and injured up to twenty people after a large procession turned violent.[95] The *New York Times* described how "the altar [was] overturned, the sacred utensils and sacerdotal robes strewed around and trampled upon—the organ broken to pieces.

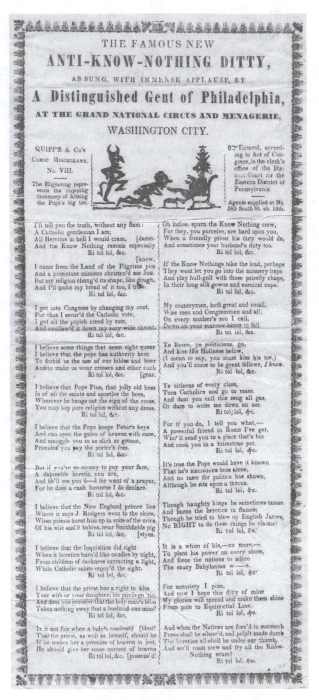

Figure 4.2   A Distinguished Gent of Philadelphia, "The Famous New Anti-Know Nothing Ditty," broadside, Philadelphia, c. 1850–870. Courtesy of the Library Company of Philadelphia.

The images, consisting of a costly Munich figure of the Madonna, and crucifix corresponding, together with the pictures, altar piece, and a splendid holy water font were also destroyed."[96] The paper noted that although "intense excitement" continued in the city, the jury found no fault with the local Know Nothings.[97]

Southern and midwestern cities likewise endured the spread of anti-Catholic nativist violence in 1854 and after. Four men were killed in New Orleans. Ten were killed in St. Louis. In the worst outbreak, nativists in Louisville, Kentucky killed twenty people on "Bloody Monday" in 1855.[98]

COMPLETION OF THE MONUMENT

In 1876 Congress created the Joint Commission on the Construction of the Washington National Monument and with that, the federal government took direct control of the project. In 1878, under Ulysses S. Grant, the Committee's findings were imposed and the US Army Corps of Engineers set to work. Colonel Lincoln Thomas Casey was put in charge of the project of completion, and Congress controlled the funds. The Monument Society was permitted to continue fundraising and advising the engineers.[99] Casey's vision for the Monument was radically different than Mills' had been fifty year's previous however.[100] The lack of clarity over who was in charge of the design created yet another set of conflicts and competing interests over the Monument. These conflicts were distinct from those that had haunted the Monument construction in previous decades. As Savage describes:

> [B]y the 1870s, Washington as symbol had lost much of his urgency. That is not to suggest that the nation was more unified. White supremacy in the South has been violently reestablished in the wake of the Civil War, and in the North the rise of monopoly capitalism was giving birth to the labor movement. Even though Washington himself was both a slave-owner and a capitalist his mythic status made him increasingly remote from those struggles in the present. Washington's heroic persona became so abstract that he no longer seemed to matter, not even in his own monument.[101]

The Washington National Monument was finally completed in 1884 and dedicated the following year.[102] Attempts were made to secure Robert Winthrop to give an oration, as he had at the laying of the monument's cornerstone forty years earlier. He was unable to do so because of poor health however, so Senator and former Massachusetts Governor Honorable John Davis Long read his oration. In 1888, the monument was formally opened to the public.[103]

In 1982, one hundred and fifty years after the Washington Monument's genesis, and one hundred twenty eight years after the destruction of the "Pope's Stone," a **replica stone** was made, and added to the obelisk. With that, the Washington Monument was finally completed.[104]

4.2 A Replica Pope's Stone

In 1982, Catholic priest Reverend James E. Grant of Spokane, Washington commissioned a replacement stone for the one that had been destroyed. In an article in a local paper, Grant claimed he was motivated to contact the National Park Service after learning about the Pope's Stone while on vacation in Washington, DC. He asked if they would install a new stone if it was provided, and they replied affirmatively. Though Grant considered asking the Vatican to commission the replacement stone, he eventually decided to do it himself. The stone, engraved "A Roma Americae" was installed in the Washington Monument at 340 feet.[105]

RELIGION AND THE DESTRUCTION OF THE "POPE'S STONE"

The city of Washington, DC is a saturated space, a symbolic representation of what some Americans have believed the nation is, the history those Americans want to remember, and what they want the nation to become. But this idea of "America" is socially constructed; it changes. What one generation chooses to remember and commemorate another ignores, for example. What remains constant however is how thoroughly the religious characteristics of nationalism are evident in the monuments and memorials in the District of Columbia. The religious significance of the city, the Washington Monument, and of course, the Know Nothing's destruction of the gifted stone were extensions of deep—and deeply religious—tensions in American society. This section will explore these.

There is nowhere in the United States where the construction and creation of myth is more evident than in Washington. After the American Revolution, the nation-building project included shaping the geography in accordance with what some American believed the "founding fathers" intended for the nation. The intentionality in the design of the capital city was evidenced from the moment L'Enfant presented his topographical plan to the president and country.[106] As Kenneth Bowling submits, L'Enfant's "long-range view of a capital of magnificent buildings and landscapes reflected America's optimistic outlook for the survival of the Union and the establishment of a Republican empire."[107] It is no surprise that George Washington championed L'Enfant's vision. But it was Thomas Jefferson's pragmatic, rationalist, ordered Roman grid that came to form the backbone of L'Enfant's baroque—even slightly histrionic—design.[108] So, the original plan of DC at once reflected a pragmatic desire for uniformity and (self?) control, and the confidence to aggressively display the ideological principles and allegedly universal human "truths" on which the new nation prided itself. Both of these aspects, as manifest in Jefferson's grid and L'Enfant's grandiosity, respectively, conveyed (and still convey) political and religious ideals, clues to how Americans imagined themselves, their place in the nation, and their nation's place in the world.

The national ethos does not only reflect and inspire an emotiveness focused on this-worldly objects, events, and persons, but rather, it evokes and contains a dedication and longing for a transcendent ideal. Scholars use the term "civil religion" to denote all those sanctified aspects of nationalism: the myths and symbols that represent and collectively shape the American national consciousness. Robert Bellah, its seminal scholar, defined civil religion as "certain common elements of religious orientation that the great majority of Americans share." Those elements, further, "have played a crucial role in the development of American institutions and still provide a religious dimension for the whole fabric of American life, including the political sphere."[109] Presidents, the "founding founders," major events, and especially wars have played an integral role in shaping the content and contours of civil religion. The American Revolution, Bellah contends, was the "final act of the Exodus" from Europe; the Declaration of Independence and the Constitution "were the sacred scriptures." The first president, George Washington, was "the divinely appointed Moses who led his people out of the hands of tyranny."[110]

No other location in the country displays the material aspects of American civil religion more conspicuously than Washington does. The District of Columbia illustrates and captures—indeed, *grounds*—American civil religion, and the monuments to individuals and particular events embody singular aspects of it. They are an integral part of the sacralization of the landscape. The entire District is a spiritual site, the mecca of American civil religion.[111] As one scholar has stated, "It is difficult to think of any other national capital that so consummately pronounces the nation-state creed in material terms."[112]

Many scholars have analyzed the journey to and around the nation's capital in religious terms. It was, and is, a pilgrimage. Cultural geographer Wilbur Zelinsky calls it a "blinding religious experience, a rite of communion."[113] Anthropologist Edith Turner, who along with Victor Turner is one of the most influential scholars of religious pilgrimage, calls it "a distinctive American gathering place." The Mall is the "carrier of the

American vision." It is in DC, she asserts, that certain "root paradigms" are observable, such as, "tradition in the making, space and time in the process of being sacralized, becoming interresonant, with harmonics."[114]

The Washington National Monument is one very significant example of the sacralization of geography and national myths in the larger landscape of the District of Columbia. In one interpretation, it both represents *and* commemorates American mythology. Zelinsky claims the Washington Monument has "transcended place and time" to become a "durable object of universal American devotion."[115] Like other symbolic structures and sites in the city, it is where the nation worships itself. It is the material display of belief in the providential sanctity of America and the trust that other nations believe also and will worship accordingly at the shrine. It is American civil religion, or theological nationalism, or what Zelinsky calls "substitute theology" in stone.

It is a polyvalent symbol; each stone reveals what the Monument meant and means to a particular population or community. During the antebellum years, its neglect represented the growing national fissures, the absence of a triumphant collective narrative. As Kirk Savage has asserted, "The stump seemed to represent a nation that had lost its way. The symbolic impact of a huge, aborted monument to the founding father cannot be overestimated."[116] Antebellum Americans could not understand themselves collectively as a unified people. The national myths that undergirded U.S. society were severely weakened by racial, ethnic, religious, and regional strife and hostility towards those who did not share them. The political process, rather than an expression of shared American ideals, became a way to channel dissent and deepen social fractures. Not even symbols of foundational American principles could inspire civic acts people could hold in common.

As we touched on in chapter 3, historians Nathan Hatch and Mark Noll have elucidated the ways in which many Protestant communities have "read" their individual and collective actions biblically and how culture is saturated with biblical meaning. Because of this, a great deal of American experience and history has been interpreted through a biblical lens. George Washington looms large in this typology of American history.[117] He was, *is*, a central figure in the Christian biblical narrative of America. The biblical typology is evidenced in both pictorial and prose representations of Washington. He is depicted as the new Moses. He is Jesus Christ, savior of the United States, in illustrations at the Washington Monument and Mall, and in Senate reports on the Park System.[118] Washington has also been imagined as the father figure in a civil holy trinity. Eminent historian John Wilson has suggested for example, that in American mythology and civil religion, Washington is God the father, Abraham Lincoln is God the son, and John F. Kennedy is God the Holy Spirit.[119]

MONUMENT'S DESTRUCTION AS RELIGIOUS ACT

Although Bellah and others have tried to argue that civil religion is not sectarian, per se, it is shot through with a recognizably Western Christian framework, and the label "Christian" has very rarely included its Catholic form in the United States. Rather, American civil religion is saturated with Protestant Christianity, which means at its genesis and to its core, it was and is a reaction against Catholicism. Civil religion is a generic pan-*Protestantism,* not a generic pan-*Christianity* in other words.[120]

Like every linear historical narrative in the Judeo-Christian tradition, civil religion is shaped by dichotomies: good versus evil; freedom versus tyranny; Christ versus anti-Christ; Jerusalem versus Babylon. As a pan-Protestant ideology, the dichotomy through which civil religion is defined and shaped is often an anti-Catholic one. This has been evident throughout the episodes under investigation here: the United States is the New Jerusalem; Rome is Babylon. In terms of Washington DC and George Washington, the same process occurs. The first president is the Christ-figure, the Catholic Pope is the anti-Christ figure, the "despot of the seven hills" and the "whore of Babylon." The United States is the benevolent, democratic Christian Eden, Rome is the evil, tyrannical snake in the garden.

In precisely the same way that those who burned the Ursuline convent and Philadelphia's Catholic churches attempted to wipe any trace of "popery" off the landscape, so too did the nativists who broke the "Pope's Stone" into pieces and threw it in the river. A Catholic stone would tarnish Washington's Monument, the symbol of all that is American, all that is pure. The stone would pollute American ideals and jeopardize the holy American project.

The "Pope's Stone" incident is an example of the destruction of sacred space. Viewed in light of the spatialization and sacralization of nationalism, it illustrated how committed nativists were to a defense of the boundaries of the sacred, of purity, and by extension, the boundaries of citizenship. The destruction of the stone is an example of one possible outcome when these boundaries are crossed and when symbols of an alternate narrative of American identity seek inclusion in the sacred national geography: the contested symbols are destroyed. To nativists, self-appointed safe guardians of the purity of all things they deemed American, the Vatican's offering of the stone was a transgressive act which required action.

Weishampel alluded to this in his "Stratagem" address and referenced the religious idioms of purity and contamination. He claimed George Washington was the "deliverer, under God, of his Country." God, Weishampel stated, "raised up our Washington." His name was "immortal"; his monument the eternal "token of salvation." Even the monument's walls were "sacred." The "pure pillar, so sacredly dedicated" to Washington would be "blemished by a foreign, despotic, and tyrannical hypocrite's hand" if the stone were included. This idea provided the religious justification for anger toward and destruction of the gift. In a rhetorical move that foreshadowed George W. Bush's post-September 11th strategies, Weishampel ended his admonition by calling the Washington Monument the "Freedom Monument."

Tellingly, nativists were angry that the stone came from the pope in his role as spiritual leader of the Catholic Church, not as political head of the Vatican States. Throughout the period of time when nativists were protesting its inclusion, other leaders and ethnic communities were sending gifts that were accepted. In 1852, for example, the Sultan of Turkey sent a stone to Washington. The following year, the Ancient Order of Hibernians did the same. Likewise, at the very same time the tension over the pope sending a stone was being reported on, artist Thomas Crawford was in Rome working on a statue of Washington for the state of Virginia's monument. The uproar over the "Pope's Stone," was not about the stone coming from another country or ethnic community; it was because it was coming from the Pope.

DESTRUCTION OF THE "POPE'S STONE" HISTORIOGRAPHY

Literature on the "Pope's Stone" is unfortunately quite sparse. With almost no exceptions, we must rely on histories of the Washington Monument, Monument Society, National Mall, and District of Columbia in order to even approach the episode. Members of the Washington Monument Society and other "gentleman historians" for example, penned narratives of both the organization and the monument in the nineteenth and early twentieth century.[121] More recently, scholars have produced informative studies of the stones and more in-depth and technical histories of the monument.[122]

There is a good body of recent scholarship on Washington DC. These include sophisticated examinations of the Washington National Monument, and sometimes explore the sacralization of the landscape I mentioned above. Kenneth Bowling's *Creation of Washington D.C.* examines how the site aside the Potomac was chosen, and what that process reveals about competing economic and political interests at stake for the new nation. He reads the creation of the capital city as a lens through which the entire history of the debate over what kind of government—centralized, federalist, limited, state-controlled, imperialist, etc.—the Constitution outlined. Although his thesis technically incorporates all of American history, from the first settlers to the present-day, his close examination of the long Revolution is instructive and sophisticated.[123]

Three other recent scholarly analyses of the Washington Monument are helpful for wrestling with the destruction of the "Pope's Stone." Kirk Savage published a sustained critical commentary on the Monument that makes use of contemporary spatial and landscape theory. In it, he examines how DC's "monumental core" was designed and created and how it "has come to define the nation and to change the character of national experience."[124] Savage's work is invaluable for both the scope of his historical content, his cultural-geographical approach, and especially, his attention to race.[125] In discussing the Monument, he claims:

> In the nativist's view, true Americans were like Washington himself: white, Protestant, of Revolutionary stock. The Know-Nothings wanted the monument to showcase the power and reach of their movement, so they restricted contributions to their own 'brethren.' Since they claimed to be the true Americans, the monument they built would issue from 'the true American heart.' When complete it would vindicate their idea that 'Americans must and shall govern America.'[126]

Inclusion of non-whites, or non-Protestants, or non-"native" Americans would call into question the nativist claim of supremacy and all the forms of dominance and power that went along with it. If Catholics were considered "brethren," they would be eligible to share that power, and claim a space in the national narrative and the right to define and use its symbols.

In *Myths in Stone*, Jeffrey Meyer examines the religious dimensions of the city of Washington. Using archeology and pilgrimage as metaphors and lenses, he listens for the "religious message" that is "implicit" in Washington's infrastructure and art. The oft-repeated message he hears is: "the Almighty stood behind the American experiment."[127] Meyer highlights additional aspects of the religiosity of DC, such as the rituals performed there, like celebrations, funerals, and popular protests, and the formalized "liturgy" of the three branches of government and presidential inaugurations.[128] He also examines the "network of symbols" that are a part of the complex development of the "foundational narratives" of the United States and their shifting meaning.[129]

As nineteenth-century folks argued about how to represent George Washington in stone, the National Park Service and upper-class white women fought bitterly over how to present his memory at the place where he was born. Seth Bruggeman unravels the motivations and perspectives of various constituents in *Here, George Washington Was Born*. Some interested parties wanted to maintain a pastoral image of Washington in a seemingly "untouched" landscape. Others proposed various replicas (of Washington's house or of the Washington National Monument, for example) be constructed. Still others championed the creation of a living history museum at the site, Bruggeman explains. An "object fetishism" became evident in these different ideas, which Bruggeman connects to religious practice and especially Christian burial rituals.[130]

Wilbur Zelinsky's work on nationalism and sacred space is also helpful as we think through the "Pope's Stone" incident. Zelinsky claims, "In every sovereign country of the modern world, the workings of the state have set their mark upon the land." Nowhere are the workings of the state to construct its narrative—what David Chidester and Edward Linenthal refer to as "the spatial orientation of American nationalism"—more visible than they are in Washington, DC. This American sacred geography is "locative" in Linenthal and Chidester's words, in that it demarcates "boundaries and borders." But it is also "utopian" because it contains a wider "appeal to a manifest destiny of territorial expansion and its aspiration to transcend all geographical limits in assuming a position of world power."[131]

A forthcoming, sustained investigation of the "Pope's Stone" draws on the work above and considers it an example of the destruction of a con-tested symbol inside a sacred landscape. It incorporates aspects of collective memory to explore how monuments are vivid representations of communal identity, desire, and longing. Work on religion and nationalism, memory (and amnesia), myth, and the creation of historical narratives provides tools to interpret the meaning of the "Pope's Stone" as part of the contested story of the American nation. What makes an analysis of the episode in the larger story of the Washington Monument fascinating is not only what it can tell us about religious conflict and national mythology at the time the Monu-ment was founded, but also how that mythology continued to evolve and was contested through the nineteenth century. In the context of nativism, like many other highly charged episodes in history, Americans attempted to effectively write out as much as they included in the national narrative. So the "Pope's Stone" tells us as much about what people wanted to remember as what they wanted to forget, how they sought to go about remembering and forgetting, and how all of it changed over time.[132]

Documents

DOCUMENT 1

The Devil is Come To You (1831), Reverend George Bourne

Source: "The Devil is Come to You," *The Protestant,* ed. George Bourne, NY: James P Requa, September 24, 1831.

Babylonish Temples. A large Masshouse is speedily to be erected at Mobile. At Pensacola an idolatrous house is now finishing. A Masshouse is to be constructed at Collins' Cross Roads, South Carolina.

ADVERSARIES. Six Jesuit Massmen are now roaming, and two others are daily expected to commence their "going about, seeking whom they may devour," in Alabama and Florida.

POPISH HIERARCHY IN THE U.S. John England[1] has issued a proclamation to the people of America, dated 29th of August, 1831 — for which we extract the following summary of Popery; in the most authentic form demonstrating that the Dragon has set up the BEAST in this Republic, and given him his power, and his seat and great authority, and that the American world are wondering after the Beast. Revelation xiii 2–4.

"Fifty years ago, there was not a diocese, a bishop, a seminary, nor a convent of the Catholic church in our Union. Now there is a perfect province, with its regular hierarchy, consisting of the Archbishop with seven suffragan Bishops, and two coadjutors, besides two exempt dioceses and their Bishops, giving an aggregate of twelve of the Episcopal body with their secular clergy: two Universities, and five or six Seminaries: a province of Jesuits with a University and Novitiate and two or three Colleges; an establishment of Sulpicians, with a University and College and Seminary; a province of Dominican friars, with their professed house and College and Novitiate; two or three establishments of Lazarists with their Colleges and Seminaries and Schools; an establishment of Augustinian friars; two flourishing Ursuline convents, Visitation Nuns, Carmelite Nuns, poor Clares, Lorretines, Sisters of Charity, and five or six other descriptions of female religious societies, with their schools and establishments, besides some Monasteries of men. Add to this, periodical presses, and continual demand for new churches and more clergymen."

The above extracts are published in the Roman papers, with the utmost exultation, and with shouts of triumph. They convey to every Christian and Philanthropist, intelligence of a most appalling character; and wring our hearts with dread anticipations. Popery is a system of idolatry and irreligion, characterized by the spirit of Truth in the most loathsome imagery, denounced in the strongest language of reprobation, and doomed by the Judge of all the earth to experience the most awful inflictions of his divinely tremendous displeasure. We do most sincerely request all Protestants to read the twelfth, thirteenth, fourteenth, fifteenth, sixteenth, seventeenth, eighteenth and nineteenth chapters of Revelation, with Scott's luminous Commentary, and then ask themselves whether it is the duty of the disciples of Jesus Christ to look with composure, much less with approbation, upon this grand artifice of the Dragon and the Beast to "deceive them who dwell upon the earth."

Popery is the implacable enemy of all civil and religious freedom. Liberty of thought, word, action, person, and possessions has never been known where Popery tyrannized.

This fact is corroborated by unerring and universal testimony; as recorded by the Popish annalists and historians. It will ever remain the same — for as soon as the walls of the Babylonish prison are overthrown, and the doors of the dungeon are opened, and the fetters of sin and darkness, are shivered, that system of pollution and slavery, like the idolatrous Jehoram, "departs without being desired, and as the sinners a hundred years old, shall be accursed."

Popery completely hardens, and extinguishes all the sensibilities of Conscience. The whole history of Europe, during the last twelve hundred years, is a melancholy and heart rending exposition of this terrifying truth. Crimes which outrage every natural feeling, have not only been invented by the Roman Priests, but were tolerated, and the price of their pardon was as well understood and as regularly paid, as any other sum given for the ordinary articles of merchandise. This is the case now in every part of the Pope's domains — and for men to talk of Conscience who either habitually perpetrate those sins, or constantly pardon and absolve, according to their impious God robbing arrogance, those "workers of iniquity," is the very climax of practical atheism, and certain murder of souls.

But if the inconceivable wickedness of Popery — and that ungodliness is inseparable from Romanism, for it is the very heart's blood and aliment of the Babylonian Priests; did not verify that Popery "sears the conscience as with a hot iron" — the indescribable cruelties and the insatiate sanguinary demands of that direful system of torture and death, demonstrates that the Mother of Harlots is "drunken with the blood of Saints, and the blood of the Martyrs of Jesus." The Jesuits may deny — Massmen may palliate — and Papists may endeavor to conceal the enormities with which the Popes, Councils, Inquisitors, and the whole Popish ecclesiastical rabblement are *branded*, which is their invariable character, and without which, the prophetical identity of "Babylon the Great" could not be *infallibly* ascertained — but all their efforts are vain — Popery is only another word for *Murder*; and the lamentable history of "the ten horns of the Beast," manifests, that every thorough going Papist is a blood thirsty enemy of all those who do not bear "the mark of the Beast," and who do not worship the monster image, which the king of the Romish Babylon, their "Lord God the Pope" hath set up for adoration. The records of the Christian Martyrs slaughtered by Dominicans, Jesuits, and all the other confederated miscreants of Rome, are only proof that the prediction of John in Revelation xiii. 15, 16, 17; and xvii. 6; and xviii. 24, have been most diabolically fulfilled with minutest exactness. But to affirm that such men have a "tender conscience, void of offence towards God and man," is as grossly deceptive and untrue; as was Satan's *"first lie"* to Adam and Eve in the Garden of Eden.

Popery not darkens, but also extirpates the powers of the mind — for by it, reason and the understanding are completely stultified. Two facts clear as meridian day, perennial as the revolutions of the 1260 years, and without exception, wherever Popery has swayed; render all additional illustration of the obscurity with which the kingdoms of Babylon have been cursed, altogether superfluous. During several centuries, the whole of the Popedom was one vast domain of ignorance, and crime — and the stars which glimmered in the profundity of that dolesome night, appeared at intervals "few and far between;" and the bestial abominations of all orders of men, the worst of whom beyond all comparison were Popes, Cardinals, Prelates and the other tribes of the *infallible horde,* were such; that it seemed as if the Papists were bereft of every quality of human nature, except the merely animal instincts.

No traveler in Germany, Ireland, or Canada, requires any instruction as it regards the religious profession of the surrounding inhabitants. These is a plain palpable difference at once obvious between the Protestant and Popish districts, which it is impossible to mistake; and as the residents are subject to the same laws and government; and have the same climate, soil and advantages — Popery alone is the efficient cause of the squalid penury and brutal ignorance which always and universally appertain to those people who idolize the Mass, and are hoodwinked by its ungodly deceitful Priests.

Popery is the avowed, unrelenting and incurable enemy of the Holy Scriptures. In every age, the Roman Priests have robbed their devotees of their heavenly birth-right — in all places, they always destroy every copy of the Scriptures which they can steal — and this they must continue to do — otherwise the craft "by which they have their gain would be destroyed; for they do evil, hate the light, and will not come to the light, lest their deeds should be reproved." John iii. 19–21.

Notwithstanding instances are continually occurring of the destruction of the Bible in this Republic, and every where else, by the Massmen; yet the Popish papers with equal frequency proclaim, that the Priests do not withhold the Bible from their blinded disciples. It is almost impossible to state which is the more heinous guilt — the open hardened robbery and burning of the Bible by Jesuits; or the unblushing impudence and mendacity, with which they deny the fact after they committed the impious crime.

All the annals of the Popedom evince, that the Roman Hierarchy originated in a deep laid, artful plot, if possible to bury mankind in superstition, idolatry, ignorance and vice; that thereby they might become the voluntary enslaved minions of a succession of ecclesiastical knavish impostors. This system has been pertinaciously prolonged by the crafty Babylonish Priests, expressly to degrade the human family; so that like the ancient Gideonites, Papists are "hewers of wood and drawers of water," for the blasphemous tyrants, whom Satan, "with all power, and signs and lying wonders, and with all deceivableness of unrighteousness," 2 Thessalonians ii. 8-12, has appointed, ordained and consecrated, "to deceive them who receive the mark of the beast, and who worship his image." Revelation xix. 19, 20.

What enlightened American citizen, what sincere Protestant, what philanthropic patriot, and what Christian can review a system thus offensive and pernicious; and not feel alarm and sorrow, at the rapid extension of its numberless evils, and at the astounding multiplication of its deluded votaries. The political dangers and mischiefs of Popery being only of temporary duration and effect, are a mere nonentity, compared with its ruinous influence in connection with the soul throughout eternity.

It is criminal in the highest degree, to veil this subject. Every man acquainted with the plain and express dictates of the divine word; and who also understands the genuine attributes of Popery, knows, that *it is impossible for a decided unequivocal Papist to be saved, according to the terms revealed in the New Testament*. We have nothing to do with the final Judgment-but we must argue according to the light of God's word; which sacred volume assures us, that considered in the aggregate, the Roman community is "*the habitation of devils, and the hold of every foul spirit, and a cage of every unclean and hateful bird*." Revelation xviii. 2. Yet by the subsequent call; "Come out of her, my people, that ye be not partakers of her sins, and that ye receive not of her plagues" — it appears, there may be some exceptions, as there was *one* righteous Lot in abominable Sodom, and *one* God fearing Obadiah in the accursed palace of Ahab and Jezebel.

But the categorical "testimony of Jesus" is — "there shall in no wise enter into it, heaven, any thing that defileth, neither whatsoever worketh abomination, or maketh a lie." Revelation xxi. 27. This denunciation may be correctly applied to that Popery which had been the peculiar topic of all the previous prophecy — what follows? That Papists resolutely living and impenitently dying in Babylon, cannot enter Paradise. — "Nothing that defileth shall enter heaven" — but to express the loathsome, awful impurity of that antichristian system; Popery is delineated as "a great whore, who has made the people drunk with the wine of her fornication" — and all history verifies, that the Popedom has always been and now is, in all its cities, and villages, streets, lanes and alleys, from the Pope's seraglio in the Vatican, to the American Priest's bed chamber for *female confession*, including the unnatural crimes of the monasteries, and the bestial licentiousness of the nunneries, one undisguised, continuous Brothel in all its variety and amplitude. In it they reside, and in it they remain, and in its defilement they die — is it not a most terrific delusion for such persons to anticipate a portion in the New Jerusalem of beatified and perfect sanctity?

Nothing "that worketh abomination" shall enter heaven — but Popery is idolatry, without dimunition, and without end — and idolatry is invariably declared in the Scriptures, to be altogether abominable. "Ahab did very abominably in following idols." — 1 Kings xxi. 26 — and we might almost suppose, that Moses had in his contemplation, not only to warn the Jews against the old Heathens, but Christians against the modern Roman Pagans. Deuteronomy vii. 25. — "The graven images of their gods shall ye burn with fire — thou shalt not desire the silver and gold on them, for it is an abomination to the Lord thy God." How therefore can an open Papist Idolator living and dying in the practice of this abomination expect admission to his glory, whose honor he has continually given to images and idols?

Nothing that "maketh a lie" shall enter heaven — but Popery is oracularly entitled, "THE LIE." 2 Thessalonians ii. 11. The Grand lie; the chief lie; the preeminent lie; that strong delusion, through the power of which men are "damned, who believe not the truth, and have pleasure in unrighteousness." This lie they credit, the talk about it, they practice it; they are willingly deceived by it; and with this "lie in thie rights hands," their souls depart from earth. To affirm, therefore, that such persons can be saved according to the express and decisive declarations of Scripture, is fostering that blindness, with which the Jesuit Massmen are leading the blindfolded Romans into the ditch of perdition, "where their worm dieth not, and the fire is not quenched." Christians! Look at these facts in all the terrifying aspects which they present to your view. The number of these idolaters is augmenting in an incalculable ratio — and a very well informed Protestant, who has been employed in gathering correct information upon this subject, assures us; that it is his deep conviction, that the Papists will have added to their numbers more bigoted partisans, during the year 1831; than the four principal Christian denominations in the United States. — Protestant Brethren! We admonish you to awake out of sleep. From compassion to perishing souls — by your profession of attachment to Jesus, the Friend of sinners — by the claim of consistency with your high and holy calling, as believers in the Son of God — and by your hope of the reward, which the Lord has promised to his faithful Servants, who "convert a sinner from the error of his way" we charge you, shake off your lethargy — Satan sleeps not — the Jesuits are wide awake — the Massmen are prowling throughout our land in all the length ad breadth of its domains, deceiving precious souls to their eternal misery. Surely, it may be hoped, that the Lord will not permit the land of the Puritans to be defiled by the Beast, and the asylum of freedom to be bewitched and captivated by the triple crowned despot of Rome — but remember you are now placed virtually in the position of the Jews, when Haman's butchering commandment was suspended over their heads; and to you may rightly be addressed the admonition of Mordecai to Esther — "if you altogether hold your peace at this time, then shall enlargement and deliverance arise from another place" — Esther iv. 14. but you!

DOCUMENT 2

The Ursuline Convent: A Poem (1835), Philemon Scank[2]

Source: Philemon Scank, *A Few Chapters to Brother Jonathan, Concerning "Infallibility, &c." Or, Strictures on Nathan L. Rice's "Defense of Protestantism,"* (Louisville, 1835), Excerpted 14–17, Printed Material, Massachusetts Historical Society, Boston, Massachusetts.

A rumor spread that in the Convent walls,
A secret ladder to a darksome prison falls,
The dwelling of repining nuns; who lie
In dismal gloom, no ray to cheer the eye;
Who groans, unheeded by their sisters, rise
Incessant; whom a scanty meal supplies,
From day to day, convey'd by cautious hand,
At midnight's silent hour; while pale they stand,
To catch the little basket's frugal stores,
Descending daily from their prison doors.
       Ten days of dark imprisonment and fast
Each imperfection shares; — when these are past,
Releasement follows if the pris'ners swear,
They never will their cruel woes declare:
Thus tyraniz'd they pine away and die;
Nor dare reveal their griefs, nor even sigh.
       Prepost'rous tale! Yet vulgar minds believ'd,
Alas! Too prone to crime, and hence to be deceiv'd
The easy dupe of knaves, to do the ill,
Their minds can plan, but hands cannot fulfill.
By these thro' all the wards the story went
Improv'd as Fancy's hundred tongues invent,
Till all the vulgar mass is in ferment.

And lest excitement lack a holy plea,
To swell the tide of Anger's raging sea;
The pulpit rang with warnings fierce and loud,
As Beecher rav'd, and fir'd the bigot crowd.
He pray'd and dung with sanctimonious face;
Then rose and spoke; and mourn'd the lack of grace,
Among the people of this favor'd land,
Who tamely suffer'd popish schools to stand; —
Where superstition, fraud and vice prevail,
And dire woes upon our race entail;
Where nuns and priests their wicked lusts enjoy,
And arts seductive on the youth employ. —
Accurs'd the land; and Freedom must expire,
Unless these Sewers be given up to fire!!!
　　　Nor he alone his pious fears disclos'd:
His sect in systematic was dispos'd —
The zealot ranks of Calvin's vip'rous brood —
To vengeance urg'd the giddy multitude;
As if the God of Armies wanted aid
To route the foes that Zion's walls invade.
Their Council met at Albany, to form
A plan of war, and help the growing storm; —
If haply all the Romish schools should yield;
And leave themselves — to reap the *golden field*.
　　　They first secure the press's giant pow'r,
(That modern battering ram of ev'ry tow'r)
To scatter round th' Atlantic shores a host,
Of Journals, "Gospel Messengers," and most,
"The Vindicator," chieftain of then all,
Proclaiming: "BABYLON THE GREAT must fall:"
To wit: the Romish church must topple down;
And shut her schools, and doff her priestly gown!
　　　The printers went to work — the presses groan'd,
As guilty jades, for fornication ston'd.
Their sland'rous columns cramm'd the public mail,
As if the bread of truth were all grown stale;
And moral taste, so oft by trash regal'd,
To know the sound, from rotten fruit had fail'd.
　　　These went the rounds from Dan to Bersabee;
And all must read that had an eye to see.
And as they read, they felt them stirr'd to wrath,
As mad dogs do, that see the running bath.

On ev'ry page they read this solemn speech:
"Hear, O ye people what the Lord would teach!
Ye must not, as ye wish your souls to live,
Ye must not to your popish neighbors give
Or civil or religious rights: — decry,
By foul and fair, by fable and by lie,
His Faith, his Morals — more than all — his schools;
For there are mainly taught the popish rules.
And see that Priests influence not your sons!
But oh! — preserve your daughters from the nuns!
    Why will ye not instruction take; and hear
A truth as clear as cloudless sun is clear: —
If ye allow these papists equal rights,
They'll soon *eclipse* the *Presbyterian lights*;
Then Freedom's flag and Calvin's faith must bow!
And Babylon look on with haughty brow: —
Indignity the Saints should never bear,
While men are brave, and woman's form is fair!
    Oh! Be not faithless to the Lord your God!
But rule these Papists with an iron rod!
Ye shall not give them rest by night or day: —
At home — abroad — at inns — or on the way.
Where'r ye find, harass their souls with grief;
No respite give, no hour of sweet relief!
Ye must not love, or call them gentle name!
But rather hate! And, if ye can, defame!
Ye may abstain from *arson* and from *blood*: —
But mind — ye must destroy them in the bid.
If not, the godliest of the godly may
Obedience own to Babylonian sway."
    So much the Press did do for Sion's cause: —
But hear another of the Council's laws.
The Rev'rend sires on Hudson's banks conven'd,
Themselves still more as Sion's friends demean'd;
When praying much and singing to the Lord;
They swore allegiance to his sacred word;
And vow'd, with cheerful hearts, they would not rest,
Till Calvinism Zion's Hills possess'd.
And each did pledge, and take his pious oath,
To take in charge the Church and country both;
And rear them to the *justest forms of truth*. —
But most of all, to caution much the youth,

What dangers in the Romish *schools* await
Their artless souls, as hooks conceal'd with bait.
    "And mind ye," said a rev'rend Preacher gray
"Remember when ye all are far away,
In town and border, when your work is found;
Your work is — popish teachers to confound.
And be not nice, about the means ye use!
Your end should be, to carry Gospel-news —
That is — to cry the Pope's religion down,
His rites, his altars; and his scarlet gown; —
To hold his priests and sacraments to scorn —
To make your popish neighbors feel forlorn.
    This last advice the common weal implies,
Which ye will not forget is ye are wise.
Yes! I repeat it: — *make them feel forlorn,*
And sighing, wish they had never been born.
But now that ye may more successful try,
(For what forbids, in such a case to lie?)
Ye must assert — assert it boldly too, —
As tho' ye did believe it true —
That they cannot the friends of Freedom be,
And yet, obedient to the Holy See.
For so their souls must scorn the people's rule;
And watch their time like some unwilling mule,
To shake the yoke indignant from their neck;
And make this happy government a wreck.
    'Tis false; but what of that? — repeat it still,
In ev'ry crowd — declare that papists will,
If we allow them favor grow so great,
As forcibly to snatch the helm of state.
And then, farewell to all that's pure and free,
To serve the Vassals of the Holy See!
    Then sit not still as tho' ye felt secure —
'Tis not a time to act the sinecure.
The people must be warn'd — arous'd — alarm'd;
Their wrath enkindled, and the vengeance arm'd;
Prepar'd to tread the papists in the dust;
For so 'tis meet — and *tread* them down we *must.*
    Then go about, thro' all the mountain glades;
The goodly towns where wealthy merchant trades;
The happy farmer's house where concord reigns: —
In short, thro'out the Union's wide domains.

Alarm the spirits of th' incautious youth;
And arm the aged in the cause of truth —
That is, to crush (not burn) the popish schools.
Now as the people may be made your tools,
Be sure ye use them! — stir them up to rage!
Tell them, 'tis theirs Jehovah's wars to wage!
For now the Beast with seven heads and horns,
This land with Schools and Colleges adorns,
With sly intent the people's hearts to gain;
And stretch his sceptre o'er this free domain; —
Then, where shall we, and all the saints abide?" —
    Thus he, when all the Council spoke and cri'd:
"We will not rest, till rage and fury drive
His Saints for Great Jehovah's cause to strive!"
Those swore they all; and thus the Council broke,
Resolv'd to place on Cath'lic necks their yoke.
    Return'd to wives, and precious babes, and home,
They loiter not about their gilded domes:
But full of rage (a holy zeal they call)
They mount their asses, order'd from the stall;
And riding to and fro, bespeak their fears —
With hideous tales alarm the peoples ears —
Repeat — enlarge — insist with fervent tone –
Then pray, and move the godlier sex to moan.
    Embolden'd thus they foam and cry amain.
Anon their hearers catch th' impassion'd strain
Then Love departs, and Vengeance arms their breasts
To burn the men that lately were their guests.
The social throng desert the festive board,
And Friendship's altar, where they erst ador'd.
The voice unkind; the brow begirt with storm;
The eye that scowls, reveal the bigot's form. —
Thus, Buzzell, vilest, hugest of thy clan! —
And Pond, too vile that we should call thee man! —
Thus Rouney, Roulstone — all ye brood of hell! —
Thus were ye fir'd by Beecher's magic spell!

Ursuline Report of the Burning of the Convent, August 11, 1834

Source: "Ursuline Report of the Burning of the Convent, August 11, 1834," Anti-Catholic Documents Collection, 1844–1930, Archives and Manuscripts, John J. Burns Library, Boston College.

The Ursulines of Boston (1817–1834) with all thy faults, I love thee still." Such were the merciful words of forgiveness which our dear mother, S. Joseph sent to that city, the cradle of her religious childhood, the first scene of her apostolic zeal and the continual object of her wishes and prayers during her life. The dying look of this ardent soul, saw doubtlessly again at this supreme moment, the painful scene.

In this moment they are all in the holy communion and from the mouth of Mary Magdalene O'Keefe of Saint Joseph we hear the heart-rending detail of the destruction of Mount Benedict. She begins her story with the words of this chapter and her voice choked with tears cries out: "Boston with all thy faults I love thee still!" Let us also listen to this story by an eyewitness.

The Fire

The moon in its first quarter gave on that evening little light, for moments it was even completely hidden behind thick clouds and it was, thanks to this partial darkness that I awakened by my Superior, could see some sinister figures hiding here and there behind the trees of the avenue.

"I see a man," said our Rev Mother to me. "I see five, I see ten," I answered her. Let all the nuns be aroused and let them dress without lights added she. The alarm was given by our dear sister Saint Ursula, who was watching a young sick sister. Cries of "Down with the pope! Down with the bishop! Down with the convent!" were distinctively heard in the street. At the same time the rioters tried to break down the iron door which closed the avenue. We had hardly had time to put on our nuns' clothes, when a furious populace spurred on by Dr. Lyman Beecher and the Protestant ministers of Boston and Charlestown had opened a way and invaded the gardens. The Mother Superior thought it prudent to make the pupils rise. Sister Saint Augustine undertook to do this. She went quietly into the dormitory which was lighted only by a light placed in the hall. And without telling them the reason, she awakened them in silence and made them dress and hid them by a distant wing which led into the garden yard where she hoped the cries of the rioters would not penetrate. Who can tell the anguish of this good sister from eleven o'clock till midnight, an hour of anxious waiting when she had in her care the hope of so many families. None of her 80 pupils went from the spot.

During this time the worthy Puritans did their work, throwing stones into the windows and although the riot made only slow progress, it was evident that if any resistance were offered the wicked designs of this cruel populace would succeed and in a few hours our dear Mt. Benedict would become the [fury] of flames.

...

Half an hour had hardly passed since we had hidden in th[e] tower, when some people knocked at the rail post of the enclosure which separated the garden where we where from the orchard. None of us answered, we even held our breath for fear of being discovered by the rioters. But soon friendly voices were heard. Mr. Carer our nearest neighbor and some well-meaning persons seeing the uselessness of their efforts to oppose the fury of the populace, who was determined burn the convent at any risk, had escaped the crowd and offered to take us to a safe place. Whilst these worthy people were endeavoring to make an opening in the enclosure which although of wood, was high and strong by made, some gentlemen had climbed on the top, took our pupils one by one and put them down on the other side, at the same time others had succeeded in breaking off some boards and the nuns could thus join their pupils.

Our place of refuge was the house of Mr. Adams on Winter Hill. He hesitated a little to receive us, fearing to attract the fury of the multitude to his property, as they were vociferating against religion and convents. These people however did not wish to take our lives, for when I went to help Sister Saint Augustine, I heard some of the rioters, who were talking together say: "Are you quite sure, that no one else is there?" They had only plotted against the life of the bishop. In order to make success the more sure they had recourse to the following stratagem: A carriage was sent for him, the coachmen took to him a message from the Mother Superior informing him of what was happening at Mount Benedict and asking him to come to that place, to prevent the destruction of the convent. But this holy bishop inspired by God or suspecting their dark plans refused to go, saying: What can one single man do during the following night they attempted to set fire to the cathedral, and it is due only to the vigilance of an Irish guard that the temple was preserved from the flames. Our hosts consented finally to receive us and we were very well treated. Mrs. Adams opened the door of her drawing room to us, where there was a sofa and some chairs. Our dear little girls sat down on the floor, where they soon fell asleep their heads resting on the knees of the ones who had a seat.

We had been about an hour under the roof of the Adams', when we saw that gentleman at the door of the drawing room. "My ladies, if some of you wish to throw a look on your convent, follow me." The Mother Superior and all the sisters, with the exception of the sick one and sister Saint Augustine, went to the upper story. The convent was already enveloped in a mass of flames. Ten minutes later we were again assembled in the drawing room, where we knelt down to repeat the Psalm: "Laudate Dominium, ommes gentes" then there was a sad silence, our hearts were sad, but our souls were submissive and resigned. Our pupils left us one by one, as the parents were informed of what had taken place. Seven or eight at most were with us, when the bishop sent some priests and carriages to take us under the hospitable roof of the good sisters of charity. When Monsignor saw us, he offered us our house in Boston, which he had bought but on which he had as yet made only one payment. Our poor Superior answered him: "Monsignor, where will you and your priests go?" "We shall board with Mr. Murphy." Mr. Murphy was a very respectable gentleman, who lived opposite the episcopal palace. We all answered him with one voice "It is better, Monsignor, that we should go and find some shelter than to disturb you and your priests." During two months our worthy bishop and the dear sisters of charity did all in their power to make our sad position easier.

But I return to some facts sadder than any I have told you. They defiled our mortuary chapel and the tombs where our dead sisters slept their last sleep, they threw the ashes of the nuns to the winds and went in their blind fury so far as to draw the teeth of some of the corpses. Then what made our hearts still more sad and is still more difficult to tell, the incendiaries had discovered the hidden tabernacle, the holy elements were profaned. But the perpetrator of the crime felt soon the effect of divine vengeance when he arrived at his home, he committed suicide by cutting his throat. His wife, terrified by this deed and by some secret power kept from touching the consecrated wafers which she found in his pocket, sent at once for the pastor of Charlestown, to whom she said: "In my husband's pocket there are some wafers, which I am afraid to touch." The minister of God understood at once and with respect took out the sacred elements.

Our souls, still much moved at the remembrance of this disastrous scene, are full of gratitude towards the generous benefactors who have come to our aid. On the Monday after this dreadful scene many ladies of Boston and Charlestown without distinction of nationality or creed offered us clothes, furniture, etc. Messrs Chickering came to offer us musical instruments on credit without limit.

Our mothers in Quebec sent to us valises with clothes and offered us at the same time a shelter under their protecting roof. Those in New Orleans did the same and added to this invitation the sum of $300.00. From the S. Sulpicians in Montreal we received a complete service for the altar. This token of generosity made us feel the benefit of our holy religion.

Our dear sick sister, the little novice Saint Henry died at Brinkley place, whither we had gone after a two months' stay with the sisters of charity. Dr. Thompson, a skillful physician who was always very devoted to us, was with her at her deathbed. Some moments before her death, the young dying girl asked to be carried to the window, to see for the last time the "ruins of Mount Benedict."

Oh my beloved sisters added the interesting narrator I have not been able to recall these scenes without emotion, my heart is full and I have only strength to add: My God pardon us our trespasses as we pardon those unfortunate fanatics.

DOCUMENT 4

Letter to the School Board (1842), Bishop Francis Kenrick

Source: Francis Patrick Kenrick, Edmund F. Prendergast, *Diary and Visitation Record of the Rt. Rev. Francis Patrick Kenrick, Administrator and Bishop of Philadelphia 1830–1851, Later, Archbishop of Baltimore* (Lancaster: Wickersham Print Company, 1916), 293-295.

To the Board of Comptrollers of Public Schools in the city and county of Philadelphia.

Gentlemen: Sympathy for a respectable lady who has been deprived for many months past of her only means of support for following the dictates of her conscience, and a solemn sense of duty to the Catholic community, whose religious interests are entrusted to my guardianship, prompt me to submit respectfully to your consideration the conscientious objections of Catholics to the actual regulations of the Public Schools.

Among them I am informed one is that the teachers shall read and cause to be read, The Bible; by which is understood the version published by command of King James. To this regulation we are forced to object, inasmuch as Catholic children are thus led to view as authoritive a version which is rejected by the Church. It is not expected that I should sate in detail the reason of this rejection. I shall only say that several books of Divine Scripture are wanting in that version and that the meaning of the original text is not faithfully expressed. It is not incumbent on us to prove either position, since we do not ask you to adopt the Catholic version for general use; but we feel warranted in claiming that our conscientious scruples to recognize or use the other, be respected. In Baltimore the Directors of the Public Schools have thought it their duty to provide Catholic children with the Catholic version. Is it too much for us to expect the same measure of justice?

The consciences of Catholics are also embarrassed by the mode of opening and closing the School exercises which, I understand, is by the singing of some hymn, or by prayer. It is not consistent with the laws and discipline of the Catholic Church for her members to unite in religious exercises with who are not of her communion. We offer up prayers and supplications to God for all men; we embrace all in the sincerity of Christian affection; but we confine the marks of religious brotherhood to those who are of the household of the faith. Under the influence of this conscientious scruple, we ask that the Catholic children be not required to join in the singing of hymns or other religious exercises.

I have been assured that several of the books used in the public schools, and still more those contained in the libraries attached to them, contain misrepresentations of our tenets and statement to our prejudice, equally groundless and injurious. It is but just to expect that the books used in the schools shall contain no offensive matter, and that books decidedly hostile to our faith shall not under any pretext be placed in the hands of Catholic children.

The School law, which provides that "the religious predilections of the parents shall be respected," was evidently framed in the spirit of our Constitution, which holds the rights of conscience to be inviolable. Public education should be conducted on principles which will afford its advantages to all classes of the community, without detriment to their conscientious convictions. Religious liberty must be especially guarded in children, who, of themselves, are unable to guard against the wiles or assaults of others. I appeal then, Gentlemen, with confidence to your justice that the regulations of the Schools may be modified so as to give to Catholic pupils and teachers, equal rights, without wounding tender consciences.

For my interpretation in this matter, besides the responsibility of my station, I have specially to plead the assurance I have received from a respectable source, that some desire had been expressed to know distinctly from me, what modification Catholics desire in the School system. It was also suggested that an appeal of this kind would receive every just consideration from the Board; and would anticipate effectually the danger of public excitement on a point on which the community is justly sensitive, the sacred rights of conscience.

With great respect, I remain, gentlemen,

Your obedient servant,

Francis Patrick, Bp. Phila

Phila.

Nov. 14, 1842.

DOCUMENT 5

Constitution and Address of the Board of Managers of the American Protestant Association (1842)

Source: "Address of the Board of Managers of the American Protestant Association With the Constitution and Organization of the Association" (Philadelphia: APA, 1843): 1–14, American Protestant Association of Pennsylvania Records, 1842–1843 Record Group 323, Microfilmed Archives, Presbyterian Historical Society, Philadelphia, Pennsylvania.

Constitution Whereas, we believe the system of Popery to be, in its principles and tendency, subversive of civil and religious liberty, and destructive to the spiritual welfare of men, we unite for the purpose of defending our Protestant interests against the great exertions now making to propagate that system in the United States, and adopt the following constitution: —

Article I. This society shall be called the American Protestant Association.

Article II. The objects of its formation, and for the attainment of which its efforts shall be directed, are —

1. The union and encouragement of Protestant ministers of the gospel, to give to their several congregations instruction on the differences between Protestantism and Popery.
2. To call attention to the necessity of a more extensive distribution, and through the study of the Holy Scriptures.
3. The circulation of books and tracts adapted to give information on the various errors of Popery in their history, tendency, and design.
4. To awaken the attention of the community to the dangers which threaten the liberties, and the public and domestic institutions of these United States from the assaults of Romanism.

Article III. This Association shall be composed of all such persons as agree in adopting the purposes and principles of this constitution, and contribute to the funds which it supported.

Article IV. The officers of the Association shall be a President, three Vice Presidents, a treasurer, a corresponding secretary, a recording secretary, and two lay directors form each denomination represented in the Association, to be elected annually; together with all the ministers belonging to it, who shall form a Board for the transaction of business, of whom any seven, at a meeting duly convened, shall be a quorum. The stated meetings of the Board to be quarterly.

Article V. The Board of Managers shall, at the first meeting after their election appoint an exec committee, consisting of a minister and a layman from each of the denominations represented in the association, of which the secretaries and treasurer shall be ex-officio members. This committee to meet as often as they may find necessary for the transaction of the business committed to them, and to report quarterly to the Board of managers. Article VI. The duties of the Board shall be, to carry out, in every way most expedient in their view, the ends and purposes for which this Association is organized; and to aid and encourage the formation of similar associations in the various parts of the United States; and to render an annual report of their proceedings to the Association, at their annual meeting on the second Tuesday in November.

Article VII. The Board of managers shall have power to enact such by-laws as may not be inconsistent with this constitution, and to fill all vacancies that may occur between the annual meetings.

Article VIII. This constitution shall be subject to amendments only at the annual meetings of the Association, by a vote of two thirds of the members present at such meeting.

The Board of Managers of the American Protestant Association deem it proper, in submitting their constitution to the consideration of their fellow citizens, to lay before them a brief exposition of the reasons which have led to this organization and of the principles on which it is to be conducted. These will be partially understood by a reference to the objects for which the Association has been formed, as set forth in the Second Article of the Constitution ... It will be seen from this article, that the Association we represent, has grown out of a conviction that our civil and religious institutions are exposed to serious danger from the secret and open assaults of Popery. We are aware that, in avowing this conviction, we may find little or no sympathy among a portion of our Protestant population. The great numerical disparity between Protestants and Romanists in our country, and the general intelligence of our citizens, furnish us, in their view, with an adequate defense against all exertions that may be made to propagate the errors of Popery in the United States. It is the prevalence of this feeling, or rather this want of feeling, among Protestants, which chiefly excites our apprehensions. We too believe that the Popery of this country is as yet a perfectly manageable thing. We should think as meanly of Protestantism as the Roman Catholics themselves do, if we questioned the plenary ability of the Protestants of this Union by moral means alone, (for all other means, in such a controversy, we abhor,) to keep Popery within narrow limits and counteract its pernicious influences. But while misapprehension, apathy, and false sympathy prevail to so great an extent among Protestants, we are free to confess that, we look with deep solicitude upon the extraordinary efforts now making by the Papal Hierarchy to obtain a firm footing in this country.

DOCUMENT 6

Our Vignette (1844), Harriet Probasco

Source: "Our Vignette," *The American Woman*, ed. Harriet Probasco (Philadelphia: September 7, 1844).

Never has there been a time since the days of the Revolution of our country, when women were so generally springing into motion, and when they were so justifiable in interposing their influence in the affairs of the government of the nation, as at the present crisis; and if the question be asked why women are so deeply interested in the present struggle, we answer because our dearest rights have been assailed by a foreign power. That the rights of the BIBLE, and of children, are particularly dear to women (especially to mothers) is acknowledged by all.

It is now no longer a matter of opinion or conjecture, what the Romanists are aiming at in our land.

The suppression of the Bible, and death to liberty of conscience is their open and avowed object (as seen in the Pope's Edict, dated at Rome, on the 8th of May last,) and if the BIBLE should be suppressed and liberty of conscience destroyed, then farewell to political liberty, for the walls of our glorious Republic would be thrown down, and the foot of Roman power be set upon the necks of our sons, and our daughters become subject to the control of the Papal priests. And shall women sit still and quietly contemplate these movements and not make an effort to arrest them? I hear the answer from a million voices, no! We will unite all our energies and efforts to repel all such interference with our rights. Let us be doubly diligent in pouring light and instruction into the mind of the rising generation; and let us strengthen the hands and encourage the hearts of our husbands, fathers and brothers, in establishing true American principles. In the name of the Lord, we bid them God speed. But our province is more especially to lay the foundation of love of country, of God, and his written word, in the hearts of the young. Let us do our work well. It is here the Pope fears the influence of woman. He knows that the son of a patriotic Christian mother will not easily become a slave to any power, for that reason he fears the Bible in the hands of "loquacious women," and well he may fear. If he really believes, as he asserts in his edict, that the "Virgin Mary has power to destroy all the heretics of the universe"—if he thinks that one Christian woman has such unlimited power, even after death, no wonder he should fear a whole nation of *living* Christian women, with the open Bible in their hands, teaching the young to fear God and keep his commandments. But we are not frightened at the announcement of any such power in the hand of a departed saint.

His information has come to the wrong country. It might do for Italy or Ireland, but not for America. The glorious light of the Gospel shines too strong for any such dogma to be palmed upon us.

We read in the good book, that all power in "Heaven and upon earth, was given into the hands of our Lord Jesus Christ," and *that* we believe, and *that* power we fear, and *that* doctrine we will teach our children, and strive to disseminate as far as our influence extends. We would then, call upon the women to speak on this subject, for no women in our land have such reason to express their sentiments as we of Philadelphia. We have had the sleepless nights and sorrowful days. We have heard the roar of the cannon, and the clashing of firearms. We have seen the dead and the mangled bodies of innocent citizens, brought to an untimely end by Romish power and policy. We have seen the lonely widow, who heart was overcharged with sorrow too big for utterance, in her helpless and dependent condition, with her orphans leaning upon her, and tears rolling down the cheek, as we talked of the father slain; and we have seen the aged and widowed mother bemourning the loss of her son—her support—the stay and the staff of her old age.

And are not these scenes sufficient to justify us in speaking out freely? We think they are. Let us, therefore, read and pray, and instruct and write, and trust in Him for success, "Who holds the wind in his fists, and who hath measured the waters in the hollow of his hand, and meted out Heaven with a span, and comprehended the dust of the earth in a measure, and weighed the mountains in scales, and the hills in a balance." It is He that "giveth power to the faint, and to them that have no might, he increaseth strength." These promises are sure, and are firmly believed by an AMERICAN WOMAN.

The Pope's Stratagem: Rome To America! (1852), John Weishampel

Source: Weishampel, John, "The Pope's Stratagem: Rome To America! An Address to the Protestants of the United States, Against Placing the Pope's Block of Marble in the Washington Monument" (Baltimore: John Weishampel, 1852), Historical Society Of Pennsylvania, Philadelphia, Pennsylvania.

Fellow Countrymen:

Permit me, an humble citizen of one of these United States, to call your attention to a subject that, as far as I have been able to learn, has failed to elicit the investigation of the Pulpit or the Press, and that to me appears to be one of no ordinary import, as touching the future destiny of our Country. It behooves us, as friends of that Country, to watch, with a jealous eye, every effort that is made by the enemies of it free institutions, under whatever pretence, to subvert its government and destroy its liberties. I have reference to the proffer, by the *Pope of Rome, of a block of marble for the Washington National Monument*, now in course of erection at the City of Washington, the Capital of the United States, which is intended to bear the intended to bear the inscription: "Rome to America." This proffer should wake up in every Protestant the spirit of inquiry as to the probable motives that actuate the Pope, and the object he may have in view. And let me seriously ask you, in the face of the history of Popery, *Is there no cause to induce suspicion and alarm?* Let us look into the matter.

The first thing that claims our attention, is the inscription upon the block: "*Rome to America.*" Is this inscription appropriate? What, I ask, is the design of erecting the Monument? I understand it to be, to perpetuate the memory of the illustrious and immortal Washington, and to transmit to posterity a worthy memorial of the high honor which the American people have always conferred upon him, as a pure patriot, a good man, and (as he is justly termed) the "father of his Country" — the deliverer, under God, of his Country from the galling yoke of foreign bondage and oppression. And this Monument is to be *American* — erected by the American people — a *National* and not a Universal memorial. But how does the inscription "Rome to America" correspond to this group? In the first place, it is a *foreign* contribution, thrust upon us without an invitation or precedent; and secondly, with an appropriate inscription. "Rome *to* America." Is it not the language of greeting from the one Country to the other? And does our Country require such a greeting from the Pope that an amicable relation be continued? Or does America need such a token of pretended respect from Rome — the Roman Power? No! Then the inscription is not appropriate; and therefore the block has no claim to a place in the Monument.

The inscription is now "Rome to America." Suppose we ask whether the Pope designs that it shall ever be altered to Rome in America. It is feared by many that the Papal throne will be removed to America. Indeed there was much talk of it in 1849. If it ever be located here, those significant words will be referred to, by his adherents, as an inspired prophecy of the change of location of that holy Power! Then the Monument would cease to be a Washington memorial — it would be converted into a trophy of Roman Papal victory — a pillar of triumph of *Rome in America*. For it is a fact that our Country is being every year more densely populated by the Pope's zealous followers, and his menials: and when we take into consideration that the Roman Power moves with deliberation, and looks far ahead, making calculations upon successes hundreds of years hence, and that it spares no means, nor "leaves *one stone* unturned" to accomplish its despotic designs, we have sufficient reasons to scan its apparent friendly approaches and guard against its encroachments in every shape and form. — We have already one Cardinal, a foreigner, a man who would, unquestionably, betray our Country into the hands of the holy *Papa*, if it were in his power to do so; soon we will have more; for his subjects are increasingly here so rapidly that it will be graciously granted as a measure of *justice* to *America*! To have a greater representation in the holy conclave in Rome! Next we may hear of his Holiness flying (under false pretense) "*to* America" for safety; and ultimately he may modestly erect his heaven-on-earth throne in Father Mathew's Cathedral in Washington, near by the base of the Monument bearing the predictive inscription "Rome *to* America." Query. Had Father Mathew an eye to that when traveling through the U. States, often in great *poverty*! Who received many gifts of charity to relieve his embarrassed situation, but who in the end was rich enough to buy the lot at a tremendous price and present it for the great Cathedral to be erected upon it?

When the great holy Potentate
Removes from Rome in royal state,
And "to America" shall come,
Where else but here will then be Rome?

So far as I have learned no other foreign power has made any similar proffer, and the likelihood is that none will, for the very good reason that the Monument is an *American* affair altogether. Especially do I suppose that none of the Emperors, Kings or Queens of other despotic or even limited monarchies will offer to do so, from the additional reason that it would be inconsistent with their character, and thus perhaps detrimental to their existing dignity at home. Their system of government is despotic, absolute, or, at best, anti-republican; ours is republican and democratic; they all, more or less, play the lord over the people, while here the people are their own lords; they curtail the people's liberties wherever they can, while our magnanimous Washington fought to *give the people liberty*; and when he had it in his power to play the game of Bonaparte's and other usurpers, he proved himself the people's true friend, by not only filling the office of President with a father's care, and with honor to his Country and himself, but by laying down precepts and examples for the future welfare of the new Republic, over which he was he first man that was called to preside — and among those precepts and examples were these: To beware of foreign influence, not to meddle with the affairs of other nations, and not to have any man serve more than two terms in the presidential chair. Their positions are so vastly different to these principles, that the thought does not probably occur to them to send blocks of stone for the Monument.

Such a man — although the monarchs of the world must do him the justice to admit his greatness and goodness — such a man they cannot so signally and perpetually honor (with *consistency*) as to place blocks of stone in the Monument, which is designed to stand to the end of time for the admiration of the people of all the nations under the sun — which shall be to our future generations the rainbow token of salvation from foreign bondage. No, they offer no such hypocritical offerings. But the subtle Pope — he passes over this inconsistency, and, as though the world were blind to it, offers to place one there. But he adopts an inscription that shall not convict him of duplicity, and one that shall for the present appear as a gracious token of friendship from "Rome to America." It says nothing of Washington — nothing of liberty — nothing of human rights. And our Monument Committee, like a certain kind of fish, that catches at any thing red, even if it be a bit of flannel on a hook, accept the proffer in great haste, and return thanks to this "god on earth" for his condescending consideration — for his hypocritical contribution. I consider that they had no right to accept it until the people had an opportunity to express their opinion upon the subject. I repeat again, that it is an *American* National Monument, and we should be jealous as to who shall be permitted to place blocks in its structure; and no despots ought to be allowed to do so under any pretence whatever.

Now let it be understood, that I am not opposing the Roman Catholic Church, but the *Politico-Religious policy of the Roman Power.* I have no objections to any church, as such, or all Protestant churches together, or Catholic and Protestant churches conjointly, in out whole country, contributing blocks or one general block of marble for this Monument. Indeed, I think it would be in good keeping with the Christian character we desire to maintain as a Nation, if they did so. Might they not all, or singly, with great propriety, furnish a block, with the inscription "To God be all the glory!" to be placed above all those bearing inscriptions? This would not detract one iota of honor from Washington. On the contrary, it would throw around his immortal name the hallowed glory of the Christian religion, in the faith of which he lived and died. We as a people believe that God raised up our Washington to lead us out of bondage, and we look to that God with gratitude, and thank him for all his good providence, by which we have been made and preserved a free and happy nation. It becomes us, but especially the people professing to be worshippers of that God, to say, in the language of the devout David of old: "Not unto us, O Lord! Not unto us, but unto Thy name give glory for they mercy's sake."

Yes, fellow citizens, I desire to oppose the approaches, under the garb of friendship, of a power that will, when it gains the designed and desired ascendancy, burn our Bibles, bind our consciences, make slaves of us, and put us to the stake, the rack, or the dungeon, for attempting to exercise the free minds which a gracious Creator has gifted us. It is true, we may not live to suffer these things; but our descendants, not many generations hence, may have cause to lament the supineness and imprudence of their too-easily duped ancestors. If I should succeed in arousing you to the consideration of this subject, and cause you to save the country from the insult referred to, I shall feel that I have done the cherished land of my birth a noble service, upon which my descendants may look with pride.

The effects of this block, if placed in the Monument, will be a mortification to nearly every American Protestant who looks upon it; and its influence upon the zealous supporters of the *Roman* hierarchy will be tremendous — especially with foreigners. They will look through it *at the Pope,* and not at Washington. I fancy I see a foreign papist winding his way up the quadrangular stairs, and he passes the hundreds of inscriptions with but little emotion; but suddenly his eyes rest upon "Rome to America."

Instantly he makes the sign of the cross, bows, and perhaps, exclaims, "Holy mother! Here is the blessed gift of his Holiness!" When he descends he will remember that inscription, though he should forget all the rest, and he will remember it for life, and ever communicate to his children and others, that the holy Pope has honored Washington with a sacred block of marble, taken from the ancient Temple of Peace at Rome. And upon that assumed fact will they base the erroneous presumption, that the Roman Power (dwelling in the Pope) is generous, liberal and friendly to human freedom and human rights. This will forever shut the ears of all the American descendants of the papist against every argument and fact relative to the despotism and tyranny of the Roman Power, and blind their eyes, so as to prevent them from seeing any danger — danger of losing *American liberty* and *human rights* —such liberty and rights as no country ever enjoys when the Papal influence sways it.

What is to be done? What can be done in this matter? Can we prevent the reception and placing the block in the sacred walls of the Monument? Perhaps not: seeing that the Committee have accepted the proffer. But we can enter our solemn protest against it. Let the Protestants everywhere in the whole land hold meetings against that measure; and if that will not induce the Committee to recall their acceptance, then let a *protest* block be furnished by us to be placed by the side of the objectionable stone, bearing an inscription by which all men may see that we are awake to the hypocrisy and schemes of that designing, crafty, subtle, far-seeing and far-reaching power, which is ever grasping after the whole World, to sway its iron sceptre, with blood-stained hands, over the millions of its inhabitants.

Will the Monument Committee heed such a protest? I am fully persuaded they would sooner incur the displeasure of the Pope, by recalling their letter, than that of a great majority of their fellow countrymen, by placing the objectionable stone in the building — which has justice for its foundation, freedom for its crowning stone, and human happiness for its glory. No, they will not, they dare not so insult the American people. I repeat, let the American Catholics put in a block of stone as a church testimonial, if they choose, and so every other church; but O keep the foreign influence, especially of avowed deadly enemies to human rights, and above all, the Roman Power, from desecrating that pure pillar, so sacredly dedicated to the memory of the good and great Washington! The friend of human rights, and the foe to despotism and tyranny! Fellow countrymen, in the name of all that you hold dear in this world, let its high-towering column not be blemished by a foreign, despotic, and tyrannical hypocrite's hand, or a hypocrite's gift!

Philadelphia, near Independence Hall
Washington's Birthday, Feb. 22, 1852.

Let every true friend to our common country aid in speedily circulating this warning throughout the land, that all may be roused before the Pope shall have placed his block in the Freedom Monument. Be wide awake! — Watch!

DOCUMENT 8

The Pope's Stone (1933), T.E. Kissling

Source: T.E. Kissling, "The Pope's Stone," *Columbia* (Washington, DC: February 1933), Special Collections, Martin Luther King Jr. Library, Washington, DC.

The most outstanding celebration of modern times — the George Washington Bicentennial — is now officially ended. Time will soon bedim the memory of the events of the commemorative year. Fortunately the history of the many tributes in honor of the Father of His Country has been preserved for posterity by the Congressional commission in charge of the observance. Search the voluminous literature of the celebration, however, and you will fail to find mention of the unique memorial in honor of General Washington contributed by His Holiness, Pope Pius IX. This gift, — of a block of marble, — was offered by the Pope in behalf of the Roman Government, of which he was then its temporal head. It was sent in response to the general invitation of the Washington National Monument Society, then in charge of its erection in the Capital City. In fact, it is the only memorial stone contributed by a foreign nation to the obelisk, which is not in the walls of the monument today. The offer of the stone and the incident of its disappearance, just seventy-nine years ago are little known today. Indeed, a complete chronicle of the affair has not hitherto appeared in print.

The first news that His Holiness intended to send a memorial stone came through the United States Legation at Rome. In a letter, dated December 24, 1851, addressed to the Secretary of the National Monument Society, Washington, Lewis Cass, Jr., at the time our Charge d'Affaires at Rome, wrote:

"I have the honor to inform you that I have been apprized by His Holiness the Pope, through Cardinal Antonelli, the Secretary of State of the Roman Government, of his intention to contribute a block of marble toward the erection of the national monument to the memory of Washington. The block was taken from the ruins of the ancient Temple of Peace, and is to receive the inscription of 'Rome to America.' As soon as the work is completed, the necessary measures will be taken to forward it to you."

This letter, quoted in full above was duly laid before the Board of Managers of the Monument Society and pursuant to their instructions, the secretary, George Watterston, wrote to Mr. Cass, under date of February 4, 1852, requesting him:

"... to tender their thanks to His Holiness for his very acceptable contribution, and to inform him that it shall be placed in a conspicuous position in the monument."

The Board of Managers ordered that this correspondence be released to the press. The complete text of the two letters appears in the *Washington Daily National Intelligencer*, February 6, 1852. Other papers throughout the country gave publicity to the proposed gift. About this time, early 1852, the first edition of Dr. Nahum Capen's "History of Democracy in the United States" was published. The letters relating to the "Pope's stone" were appended to the volume, prefaced by the comment:

What a sublime democracy does the following correspondence indicate! The ruins of an Empire to perpetuate the glory of a Republic, and a voluntary tribute of the Supreme Pontiff to aid in rearing a monument in honor of the achievements of the people!"

Although a similar offer from the Swiss Government had been made a short time previous to the one from Rome, the latter received an unusual amount of publicity and discussion, — and for reasons that were soon apparent. It was that period of our national history when the self-styled "Know-Nothing Party" endeavored to gain ascendancy in American Politics. This party openly professed sentiments hostile to aliens and particularly to the Roman Catholic Church. Indeed, it was not long before certain members of that party found something sinister in the Pope's gift.

Two weeks following the publication of the Cass correspondence there appeared a widely circulated penny pamphlet of eight pages, entitled: "The Pope's Stratagem: 'Rome to America'—An Address to the Protestants of the United States Against Placing the Pope's Block of Marble in the Washington Monument. Containing also important Suggestions to both the Roman Catholic and Protestant Churches in our Country, relative to the monument. — by John Weishampel, Sr., of Baltimore, Md." The address was dated, "Philadelphia, *near Independence Hall*, Washington's Birth-day, Feb. 22, 1852."

In the appeal to his "Fellow Countrymen," Mr. Weishampel vehemently denounced the Board of Managers of the Monument Society for their acceptance of the proffer of the Pope. The main objections were that the stone was "a *foreign* contribution thrust upon us without invitation or a precedent"; that "the Monument is to be *American* — erected by the American people — a *National* and not a Universal memorial ..."; that the inappropriate inscription said "nothing of Washington — nothing of liberty — nothing of human rights"; and that, indeed, the Pope's "gracious token of friendship" might be a part of a plot to "erect his heaven-on-earth throne in Father Mathew's Cathedral in Washington, near by the base of the Monument." (The reference is to the old St. Mathew's Church, formerly located on the northeast corner of H and 15th Streets.)

The address concluded with recommendations that protest meetings be held, and that if the acceptance of the Pope's offer was not recalled, then a "*protest* block," bearing a suitable inscription, should be placed by the side of the objectionable stone. The first protest meeting was held, March 8, 1852, "in old Southwark," Philadelphia. Several other meetings followed in that city and in New York, Boston, Baltimore, in New Jersey and elsewhere. Editorials from a portion of the daily press, many long petitions, resolutions and protest letters came to the attention of the Board of managers of the Monument Society, from "an insulted and indignant people."

A forceful rebuke to Mr. Weishampel was soon broadcast from Washington, under date of May 7, 1852, and signed, "A Protestant and a Member." (A copy of the same is inserted in the Library of Congress copy of the eighth edition of the Weishampel pamphlet.) Among other facts, the defender of the Monument Society revealed that all of the members of the Board of Managers were Protestants, except one; that the American people were slow to contribute to the Monument fund; that the society had accepted a stone offered by the Swiss Government, and that other "foreign powers" desired to contribute. In fact, the Monument today contains stones contributed by the governments of Switzerland, Turkey, Bremen, Japan, China, Greece, Wales, Brazil and Siam. But the block of marble from Rome did not find its place in the memorial shaft, and herewith lies an unfortunate chapter in the history of the monument.

Although the Monument Society did not recall its acceptance of the Roman stone,

expressed in its letter of February 4, 1852, — it was not until a year and a half later, when the storm of protest had somewhat abated, that the block of marble actually began its journey from Rome. It arrived in New York, the last week of September, 1853. The *Washington Daily Evening Star*, of November 4, 1853, briefly reports the arrival, in the Capitol City, of the stone from Rome, and a block of lava from Mount Vesuvius, the latter bearing the donor's inscription, "Wm Terrill, Geo." The tribute from the government of Rome was described as a block of African marble of beautiful texture; length, three feet; height, eighteen inches; and thickness, ten inches. It originally stood in the Temple of Concord, at Rome. The inscription *Rome to America*," appeared on its face upon arrival here.

That the stone would never find its place in the National Monument in memory of George Washington was certainly not in the minds of the parishioners of St. Patrick's, St. Mathew's, and St. Mary's churches in Washington, when they so generously contributed to the Monument Society fund, at their Thanksgiving Day services in 1853. Though the Catholic church at nearby Rockville, Maryland, had been desecrated and other acts of violence committed against Catholic church property in other parts of the country, during the Know-Nothing excitement, apparently no direct threat against the "Pope's Stone" was made in these anti-Catholic demonstrations.

In the meantime however, the newly appointed Apostolic Nuncio to Brazil, Monsignor Cajetan Bedini, titular Archbishop of Thebes, arrived in Washington, in July, 1853, commissioned by the Holy Father to examine the state of ecclesiastical affairs in the United States, and to present a letter to the President, who received him with great courtesy. This letter conveyed the desire of the Head of the Roman Government "to maintain and cherish the existing friendly relations between that country and the United States" — sentiments reciprocated by President Peirce in his interview with the Pope's messenger. (The United States maintained diplomatic relations with the Papal States from 1848 to 1863.)

For six months, Monsignor Bedini visited throughout the United States, returning to Washington in January, 1854, soon after the apostate priest, Father Gavazzi, had appeared there and rendered an anti-Catholic lecture, in which he denounced the Nuncio. Upon the departure of the Archbishop from this country, the Hon. William L. Marcy, Secretary of State, communicated with our agent in Rome, under date of January 30, 1854, in part, as follows:

"Though he (Bedini) was here received (in Washington) with all the respect and consideration due to his person and the occasion, it is a matter of sincere regret that in other places he has since visited he has been subjected to annoyances, on the part of a few individuals, which have been discountenanced by the Government and very generally reprobated by our citizens."

Mr. Cass was instructed to express the regret of the President, "... that any part of the people should have forgotten in moments of excitement what was due to a distinguished functionary charged with a friendly mission from a foreign power with which this country has hitherto maintained, and is still desirous of maintaining, amicable relations." (Dept. of State Archives, *Instructions to Lewis Cass, Jr., 1849–61*, No. 25.)

This message was conveyed by Mr. Cass to the Minister of Foreign Affairs, at Rome, and was duly acknowledged by Cardinal Giacomo Antonelli, Secretary of State, under date of February 27, 1854. The reply was received in Washington on April sixth.

Meanwhile, an act occurred in the Federal City which created considerably indignation and excitement and was the subject of much public discussion. The block of marble contributed by the Roman Government, through His Holiness, Pope Pius IX, disappeared from the Monument Grounds, early Monday morning, March 6, 1854.

The first mention of this act of "outrageous vandalism" appeared in the afternoon *Star,* of March 6. At a meeting held on Tuesday, March 7, a resolution was passed by the Board of Managers of the Monument Society offering a reward of $100 for the apprehension of the perpetrators of the deed. A full investigation of the affair was immediately launched by the Building Committee, and their findings were released to the press. A perusal of the contemporary accounts reveals the following facts.

Some time between one and two o'clock on the morning of March 6, 1854, a group of men, estimated from four to ten in number, suddenly surrounded the night watchman in his hut at the Monument Place. A heavy cord was passed around the watch-box, stones were piled against the door, and papers were pasted over the windows. After thus imprisoning the watchman, and threatening him, the intruders went to the lapidarium near by on the premises. Forcing an entrance into the shed, they found the block of marble from Rome, stored by the side of the one from Deseret (Utah), the latter inscribed, "Holiness to the Lord."

Placing the block on a hand-cart, they moved it to the riverside, less than a quarter of a mile off. Here it was pitched down the steep bank, to the beach, where they apparently enjoyed defacing it and attempted to break it up, before taking it in a boat to the middle of the Potomac, where it was jettisoned.

No effective remonstrance was made by the watchman on duty, who was equipped with a double-barreled gun, loaded with buck-shot. In fact, it was not until several hours later that he opened a window of his shed, burnt the rope imprisoning him and crawled out to the ground. His faithful watchdog had been poisoned. It was not till then, four o'clock, that he roused Mr. Hilton, the day watchman, who lived on the premises, and the alarm was given. Suspected of collusion, the night watchman, Mr. John C.

Stewart, was immediately suspended, and a week later he was dismissed for "negligence of duty."

That the block was evidently mutilated beyond recognition, before it was thrown in the water, was the belief of the investigators who found fragments on the banks of the Potomac, the morning after it disappearance. The *Washington Sentinel*, of March 8, 1854, mentioned the "many fragments of this stone at the office of the association in the City Hall." The Sunday following the destruction of the "Pope's stone," souvenir hunters flocked to the scene. As reported in the *Evening Star*, of March 13:

"Great numbers of persons visited the Monument Grounds yesterday, all apparently anxious to obtain information about the shattered block, and looking for pieces of it. Five dollars an inch was offered for pieces of the genuine, and hundreds of persons went to the river shore to gather chips; some were wading in the water, others scratching in the sand in hopes of success."

At a meeting of the Board of Aldermen, Monday evening, March 13, a resolution was passed authorizing a reward for the discovery of the perpetrators of the vandal act. But this order was not concurred in by the Board of Common Council, where the resolution was rejected. On April fifth, the Board of Managers of the Washington National Monument Society unanimously resolved to increase their reward to $500. However, this action proved fruitless.

The Grand Jury, then in session, examined the testimony of two hackmen and other witnesses, and had the case before them for several days. They found nothing of consequence, despite a diligent effort on the part of the public prosecutor. On the first of April, the grand jurors were discharged, having faithfully completed their term of service.

The incident of the disappearance of the "Pope's stone" was characterized by the *Daily National Intelligencer* of Washington on March 8, 1854 as a "deed of barbarism ... which will be considered as belonging rather to some of the centuries considerably in our rear than to the better half of the boasted nineteenth." The *Philadelphia Sun* took a contrary view. But for the most part, the press of the country deplored the "disgraceful affair."

A search, by the writer, of the archives of the Department of State, failed to reveal any mention whatever of the destruction of the stone from Rome. No word of apology or explanation was apparently communicated to the Roman Government such as was dispatched in the Monsignor Bedini episode. The construction of the Monument, at that time, was an entirely private undertaking, and the government evidently chose to let the matter rest with the Monument Society and the authorities of the city of Washington.

In the official "History of the Washington National Monument and the Washington National Monument Society," Mr. Frederick L. Harvey, Secretary, declares:

"The immediate effect of the destruction of the 'Pope's stone' was to anger a large body of the citizens of the country... then, and for a long time afterward, to estrange any interest they had had in the building of the Monument, and to this extent impair the field for the collection of funds for the Monument."

The monument at this time, 1854, had reached a height of 153 feet. For lack of funds, all construction work ceased at this point. In 1876, the government took over the task of completing the memorial shaft, and the capstone was finally set, December 6, 1884. Since the opening of the Monument to the public, in 1888, several memorial stones have been inserted, — the latest being the one from Idaho in 1928. According to the present policy of the Washington National Monument Society, "stones presented by the States and Territories of our Federal Union, or by foreign countries" are still acceptable.

In 1865, a stone from the wall of Servius Tullius was sent to Washington, by the citizens of Rome, in honor of President Abraham Lincoln. This stone reposed here in the crypt of the Capitol, without incident, until 1870, when it was transferred to Springfield, Illinois, to be placed in the Lincoln Memorial there.

On February 22, 1932, the City of Rome dedicated a beautiful thoroughfare, named "Viale Giorgio Washington," in memory of this illustrious American patriot, in the bicentennial year of his birth.

DOCUMENT 9

Letter to Brethren of the American Party (1855)

Source: "Brethren of the American Party," Letter, *Scrapbook,* Textual Records from the Washington National Monument Society, Records of the Office of Public Buildings and Public Parks of the National Capital, 1790–1992, Group 42, National Archives, Washington, DC.

Dear Brethren of the American Party,
For twenty years' past a voluntary association has existed in this city, armed for the purpose of raising funds to erect a monument to Washington. It was founded on the scheme of voluntary contributions among the people of the United States, and such sums as would enable every citizen to contribute towards it. After years of patient waiting, a sufficient amount was accumulated to justify them in adopting a plan and beginning the work. A plan was adopted of a single shaft of white marble, of four equal sides, having a base 55 feet square, and rising to the height of six hundred feet, diminishing gradually from base to top, and to be 33 feet square at the top. The base is to be a pantheon, surrounded by columns and ornamented by statues. The interior of the monument is a square chamber; the walls, fifteen feet in thickness, are composed of the solid blue stone of the Potomac in large masses; faced on the outside with white marble eighteen inches thick, firmly bonded at every course into the blue stone. The corner stone was laid on the 4th of July, 1848. The structure has reached the height of one hundred and seventy feet, at a cost of upward of 230,000 dollars. — And it appears to be firm as the materials of which it is composed.

Last year, the contributions were wholly insufficient to keep up the ordinary progress of the work, and the managers were constrained to apply to Congress for aid. In the course of its construction they had thought it expedient and proper to receive not only contributions in money from every quarter of the globe, but they invited contributions in ornamented stones, to be placed, under the direction of the architect, in the face of the wall of the chamber. Among others, a stone was sent from the Pope of Rome, and was received by the managers, to be placed, as the others, in some conspicuous place.

It was an American monument, and its construction and management was said to be mainly in the hands of Catholics and Foreigners. Complaints were also made of the administration of the association, and of the expenditures and losses in the collection of funds. For these and divers other causes, the Americans of this District resolved in their respective Councils, that this work ought to be, typical of their government, completed by the free act of the People, under the direction and by the hands of the natives. Accordingly, at the election held on the 22nd of February last, they nominated and elected a ticket of their own Order, who now have the control of the work.

It will require at least one million of dollars to complete it as it was originally designed, and that sum must be raised by the Councils of our Order, or we must suffer indelible disgrace and become a bye-word. There are enrolled in the Order, at this time, not less than two millions of freemen. A contribution of fifty cents from each, a sum within the reach of every member, will effect it. There may be some too poor — there cannot be any man too mean or insensible to the obligation upon them — to give this sum. If this shall be so, we have adopted a plan by which that difficulty may be met. For every contribution of one dollar, a certificate of membership is to be issued to the person in whose name the subscription is made. It is therefore proposed that the collections shall be made in each Council, throughout the nation, in such manner as each may deem most expedient, and the money remitted to John M. McCalla, Esq., Treasurer of the National Monument, accompanied by a letter to Chas. C. Tucker, Secretary of the National Monument, stating the amount thus forwarded, and transmitting a list of the names to whom a certificate for each dollar, thus paid in, is to be sent. For each single subscription of five dollars, a handsome engraved plate of the monument, of large size, will be sent.

But Brethren, while the sum of fifty cents for each member of the Order may be hardly sufficient to complete the structure, it will take as much more to finish the work, and the grounds, and leave a surplus to be invested, and yield an interest to keep it in repair, and defray the incidental annual expenses.

We have pledged the American party to this work. We have taken the great step of overthrowing on this pledge, the administration which has preceded us, and which not only failed, but went as beggars to Congress to ask legislative aid for that which loses all merit, unless it be the free-will offering of grateful hearts.

Have we done right?

Brothers, — We come to you to demand your aid in this great work to which we have been appointed, and to which, through us, you are pledged. We do not come alone. Our brethren in the District of Columbia, beneath the walls of the Presidential Mansion, from which a frowning brow is ever turned upon us — these brethren, moved by the sacred fire that ever burns in their hearts, the altars of patriotism, defying the scorn and contumely and lust of those temporarily in power, have come up freely to our aid. They have set to you, the free citizens of free states, with power to remove and bring to account those who dare to turn a wrathful eye on the movements of those native to the soil — to you in every sense Freemen — they have set a bright and glorious example. May you walk by its light. The Councils in this the heart of the nation — yet not one of its members — our Councils have with wondrous unanimity resolved to contribute *one dollar* for each member enrolled in each separate Council. Let it go forth — publish it wherever in this broad land, those born beneath the stars and stripes, the glorious banner of our Union, have met, or shall meet, to resolve that Americans must and shall govern America. — Ring it in the ear of the slothful — breathe it into the heart of the earnest — the native Americans, in Council, in the District of Columbia, have resolved to contribute a dollar for each member toward the completion of the work; and they have already begun their contributions.

Brethren it is a national work. — it is the heaped up offering of a mighty people — it is the work of the age. To it, from every kindred and nation, offerings have been brought — the tribute of far off lands to that name which stands single, alone, mighty, majestic in the history of the world, as though it were written in letters of starry light in the high heavens, to be read by all men. These are but the homage paid to virtue and renown, while the heart is cold, or hostile.

But to you, Brethren, his name is a household word. It was breathed over you on a mother's bosom, and graven on your heart by a mother's love. — It was taught you by a father's watchful care, and has been held ever before you as your beacon and your guide by a father's ceaseless anxiety. It was your watchword in the sports of youth — It is, it must be your polar star in the mazes of a maturer life. — It is the name for patriotism — it is little less than that of a god. Oh the heart — the true American heart — the heart that beats responsive to the call of country — the heart that thrills at those words of wisdom and warning which fell from his lips, teaching us the dangers of foreign influence — the heart that swells with gratitude to the great human benefactor, who, having led us through the perils of the terrible conflict of the Revolution, and guided us through the scarcely less perilous history of the federation, and presided over that grand and august assembly which framed our matchless Constitution, laid in practice the deep foundations of this mighty nation- the heart of the native born American leaps up with joy, to testify its deep love and veneration for him, and seeks some adequate means to express it, And, Brethren and Countrymen, we bring it to you; we give you, by the means now spread before you, an opportunity to enroll your names in the book where is found the mighty company who have contributed to this the most remarkable monument ever erected to man, which, as his name, shall stand unique, lofty, towering above all others known among men.

Brethren, come to our aid.

By order of the Board:

Chas C. Tucker, Secretary

Washington, D.C., May, 1855.

Officers of the Society: Franklin Pierce, President of the United States and ex-officio President; Vespasian Ellis, First Vice President; John T. Towers, Mayor of Washington and ex-officio Second Vice President; George H. Plant, Third Vice President; John M. McCalla, Treasurer; Chas C. Tucker, Secretary.

Managers: Henry Addison, Charles R. Belt, French S. Evans, Charles W. Davis, John N. Craig, Samuel E. Douglas, Thomas D. Sandy, Joseph H. Bradley, Samuel C. Busey, James Gordon, Robert T. Knight, Joseph Libby, Sr., Thomas A. Brooke

Notes

1 Creating a Christian America

1. Scholars of critical race theory in particular have produced an elegant body of scholarship of this coded language. See the seminal Henry Louis Gates, *"Race,"* *Writing, and Difference* (Chicago: University of Chicago Press, 1986).

2. As more than a few journalists and bloggers have recently documented, the word "weird" was consciously chosen to "accidentally" slip out of the mouths of Obama staffers. See Ben Smith and Jonathan Martin, "Obama Plan: Destroy Romney," *Politico*, September 9, 2011.

3. James Aho, *This Thing of Darkness: A Sociology of the Enemy* (Seattle: University of Washington Press, 1994) and Vilho Harle, *The Enemy with a Thousand Faces: The Tradition of the Other in Western Political Thought and History* (Westport, CT: Praeger, 2000).

4. See Daniel A. Cohen, "Alvah Kelly's Cow: Household Feuds, Proprietary Rights, and the Charlestown Convent Riot," *New England Quarterly* 74:4 (December 2001): 531–79.

5. Gary Nash, *First City: Philadelphia and the Forging of Historical Memory* (Philadelphia: University of Pennsylvania Press, 2002), 171.

6. See Frederick L. Harvey, *History of the Washington National Monument and of the Washington National Monument Society* (Washington, DC: Norman T. Elliott Printing Co, 1902), and George J Olszewski, *A History of the Washington Monument, 1844–1968, Washington, D.C.* (Washington, DC: Office of History and Historic Architecture, Eastern Service Center, 1971).

7. Communists and socialists were (and are) likewise persecuted for ascribing to a faith that is commonly associated with atheism. The percentage of Americans who claim they will not vote for an atheist is in fact lowest of all possible choices. The myth that President Obama is both a Muslim and a socialist, coupled with his African parentage, is a fusion of three faiths about which too many Americans are ignorant and/or intolerant. See the Pew 2004 study in which 38% of U.S. adults claimed they would be reluctant to vote for a Muslim, and 52% for an atheist. "Religion and Politics: Contention and Consensus" (2003) Pew Research

Center for the People and the Press, available electronically at http://www.peo-ple-press.org/2003/07/24/religion-and-politics-contention-and-consensus.

8. The builders of many Catholic churches employed various strategies to conceal, disguise, or otherwise protect them from harm. See Katie Oxx, "'Sprung Forth as if by Magic:' Saint John the Evangelist Catholic Church as a Model for a Spatial Analysis of Early National Philadelphia," *American Catholic Studies* 119, no. 4 (Winter, 2009). Likewise, individual Catholics hid their identity at times for safety, and religious men and women removed their identifying garments.

9. This "Roman question" was crucially important to both American Catholics and American Protestants. The increase in anti-Catholicism paralleled the increased visibility of the pope, and the power of the papacy grew as ultramontanist influence prevailed. See especially Peter D'Agostino's unparalleled *Rome in America Transnational Catholic Ideology from the Risorgimento to Fascism* (Chapel Hill: University of North Carolina Press, 2004). Prior to the nineteenth century, clergy in America belonged to orders without a recognizable figurehead, but as the church grew, "secular" clergy—under the direct jurisdiction of the pope—were ordained and placed in leadership roles. The Jesuits, on the other hand, were suppressed. Non-Catholic perceptions of the papacy's power in the U.S. were probably closer to the truth than Catholic apologists would have us believe. Both the perception and reality of this power likely *saved* Catholics from significantly worse anti-Catholic violence.

10. See Jon-Christian Suggs, "Romanticism, Law, and the Suppression of African-American Citizenship," in *Race and the Production of Modern American Nationalism*, edited by Reynolds J. Scott-Childess (New York: Garland, 1999).

11. See Stephen Newcombe's *Pagans in the Promised Land: Decoding the Doctrine of Christian Discovery* (Golden, Colo.: Fulcrum, 2008). As always, my thinking through these sections has been shaped and expanded by Fay Botham's ideas and works.

12. A voluminous body of inter and transdisciplinary scholarship explores this. Most helpful to my thinking has been the collected essays in Henry Goldschmidt and Elizabeth McAlister, eds. *Race, Nation, and Religion in the Americas* (New York: Oxford University Press, 2004); Luis D. León, *La Llorona's Children: Religion, Life, and Death in the U.S.-Mexican Borderlands* (Berkeley: University of California Press, 2004), and Robert J.C. Young, *Colonial Desire: Hybridity in Theory, Culture and Race* (New York: Routledge, 1995).

13. See John Corrigan and Tracy Levealle, with Art Remillard, "French and Spanish Missions in North America" at the Electronic Cultural Atlas Initiative, http://ecai.org/na-missions/ for a spatial overview of Catholic missions. For the history of Spanish North America, see especially David J. Weber, *The Spanish Frontier in North America* (New Haven: Yale University Press, 2009).

14. Any study of Puritans and Puritanism begins and ends with Perry Miller. See *The New England Mind: The Seventeenth Century* (Boston: Beacon Press, 1961) and *Orthodoxy in Massachusetts, 1630–1650* (Boston: Beacon Press, 1959). See also Patrick Collinson, Peter Lake and Steven C. A. Pincus on British Puritans; Michael Winship and Andrew Delbanco for American varieties, and Francis Bremer and Stephen Foster for a transatlantic perspective. Collinson, *The Elizabethan Puritan Movement* (New York: Oxford University Press, 1990) and *The Religion of Protestants: The Church in English Society, 1559–1625* (Oxford: Claren-

don Press, 1982); Lake and Pincus, *The Politics of the Public Sphere in Early Modern England* (New York: Palgrave, 2007); Winship, *Seers of God: Puritan Providentialism in the Restoration and Early Enlightenment* (Baltimore: Johns Hopkins University Press, 1996); Delbanco, *The Puritan Ordeal* (Cambridge: Harvard University Press, 1989)); Bremer, *The Puritan Experiment: New England Society from Bradford to Edwards* (Hanover, NH: University Press of New England, 1995); and Foster, *The Long Argument: English Puritanism and the Shaping of New England Culture, 1570–1700* (Chapel Hill: University of North Carolina Press, 1991

15. Charles Lloyd Cohen, *God's Caress: The Psychology of Puritan Religious Experience* (New York: Oxford University Press, 1986), 4.

16. Scholarship on Puritans and New England religion is vast. See Patricia U. Bonomi, *Under the Cope of Heaven: Religion, Society and Politics in Colonial America* (New York: Oxford University Press, 1986), and Jonathon Butler, *Awash in a Sea of Faith: Christianizing the American People* (Cambridge: Harvard University Press, 1990); David Chidester's, *Patterns of Power: Religion and Politics in American Culture* (Englewood Cliffs: Prentice Hall, 1988), especially pages 303–4; and David D. Hall's *Worlds of Wonder, Days of Judgment: Popular Religious Belief in Early New England* (Boston: Harvard University Press, 1990) are also informative. For a historian of law's perspective see Thomas Curry, *The First Freedoms: Church and State in America to the Passage of the First Amendment* (New York: Oxford University Press, 1986), especially chapter 1.

17. Scholarship on the influence of Islam on southern American Christianity (both European and African denominations) is fascinating. See Sylviane Diouf, *Servants of Allah: African Muslims Enslaved in the Americas* (New York: New York University Press, 1998). On Puritan's conceptions of Africans and Muslims, see Mukhtar Ali Isani's "Cotton Mather and the Orient" *New England Quarterly* 43:1 (March 1970) 46–58 and Moulay Ali Bouânani, "Propaganda for Empire: Barbary Captivity Literature in the US," *Journal of Transatlantic Studies*, 7:4 (December 2009) 399–412. Both articles offer a compelling analysis of the extent of influence of African and Muslim cultures and religions on New England Puritans in general and Cotton Mather in particular. This is an area of scholarship that demands much more attention. The quotes are from Isani, 51–52.

18. Sydney E. Ahlstrom, *A Religious History of the American People* (New Haven: Yale University Press, 1972), 156.

19. Larzer Ziff, *Puritanism in America: New Culture in a New World* (New York: Viking Press, 1973), 90-92.

20. Edmund S. Morgan, *Roger Williams: The Church and the State* (New York: W. W. Norton & Company, 2007).

21. The Avalon Project at Yale University, "Constitution of Pennsylvania – September 28, 1776," 1996–2003; http://www.yale.edu/lawweb/avalon/states/pa08.htm, accessed August 2, 2005.

22. Early Pennsylvania history is covered in Randall M. Miller and William A. Pencak, eds., *Pennsylvania: A History of the Commonwealth* (Centerville: Pennsylvania State University Press, 2002), and a number of essays in *Philadelphia: A 300-Year History*, edited by Russell F. Weigley (New York: W.W. Norton & Company, 1982), especially Mary Maples Dunn and Richard S. Dunn, "The Founding, 1681–1701."

23. See Maura Jane Farrelly's new *Papist Patriots: The Making of an American Catholic Identity* (New York: Oxford University Press, 2012) for a description of this.

24. Additional colonial Maryland history is recounted in Jon Butler, "Religion in Colonial America" in *Religion in American Life: A Short History* (New York: Oxford University Press, 2011), 1–145, and Jay Dolan, *The American Catholic Experience: A History from Colonial Times to the Present* (Garden City: Doubleday, 1985), 71–76.

25. Butler, 78–83.

26. It was not until the Second Vatican Council in 1965 for instance, that the Roman Catholic Church formally decried this idea.

27. Classic studies of the Great Awakening include: Richard L. Bushman, *From Puritan to Yankee: Character and the Social Order in Connecticut, 1690–1765* (Cambridge: Harvard University Press, 1967), and Alan Heimert, *Religion and the American Mind: From the Great Awakening to the Revolution.* (Cambridge: Harvard University Press, 1966). More recently, Thomas S. Kidd, *God of Liberty: A Religious History of the American Revolution* (New York: Basic Books, 2012).

28. D. W. Bebbington, *Evangelicalism in Modern Britain: A History from the 1730s to the 1980s* (London: Unwin Hyman, 1989), 4.

29. See Michael O. Emerson and Christian Smith, *Divided by Faith: Evangelical Religion and the Problem of Race in America* (New York: Oxford University Press, 2000); Mark A. Noll, *American Evangelical Christianity: An Introduction* (Oxford: Blackwell, 2001) and *Between Faith and Criticism: Evangelicals, Scholarship, and the Bible in America* (New York: Harper & Row, 1986).

30. Jon Butler is the strongest challenger of Great Awakening proponents. See "Enthusiasm Described and Decried: The Great Awakening as Interpretive Fiction," *Journal of American History* 69, (no. 1982-3), and "Historiographical Heresy: Catholicism as a Model for American Religious History," in *Belief in History: Innovative Approaches to European and American History*, edited by Thomas Kselman (Notre Dame: University of Notre Dame Press, 1991).

31. Islamic educator and intellectual Hamza Yusuf has recently shown that although it has long been overlooked by scholars, the evolving understanding of state and self as shaped by John Locke and other *philosophes* was influenced by Muslims. See Ed Husain, "Forgotten History: US Founding Fathers and Muslim Thought." The Arab Street (Council on Foreign Relations) (March 6, 2102). My thanks to Hamid Zambrano for pointing this out and thinking through it with me.

32. Henry F. May, *The Enlightenment in America* (New York: Oxford University Press, 1976).

33. Like the Great Awakening, scholars debate this. See Ruth H. Bloch, "Religion and Ideological Change in the American Revolution" in *Religion and American Politics from the Colonial Period to the 1980s*, edited by Mark A. Noll (New York: Oxford University Press, 1990), 44–61.

34. The Anglican Church lost approximately seventy percent of clergy, for example. Butler, "Religion in Colonial American," 150.

35. Grant Wacker, "Religion in Nineteenth-Century America" in *Religion in American Life: A Short History*, 155–310 (New York: Oxford University Press, 2011), 156–59.

36. Ibid., 158.

37. "Constitution of Pennsylvania," 1776. Interestingly, Benjamin Franklin, president of the Pennsylvania Constitutional Convention, was against this measure, but acceded to public and ministerial pressure. See Curry, 161.

38. See Garry Wills, *Under God: Religion and American Politics* (New York: Simon and Schuster, 1990), 379 and Leonard W. Levy, *The Establishment Clause: Religion and the First Amendment* (Chapel Hill: The University of North Carolina Press, 1994), 34.

39. See Mark Douglas McGarvie, *One Nation Under Law: America's Early Struggles to Separate Church and State* (Northern Illinois University Press, 2005), 17-18 for disestablishment. Unitarians will be discussed in chapter 2.

40. This was a much more complicated process than can be addressed here. See Daniel Walker Howe, *What Hath God Wrought: The Transformation of America, 1815–1848* (New York: Oxford University Press, 2009), and Gordon S. Wood, *Empire of Liberty: A History of the Early Republic, 1789–1815* (New York: Oxford University Press, 2009).

41. This categorization raises the same issues as does using "Great Awakening." See Terry Bilhartz, *Urban Religion and the Second Great Awakening: Church and Society in Early National Baltimore* (Rutherford: Fairleigh Dickinson University Press, 1986). He asserts that based on what evangelicals wanted to accomplish versus what they did accomplish, the Second Great Awakening existed, but was a failure. Nathan Hatch contends, however, "The wave of popular religious movements that broke upon the United States in the half century after independence did more to Christianize American society than anything before or since." He uses the Methodist and Baptist denominations in particular to support his argument. See Hatch, *The Democratization of American Christianity*, 3. Also see Donald Mathews, "The Second Great Awakening as an Organizing Process, 1780–1830: An Hypothesis," *American Quarterly* XXI, no. 1 (1969).

42. See Paul Boyer, *Urban Masses and Moral Order in America, 1820–1920* (Boston: Harvard University Press, 1978).

43. On the evangelical positions towards those they were helping, see Boyer, 54–64.

44. Derek Chang, *Citizens of a Christian Nation: Evangelical Missions and the Problem of Race in the Nineteenth Century* (Philadelphia: University of Pennsylvania Press, 2010), 8.

45. See especially Sacvan Bercovitch, who describes a "synthesis" of "evangelical Protestant religion, republican political ideology, and commonsense moral reasoning." *Puritan Origins of the American Self* (New Haven: Yale University Press, 1975).

46. See James H. Moorhead, "Prophecy, Millennialism, and Biblical Interpretation in Nineteenth-Century America" in *Biblical Hermeneutics in Historical Perspective* (Grand Rapids, MI: Eerdmans, 1991), Ernest R. Sandeen, *The Roots of Fundamentalism: British and American Millenarianism, 1800–1930* (Chicago: University of Chicago Press, 1968), and Ernest Lee Tuveson, *Redeemer Nation: The Idea of America's Millennial Role* (Chicago: University of Chicago Press, 1980), 125.

47. Lyman Beecher, *Autobiography* (Cambridge: Belknap Press of Harvard University Press, 1961; 1864), Vol II, 167.

48. James Axtell, *The Invasion Within: The Contest of Cultures in Colonial North America* (New York: Oxford University Press, 1985); Richard Callahan, ed., *New Territories New Perspectives: The Religious Impact of the Louisiana Purchase* (University

of Missouri, 2008); and Tracy Leavelle, "Geographies of Encounter: Religion and Contested Spaces in Colonial North America," *American Quarterly* 56, no. 4 (2004): 913–43.

49. The Louisiana Purchase doubled the size and population of the United States. The territory extended from the Gulf of Mexico to the Canadian border and from the Mississippi River to the Rocky Mountains, what is today the center of Montana. See James M. Volo and Dorothy Denneen Volo, "Louisiana Purchase" in *Encyclopedia of the Antebellum South* (Santa Barbara, CA: ABC-CLIO, 2000).

50. "Federal Constitution of the United Mexican States" (1824). Available on line at http://tarlton.law.utexas.edu/constitutions/text/1824index.html.

51. Some U.S. immigrants supported Texan independence, some desired statehood in Mexico, some Mexicans desired independence, and some sought U.S. statehood.

52. Of those that will not be singled out here, seminal works include: Thomas J. Curran, *Xenophobia and Immigration, 1820–1930* (Boston: Twayne Publishers, 1975); Roger Daniels, *Coming to America: A History of Immigration and Ethnicity in American Life* (New York: Perennial, 2002); David Brion Davis, *The Slave Power Conspiracy and the Paranoid Style* (Baton Rouge: Louisiana State University Press, 1969); Joe R. Feagin, "Old Poison in New Bottles: The Deep Roots of Modern Nativism," in *Immigrants Out! the New Nativism and the Anti-Immigrant Impulse in the United States*, edited by Juan F. Perea (New York: New York University Press, 1996); Marie Léonore Fell, *The Foundations of Nativism in American Textbooks, 1783–1860* (Washington, DC: Catholic University of America Press, 1941); Jack Fong, "American Social 'Reminders' of Citizenship After September 11, 2001: Nativisms and the Retractability of American Identity," *Qualitative Sociology Review* 4, no. 1 (2008); Jon Gjerde, *Major Problems in American Immigration and Ethnic History: Documents and Essays* (Boston: Houghton Mifflin, 1998); Mary Saint Henry, *Nativism in Pennsylvania with Particular Regard to its Effect on Politics and Education, 1840–1860* (Philadelphia: Dolphin Press, 1936); Richard Hofstadter, *The Paranoid Style in American Politics, and Other Essays* (New York: Vintage Books, 1967); Dale T. Knobel, *Paddy and the Republic: Ethnicity and Nationality in Antebellum America*, 1st ed. (Middletown, CT: Wesleyan University Press; Distributed by Harper & Row, 1986); Ira M. Leonard and Robert D. Parmet, *American Nativism, 1830–1860* (New York: Van Nostrand Reinhold Company, 1971); Walter Benn Michaels, *Our America: Nativism, Modernism, and Pluralism* (Durham: Duke University Press, 1995); John R. Mulkern, *The Know-Nothing Party in Massachusetts: The Rise and Fall of a People's Movement* (Boston: Northeastern University Press, 1990), 236.

53. Unfortunately, some scholars still overlook and undervalue religion as a dominant historical force. This is changing though. See Scott Jaschik, "Religious Revival," *Inside Higher Ed*, December 21, 2009, http://www.insidehighered.com/news/2009/12/21/religion.

54. John Higham, *Strangers in the Land: Patterns of American Nativism, 1860–1925* (New Brunswick: Rutgers University Press, 2002), 4.

55. Ibid., 5.

56. Ibid., 6–7.

57. Ibid.,10.

58. Higham, 26. The assumptions about Irish piety that Higham privileged have

been disproven though. Both Kerby Miller and following him, Michael Carroll, have found that nativism was and is a *cause* of Irish loyalty to the institutional church, not a *result*. And the years Higham claims that anti-Catholic nativism emerged were well before the immigration of the predominantly Catholic famine Irish. In other words, the Irish in America in the late 1830s and 1840s were not poor and were most likely Protestant if churched at all. Distrust of ethnic immigrants could not have led nativists to conflate their xenophobia with anti-Catholicism, then; it existed on its own. A useful alternative to either Higham's overemphasis on "foreignness" as the genesis of nativist hostility (and by extension, Irish American Catholic identity) and Carroll's emphasis on the "Americanness" of Irish American Catholic identity (and by extension, the emergence of nativism) is discussed by Kerby Miller. See "Class, Culture, and Immigrant Group Identity in the United States: The Case of Irish-American Ethnicity," in *Immigration Reconsidered*, edited by Virginia Yans-McLaughlin (New York: Oxford University Press, 1990), and Michael P. Carroll, *American Catholics in the Protestant Imagination: Rethinking the Academic Study of Religion* (Baltimore: Johns Hopkins University Press, 2007).

59. Many of these bear a striking resemblance to ideas shaping 2012 America.

60. David Brion Davis, *The Fear of Conspiracy: Images of Un-American Subversion from the Revolution to the Present* (Ithaca: Cornell University Press, 1971), xix.

61. Ibid., xviii–xxiii.

62. David Harry Bennett, *The Party of Fear: From Nativist Movements to the New Right in American History* (Chapel Hill: University of North Carolina Press, 1988), 40.

63. Ibid., 2, 4.

64. Ibid., 13.

65. Ibid., 81, 85.

66. Ibid., 94.

67. He claims, "*What allowed nativist ideology to provide apparently simple explanations for mystifying events in a complex world was...the particular intellectual inheritance of the early American nation and the particular anxieties associated with building a nation.* And what allowed nativist ideology to become bound to organizations was a sense—shared by numbers of citizens during the first half-century of the United States—that personal identity as Americans required participation in voluntary associations." Knobel, *America for the Americans: The Nativist Movement in the United States* (New York: Twayne Publishers; Prentice Hall International, 1996), xxxviii. (Knobel's italics).

68. Tyler Gregory Anbinder, *Nativism and Slavery: The Northern Know Nothings and the Politics of the 1850's* (New York: Oxford University Press, 1992), 330. Other important works on nativism that consider race include: Najia Aarim-Heriot, *Chinese Immigrants, African Americans, and Racial Anxiety in the United States, 1848–82* (Urbana: University of Illinois Press, 2003); Kristofer Allerfeldt and Jeremy Black, *Race, Radicalism, Religion, and Restriction: Immigration in the Pacific Northwest, 1890–1924* (Westport, Conn.: Praeger, 2003); Katrina Irving, *Immigrant Mothers: Narratives of Race and Maternity, 1890–1925* (Urbana: University of Illinois Press, 2000); Michaels, *Our America;* Forrest G. Wood's *The Arrogance of Faith: Christianity and Race in America from the Colonial Era to the Twentieth Century*, 1st ed. (New York: Knopf, 1990), though not on nativism exclusively, is a profound examination of the intersection of Christianity and race throughout

American history. Chapter 6, "Thy Kingdom Come, Thy Will Be Done," is especially insightful. Also see Derek Chang, *Citizens of a Christian Nation: Evangelical Missions and the Problem of Race in the Nineteenth Century* (Philadelphia: University of Pennsylvania Press, 2010) and a number of essays in Richard J. Callahan, *New Territories, New Perspectives: The Religious Impact of the Louisiana Purchase* (Columbia: University of Missouri Press, 2008).

69. Ibid., xv.

70. Peter Schrag, *Not Fit for our Society: Nativism and Immigration* (Berkeley: University of California Press, 2010), 32.

71. See Ahlstrom, *A Religious History*; Charles I. Foster, *An Errand of Mercy: The Evangelical United Front, 1790–1837* (Chapel Hill: University of North Carolina Press, 1960); Martin E. Marty, *Righteous Empire: The Protestant Experience in America* (New York: The Dial Press, 1970).

72. Jon Butler, "Historiographical Heresy," 286; Mark A. Noll, *America's God: From Jonathan Edwards to Abraham Lincoln* (New York: Oxford University Press, 2002), 31–50.

73. In the twentieth century, Sidney Mead, Sydney Ahlstrom, William Warren Sweet, Winthrop Hudson and Robert Handy continued to analyze American religious history with mainline Protestantism at its center. See Ahlstrom, *A Religious History*, Robert T. Handy, *A Christian America: Protestant Hopes and Historical Realities* (New York: Oxford University Press, 1984); Winthrop S. Hudson, *Religion in America* (New York: Charles Scribner's Sons, 1965); Sidney Earl Mead, *The Lively Experiment: The Shaping of Christianity in America* (New York: Harper and Row, 1963); William Warren Sweet, *The Story of Religion in America* (New York: Harper & Brothers, 1939).

74. See Jon Butler's *Awash in a Sea of Faith,* in which he emphasizes the institutional power-plays denominations made in order to develop or retain power. (See especially chapter 9, "Christian Power in the American Republic," pp. 257–288). Also see Gordon Wood, who discusses what might be called a "cultural disestablishment." John Higham and Harry Stout suggest that disestablishment led to Protestants' discovery of a "communal identity." See Higham, "Ethnicity and American Protestants: Collective Identity in the Mainstream," in *New Directions in American Religious History*, edited by Harry S. Stout and D.G. Hart (New York: Oxford University Press, 1997), 239–59; Harry S. Stout, "Ethnicity: The Vital Center of Religion in America," *Ethnicity* 2 (1975): 49; and Gordon S. Wood, "Religion and the American Revolution," in Stout and Hart, *New Directions,* 173–205, passim.

75. More recently, this has been called the "Protestant moral establishment" by historian David Sehat, who demonstrates how outsider religious groups have nearly always lost their battles with this establishment, betraying the common American belief in the sovereignty of the First Amendment. See *The Myth of American Religious Freedom* (London: Oxford University Press, 2011).

76. See R. Laurence Moore, *Religious Outsiders and the Making of Americans* (New York: Oxford University Press, 1986), especially 3–21. Moore looks at the understanding of religious pluralism in the American context. He claims that "until relatively recently, American church history continued to emphasize themes of Protestant unity rather than themes of diversity and unsettled pluralism." He then examines the fear and subsequent desire felt by (mainline)

Protestant groups as they lost "control" and attempted to halt the unraveling of their consensus if not on the ground then at least historiographically. Also see Catherine L. Albanese, *America: Religions and Religion*, 1st ed. (Belmont, CA: Wadsworth, 1983; reprint, 1998); Robert Bruce Mullin and Russell E. Richey, *Reimagining Denominationalism: Interpretive Essays* (New York: Oxford University Press, 1994); Harry S. Stout and D.G. Hart, eds., *New Directions*; Thomas A. Tweed, ed., *Retelling U.S. Religious History* (Berkeley: University of California Press, 1997). Also see John Corrigan and Lynn Neal's recent edited volume, *Religious Intolerance in America: A Documentary History* (Chapel Hill: UNC Press, 2010), for historical and contemporary sources and valuable insight.

77. See Nathan O. Hatch, *The Democratization of American Christianity* (New Haven: Yale University Press, 1989), 220. Scholars who have taken up the call include Bilhartz, *Urban Religion and the Second Great Awakening* and Jonathan D. Sassi, *A Republic of Righteousness: The Public Christianity of the Post-Revolutionary New England Clergy* (New York: Oxford University Press, 2001).

78. Mark A. Noll, *The Civil War as a Theological Crisis* (Chapel Hill: University of North Carolina Press, 2006) and see also the collected essays in Randall M. Miller and Jon L. Wakelyn, *Catholics in the Old South: Essays on Church and Culture* (Macon, GA: Mercer University Press, 1983).

79. Bruce Dorsey, *Reforming Men and Women: Gender in the Antebellum City* (Ithaca: Cornell University Press, 2002), 196.

80. Ibid., 197.

81. Ibid., 198.

82. Ibid., 199–202.

83. The rhetorical strategies of Catholics and Protestants and how those strategies shaped each of their understanding and misunderstanding of the other is the subject of communication scholar Jody Roy's text as well. She examines Protestant polemics and alleged "exposés" as part of the development of a culture of conspiracy, and takes varied Catholic responses to that literature into consideration. Catholicism and anti-Catholic function alongside one another, they shaped and were shaped by "competing understandings of what it meant to be both Catholic and American in the nineteenth century. Margaret DePalma also looks at the communities in dialogue. She claims they shared a "mutual necessity" on the frontier through which they learned from each other and that Catholicism in America "kept pace"—both structurally and culturally—with the development of the nation. While disagreements existed, so too did an "amiable" relationship and a "core dialogue" that sustained it. DePalma attributes this to the fact that members of both religious groups were present at the "founding" of the West, and that the personalities of those who worked on the frontier were accommodationist. William Shea has compared Catholic and Protestant theological histories and categorized the communities on a continuum between "biblical" and "liturgical" using nineteenth-century apologetics. He admits that almost all churches are *both* biblical and liturgical; it is a matter of degree. The accusations by Protestants that Catholicism is not biblical, and the Catholic accusation that Protestants are not liturgical illustrates that "neither is enough of what it should be in the eyes of the other" more than they reveal theological distinctions between them. Drawing on Ray Billington's work he takes a transatlantic historical view of the conflict between evangelicals and Catholics in the antebellum

period, and adds that the Catholic church hierarchy was anathema to the Puritans of the colonial period. He divides into "currents" three aspects of the interaction between Catholics and evangelicals: "American nativism, political fear of Rome, and evangelicalism." The theology of evangelicalism, Shea claims, is not inherently nativist, since nativism is "ethnic and political xenophobia," but what has joined them throughout history, he believes, is "a rabid political fear of popery." See Jody M. Roy, *Rhetorical Campaigns of the Nineteenth-Century: Anti-Catholics and Catholics in America* (Lewiston, NY: Edwin Mellen Press, 1999), 19, and Margaret C. DePalma, *Dialogue on the Frontier: Catholic and Protestant Relations, 1793–1883* (Kent, OH: Kent State University Press, 2004), xi, xiii, xv; and William M. Shea, "Biblical Christianity as a Category in Nineteenth-Century American Apologetics," *American Catholic Studies* 115, no. 3 (2004): 2 and *The Lion and the Lamb: Evangelicals and Catholics in America* (New York: Oxford University Press, 2004), 57.

84. Jenny Franchot, *Roads to Rome: The Antebellum Protestant Encounter with Catholicism* (Berkeley: University of California Press, 1994), xxii.

85. Ibid., 350. As I read her though, she specifically means that the Catholic narrative is a categorical crisis for Protestantism, so in the end her text still traces Protestants' gaze on Catholics as "other."

86. Elizabeth A. Fenton, *Religious Liberties: Anti-Catholicism and Liberal Democracy in Nineteenth-Century U.S. Literature and Culture* (New York: Oxford University Press, 2011).

87. Philip Hamburger, *Separation of Church and State* (Cambridge: Harvard University Press, 2002), 194.

88. Tracy Fessenden, *Culture and Redemption: Religion, the Secular, and American Literature* (Princeton: Princeton University Press, 2007), 5.

89. Ibid., 6.

90. Cain Hope Felder, ed., *Race, Racism and Biblical Interpretation* (Minneapolis: Fortress Press, 1991); Randall M. Miller, Harry S. Stout, and Charles Reagan Wilson, eds, *Religion and the American Civil War* (New York: Oxford University Press, 1998); Eugene D. Genovese, *Roll, Jordan, Roll: The World the Slaves Made* (New York: Vintage Books, 1974); Elizabeth Fox-Genovese and Eugene D. Genovese, *Slavery in White and Black: Class and Race in the Southern Slaveholders' New World Order* (Cambridge: Cambridge University Press, 2008); George C. Rable, *God's almost Chosen Peoples: A Religious History of the American Civil War* (Chapel Hill: University of North Carolina Press, 2010).

91. Handy, *A Christian America*, 51.

92. See Robert P. Swierenga, "Ethnoreligious Political Behavior in the Mid-Nineteenth Century: Voting, Values, Cultures," in *Religion and American Politics From the Colonial Period to the 1980s,* edited by Mark A. Noll (New York: Oxford University Press, 1990), 146.

93. Billington, 2.

94. Ibid., 1.

95. Ibid., 39–40.

96. Ibid., 142.

97. Randall M. Miller et al., *Religion and the American Civil War* (New York: Oxford University Press, 1998), Idem. and Jon L. Wakelyn, *Catholics in the Old South.*

98. Richard R. Duncan, "Catholics and the Church in the Antebellum Upper South," in *Catholics in the Old South*, 86.

99. This was a complicated position though. As Duncan notes, prominent Catholic clergy held slaves and provided the theological scaffolding for slavery's defense, though they might have lamented its existence. The Jesuit order in Maryland moreover, owned more slaves than most others. See Duncan, "Catholics and the Church," 87–89 and Kirby Miller, "Class, Culture and Immigrant Group," 17.

100. Randall M. Miller, "A Church in Cultural Captivity: Some Speculations on Catholic Identity in the Old South" in *Catholics in the Old South*, 35.

101. Miller, "Church in Captivity,"28; Duncan, "Catholics and the Church," 91.

102. Mark Stephen Massa, *Anti-Catholicism in America: The Last Acceptable Prejudice* (New York: Crossroad Pub, 2003), 3. See also Massa's insightful and historiographical essay, "The New and Old Anti-Catholicism and the Analogical Imagination," *Theological Studies* 62, no. 3 (September 2001): 549.

103. Massa, *Last Acceptable Prejudice*, 3. On American civil religion generally, see Robert Bellah's seminal "Civil Religion in America," *Daedalus* 134, no. 4 (Winter 1967): 40–55.

104. Philip Jenkins, *The New Anti-Catholicism: The Last Acceptable Prejudice* (New York: Oxford University Press, 2003), 2.

105. Ibid., 20.

106. Secularization theorists claimed that as societies "develop" (industrialize, Westernize) they become less religious. See the important James A. Beckford, *Religion and Advanced Industrial Society* (London and Boston: Unwin Hyman, 1989); Bryan S. Turner, *Religion and Modern Society: Citizenship, Secularisation and the State* (Cambridge: Cambridge University Press, 2011); and Bryan R. Wilson, *Religious Toleration & Religious Diversity* (Santa Barbara, CA: Institute for the Study of American Religion, 1995). But it was not the case. See the recants by former proponents of the secularization theory: Peter L. Berger, *The Desecularization of the World: Resurgent Religion and World Politics* (Washington, DC: W.B. Eerdmans, 1999), and Harvey Gallagher Cox, *Religion in the Secular City: Toward a Postmodern Theology* (New York: Simon and Schuster, 1984).

107. Jenkins, *The New Anti-Catholicism,* 7-10.

2 Burning of the Charlestown Convent

1. The abhorrent incident was videotaped and is available for viewing at the Council on American-Islamic Relations website (www.cair.com) and on you tube at http://www.youtube.com/watch?v=NutFkykjmbM&lr=1&uid=c697vMbAwc Uut6DQmfNGdQ*.

2. Smaller incidents had taken place throughout the colonial and revolutionary periods.

3. Lyman Beecher, "A Plea for the West," (1835), 10–11.

4. *Proceedings of the First Ten Years of the American Tract Society* (Boston: Flagg and Gould, American Tract Society, 1824). Available at http://archive.org/details/proceedingsfirs02socigoog.

5. Elizabeth Hansot and David Tyack, *Managers of Virtue: Public School Leadership in America, 1820–1980* (New York: Basic Books, 1982), 38.

6. Charles I. Foster, *An Errand of Mercy: The Evangelical United Front, 1790–1837*

(Chapel Hill: University of North Carolina Press, 1960), 157–67; David Paul Nord, *Faith in Reading: Religious Publishing and the Birth of Mass Media in America*, edited by Harry S. Stout (New York: Oxford University Press, 2004), 81–82.

7. Foster, *Errand of Mercy*, 227.
8. Nord, *Faith*, 5–12.
9. Ibid., 82.
10. Ray Allen Billington, *The Protestant Crusade 1800–1860: A Study of the Origins of American Nativism* (Chicago: Quadrangle Books, 1938), 57.
11. *Catholic Telegraph*, June 9, 1832.
12. Ibid.
13. *Kingston Patriot*, December 1830. (emphasis theirs).
14. Kathryn Kish Sklar, *Catharine Beecher: A Study in American Domesticity* (New Haven: Yale University Press, 1973); Susan Hill Lindley, *"You have Stepped Out of Your Place:" A History of Women and Religion in America*, paperback ed. (Louisville, KY: Westminster John Knox Press, 1996), especially chapter 6, "The Ideal American Woman."
15. See Carol Coburn and Martha Smith, *Spirited Lives: How Nuns Shaped Catholic Culture and American Life, 1836–1920* (Chapel Hill: University of North Carolina Press, 1999); Jo Ann McNamara, *Sisters in Arms: Catholic Nuns through Two Millennia* (Cambridge: Harvard University Press, 1996).
16. Jenny Franchot, *Roads to Rome: The Antebellum Protestant Encounter with Catholicism* (Berkeley: University of California Press, 1994), xxv.
17. Ibid, 144.
18. See Elizabeth A. Fenton, *Religious Liberties: Anti-Catholicism and Liberal Democracy in Nineteenth-Century U.S. Literature and Culture* (New York: Oxford University Press, 2011); Tracy Fessenden, "The Convent, the Brothel, and the Protestant Woman's Sphere," *Signs* 25, no. 2 (2000); Franchot, *Roads to Rome*; Susan M. Griffin, *Anti-Catholicism and Nineteenth-Century Fiction* (Cambridge: Cambridge University Press, 2004); Catherine McGowan, "Convents and Conspiracies: A Study of Convent Narratives in the United States, 1850–1870" (Ph.D. diss., University of Edinburgh, n.d.); Jeanne Hamilton, "The Nunnery as Menace: The Burning of the Charleston Convent, 1834," *U.S. Catholic Historian* 14, no. 1 (Winter, 1996); Nancy Lusignan Schultz, "Introduction," in *Veil of Fear: Nineteenth-Century Convent Tales* (West Lafayette, IN: Purdue University Press, 1999).
19. Ray Allen Billington, "The Burning of the Charlestown Convent," *New England Quarterly* 10, no. 1 (March, 1937), 10.
20. Interestingly, Thayer's conversion from Congregationalism was bound and published with a conversion narrative written by John Hughes. Hughes' story was a fiction that intentionally replicated popular Protestant conversion narratives of the time.
21. Hamilton, "Nunnery as Menace," 35–36.
22. Robert H. Lord, "Religious Liberty in New England: The Burning of the Charlestown Convent," *Historical Records and Studies United States Catholic Historical Society* 22 (1932), 7–9.
23. Hamilton, "Nunnery as Menace," 36–38.
24. Ibid., 39.
25. Daniel A. Cohen, "Alvah Kelley's Cow: Household Feuds, Proprietary Rights,

and the Charlestown Convent Riot," *New England Quarterly* 74, no. 4 (Dec., 2001), 155.

26. Hamilton, "Nunnery as Menace," 41.

27. *The Jesuit*, July 23, 1831, quoted in Lord, 14.

28. Nancy Lusignan Schultz, *Fire and Roses: The Burning of the Charlestown Convent, 1834* (New York: Free Press, 2000), 113–15.

29. Ibid., 108, 113–15; Lord, "Religious Liberty," 12.

30. *Christian Watchman*, Aug 15, 1834, as quoted in Schultz (2000), 166.

31. Beecher biographers are the only naysayers though. Milton Rugoff claimed it was "unlikely." Stuart Henry claimed, "Beecher cannot be blamed exclusively for the Charlestown fire." Demographics provide some defense for the preacher also. The crowds who burned the Ursuline convent have been shown to be primarily working class men, while the members of congregations that Beecher preached to were probably middle- and upper-class folks. Stuart C. Henry, *Unvanquished Puritan; a Portrait of Lyman Beecher* (Grand Rapids, MI: W. B. Eerdmans Pub. Co, 1973), 164n52; Milton Rugoff, *The Beechers: An American Family in the Nineteenth Century* (New York: Harper & Row, 1981), 153.

32. Scank was the pseudonym of Bishop George Elder of Bardstown, Kentucky, who was embroiled in debates over Catholic and Protestant doctrine with Protestant minster Nathan Rice. See Philemon Scank, *Ursuline Convent: A Poem* (Louisville, KY: 1835). For the Rice-Elder debates, see C. Walker Gollar, "The Alleged Abduction of Millie McPherson and Catholic Recruitment of Presbyterian Girls," *Church History: Studies in Christianity and Culture* 65 (1996).

33. Quoted in Schultz, *Fire and Roses*, 116–17.

34. Louisa Goddard Whitney, *The Burning of the Convent a Narrative of the Destruction by a Mob of the Ursuline School on Mount Benedict, Charlestown, as Remembered by One of the Pupils* (Cambridge, MA: Welch, Bigelow, 1970), 7.

35. Lyman Beecher, *Autobiography* (Cambridge: Belknap Press of Harvard University Press, 1961), Vol. I: 186.

36. Ibid., vol. II: 250.

37. Billington claimed, "All the hatreds bred of the struggle ... were centered on the Ursuline convent. To the lower classes, for whom Congregationalism was a sacred creed, Catholics and Unitarians seemed to be combining against their community religion." Billington, "Burning," 7.

38. Beecher, *Autobiography*, 542.

39. Schultz, *Fire and Roses*, 159 and 296n27. Schultz references the *Mercantile Journal*, August 8, 1834, and a letter from Anna Loring to Mary Pierce, in the Somerville Library Collection

40. See the very helpful list at the beginning of Schultz' narrative, *Fire and Roses*, ix–xi and Hamilton, "Nunnery as Menace," 36–40.

41. Hamilton, "Nunnery as Menace," 41.

42. Lord, "Religious Liberty," 15–16.

43. Daniel A. Cohen, "Miss Reed and the Superiors: The Contradictions of Convent Life in Antebellum America," *Journal of Social History* 30 (Fall, 1996), 161; Lord, 16.

44. Schultz, *Fire and Roses*, 162.

45. Whitney, *The Burning of the Convent*, 17; Schultz, *Fire and Roses*, 171.

46. Whitney, *The Burning of the Convent*, 73.

47. Schultz, *Fire and Roses,* 163.
48. Cohen, "Miss Reed," 161.
49. Unknown source, Scrapbook (original) 1834–1894, CUA Archives, http://dspace.wrlc.org/view/ImgViewer?img=3&url=http://dspace.wrlc.org/doc/manifest/2041/2519
50. Schultz, *Fire and Roses,* 161.
51. Whitney, *The Burning of the Convent,* 85–87.
52. Lord, "Religious Liberty," 22.
53. Schultz, *Fire and Roses,* 172.
54. Ibid., 107–12.
55. See especially Philip J. Deloria, *Playing Indian* (New Haven: Yale University Press, 1999).
56. Lord, "Religious Liberty," 23.
57. Whitney, *The Burning of the Convent,* 126.
58. Ibid., 128; *The Gleaner,* Aug 16, 1834.
59. Whitney, *The Burning of the Convent,* 134–38, 140–42.
60. Letter from Theodore Russell to Charles Russell, August 31, 1834, Charles Russell Collection, Massachusetts Historical Society, quoted in Schultz (2000), 188. (Emphasis Schultz or Russell.)
61. Creasy later bragged about it, and then committed suicide in a local bar. See Patrick Donohue, "The Charlestown Convent; Its Destruction by a Mob" (1870).
62. Whitney, *The Burning of the Convent,* 181–82.
63. Billington, "Burning," 17.
64. Mother Superior, Letter to the *Boston Recorder,* August 15, 1834.
65. *Records of the American Catholic Historical Society* Vol. 13 (1919), 106–12.
66. Patrick Donohue, "The Charlestown Convent," 18.
67. Ibid., 20.
68. Bisson claimed the militia prevented more violence; Donohue claimed there was no force present. See Wilfred J. Bisson, *Countdown to Violence: The Charlestown Convent Riot of 1834* (New York: Garland 1989), 115, and Donohue, "The Charlestown Convent," 20.
69. *Boston Recorder,* August 14, 1834 and Donohue, "The Charlestown Convent," 21.
70. Donohue, "The Charlestown Convent," 21.
71. Bisson, *Countdown to Violence,* 118.
72. *Trial of John Buzzell Before the Supreme Judicial Court of Massachusetts for Arson and Burglary in the Ursuline Convent at Charlestown* (Boston: Russell, Odiorne & Metcalf, 1834). Available at http://catalog.hathitrust.org/Record/009733388.
73. Donohue, "The Charlestown Convent," 31.
74. Ibid., 24–26
75. Bisson, "Countdown to Violence," 116, 119–20; Schultz, *Fire and Roses,* 229.
76. "Account of the Conflagration," by a Friend, 3. Avaialble at http://www.archive.org/stream/accountofconflag00bost#page/n9/mode/2up (retrieved December 10, 2011).
77. Caleb Stetson, *A Discourse on the Duty of Sustaining the Laws Occasioned by the Burning of the Ursuline Convent* (Boston: Hilliard and Gray, 1834), 14–15.
78. Ibid., 15.

79. "Scrapbook," Ursuline Convent Collection, Archives of the Catholic University of America (1834), 43.

80. "Roxbury Committee of Vigilance Records, 1834–1835," *Records of the Massachusetts Historical Society* (June 1920), 327.

81. Lord, "Religious Liberty," 28.

82. Ibid., 27.

83. Caroline Howard Gilman, *The Poetry of Travelling in the United States*, (1838), 187–89. Available at http://www.archive.org/stream/poetryoftravelli00gilm#page/186/mode/2up

84. Theodore Dwight, *Open Convents, Or Nunneries and Popish Seminaries Dangerous to the Morals and Degrading to the Character of a Republican Community* (New York: Van Nostrand, 1936), 123–24.

85. John R. Mulkern, *The Know-Nothing Party in Massachusetts: The Rise and Fall of a People's Movement* (Boston: Northeastern University Press, 1990), 103.

86. Ibid., 117.

87. Ibid., 145.

88. See Ray Allen Billington, "Maria Monk and Her Influence," *Catholic Historical Review* (October 1936), 287; McGowan, 45–48; and Schultz, "Introduction," xvi. Monk's story was first refuted by William Stone, a noted (though mild) anti-Catholic. Stone's refutation was challenged by Monk, her ghost writers, and others. See *Evidence demonstrating the falsehoods of William L. Stone concerning the Hotel Dieu Nunnery of Montreal* (New York: s.n., 1837) Widener Library, Harvard University. Available electronically at http://nrs.harvard.edu/urn-3:FHCL:5156121.

89. Franchot, *Roads to Rome,* 148.

90. Rebecca Theresa Reed, *Six Months in a Convent, Or, the Narrative of Rebecca Theresa Reed* (Boston: Russell, Odiorne & Metcalf, 1835), 186.

91. Ibid., 160.

92. Schultz, "Introduction," 13.

93. "Religious Instruction," *Boston Recorder*, December 1834.

94. Samuel K. Williams, *Boston Recorder*, December 1834.

95. *Trial of John Buzzell.*

96. "Scrapbook," 31–32.

97. Nancy F. Cott, *The Bonds of Womanhood: "Woman's Sphere" in New England, 1780–1835*, (New Haven: Yale University Press, 1997).

98. "Prove All Things," Letter to the Editor, *Boston Recorder*, August 1834.

99. Ibid.

100. *Recorder*, 13.

101. Franchot, *Roads to Rome,* xxv.

102. Ibid., 88.

103. Harry Hazel, *The Nun of St. Ursula, or, The Burning of the Convent: A Romance of Mount Benedict.* (Boston: F. Gleason, 1845).

104. James Phinney Munroe, *The Destruction of the Convent at Charlestown, Massachusetts, 1834.* (Boston: New England Magazine Co, 1901).

105. In addition to those mentioned here see John T. Galvin, *Mob Violence and Economic Class in Jacksonian Boston: The Burning of the Ursuline Convent and the Garrison Mob* (1971).

106. E. Digby Baltzell, *Puritan Boston and Quaker Philadelphia*, 3rd. ed. (New Brunswick: Transaction, 1979), 425. Primary sources support this claim.

107. Ibid.

108. See Joseph Mannard, "The 1839 Baltimore Nunnery Riot," *Maryland Historian* (1988) and "Protestant Mothers and Catholic Sisters: Gender Concerns in Anti-Catholic Conspiracy Theories, 1830–1860," *American Catholic Studies* III (2000).

109. Mannard, "Baltimore Nunnery Riot," 13.

110. In addition to those mentioned, Nancy Lusignan Schultz reconstructed the convent burning, the events leading up to it, and the aftermath in *Fire and Roses,* a narrative with much historical detail. In 1997, she also co-curated "Lifting the Veil," an exhibition on the burning for the Somerville Museum in Boston. Artifacts from the convent and related material were on display and a corresponding website was produced. Through all these media, Schultz has brought the event to life with valuable textual and material sources. See Nancy Natale and Nancy Lusignan Schultz, "Lifting the Veil: Remembering the Burning of the Ursuline Convent," Somerville (Massachusetts) Museum, April 20-December 1997; and Schultz, "Introduction," and *Fire and Roses.*

111. Franchot, *Roads to Rome,* 148.

112. Cohen, "Miss Reed," and "The Respectability of Rebecca Reed: Genteel Womanhood and Sectarian Conflict in Antebellum America," *Journal of the Early Republic*, 16 (Fall 1996): 422. Here, Cohen primarily confronts Billington's narrative of Reed. In addition to those noted here, he also examines local rivalries between families as an integral part of the conflict in one article and the role of local firemen in the incident in another. See the aforementioned Cohen "Alvah Kelly" and "Passing the Torch: Boston Firemen, 'Tea Party' Patriots, and the Burning of the Charlestown Convent," *Journal of the Early Republic* 24, no. 4 (2004): 527–87.

113. Hamilton, "Nunnery as Menace," 35–65.

114. Fessenden, "Convent and Brothel," 457 and 463. She is referring here to the large body of scholarship that began with Ann Douglas, *The Feminization of American Culture* (New York: Avon Books, 1978).

115. Bruce Dorsey, *Reforming Men and Women: Gender in the Antebellum City* (Ithaca: Cornell University Press, 2002), 238.

116. Ibid., 220.

117. David Harry Bennett, *The Party of Fear: From Nativist Movements to the New Right in American History* (Chapel Hill: University of North Carolina Press, 1988), 42–47.

118. Marie Anne Pagliarini, "The Pure American Woman and the Wicked Catholic Priest: An Analysis of Anti-Catholic Literature in Antebellum America," *Religion and American Culture: A Journal of Interpretation* 9, no. 1 (Winter, 1999), 97–128.

3 The Philadelphia Bible Riots

1. "Quran Burning Issue: Terry Jones vs. World," http://www.youtube.com/watch?v=MfPPtHtUfmQ.

2. "Worldwide Burning of Korans and Muhammad by Dr. Terry Jones," http://www.youtube.com/watch?v=tZk8do68JwE.

3. See Fay Botham's "Epilogue: A Postmodernist's Reflections on History and Knowledge" for a sophisticated discussion of this dialectic between epistemology and hermeneutics in *Almighty God Created the Races: Christianity, Interracial Marriage, & American Law* (Chapel Hill: University of North Carolina Press, 2009).

4. Michael Feldberg, *The Philadelphia Riots of 1844: A Study in Ethnic Conflict* (New York: Greenwood Press, 1975), 116.

5. For more on the violence in the city in the early nineteenth century, see Elizabeth M. Geffen, "Violence in Philadelphia in the 1840s and 1850s," *Pennsylvania History* 36 (1969), 381–410.

6. Ray Billington is the foremost proponent of this historical transatlantic view.

7. The United States was considered a "mission field" until 1908.

8. Frank J. Coppa, *The Modern Papacy since 1789* (New York: Addison Wesley Longman., 1998), 79–83.

9. Pope Gregory XVI, *Inter Praecipuas*, May 8, 1844.

10. See Dale B. Light, *Rome and the New Republic: Conflict and Community in Philadelphia Catholicism between the Revolution and the Civil War* (Notre Dame: University of Notre Dame Press, 1996) and "The Reformation of Philadelphia Catholicism, 1830–1860," *Pennsylvania Magazine of History and Biography* CXII, no. 3 (July, 1988); Rodger Van Allen, "Communal Bishops and the Future of Catholicism," *Theology Today* 65, no. 4 (2009); Patrick W. Carey, *People, Priests and Prelates: Ecclesiastical Democracy and the Tensions of Trusteeism* (Notre Dame: University of Notre Dame Press, 1987).

11. "Wresting the Scripture's," *Youth's Penny Gazette*, April 5, 1843.

12. See Jon Gjerde, Jon, and S. Deborah Kang, *Catholicism and the Shaping of Nineteenth-century America* (New York: Cambridge University Press, 2012), especially chapter 4, and Paul C. Gutjahr, *A History of the Good Book in the United States: 1777–1880* (Stanford University Press, 1999), 120–24.

13. John Dowling, *Burning of the Bibles: Defense of the Protestant Version of the Scriptures Against the Attacks of the Popish Apologists for the Champlain Bible Burners* (Nathan Moore, 1843), 21 (accessed April 10, 2012, http://books.google.com/books?id=d3Q2AAAAMAAJ&printsec=frontcover&source=gbs_ge_summary_r&cad=0#v=onepage&q&f=false). For a description of the "Champlain Bible Burning," see Ray Allen Billington, *The Protestant Crusade 1800–1860: A Study of the Origins of American Nativism* (Chicago: Quadrangle Books, 1938), 157–58.

14. Judith Amanda Hunter, "Before Pluralism: The Political Culture of Nativism in Antebellum Philadelphia" (Ph.D. diss., Yale University, 1991), 57–58. David Montgomery has explained, "The whole Protestant edifice of churches, Bible societies, temperance societies, and missionary agencies was thus interposed against Catholic electoral maneuvers in the name of 'non-sectarian politics' at the very moment when those maneuvers were enjoying some success." See David Montgomery, "The Shuttle and the Cross: Weavers and Artisans in the Kensington Riots of 1844," *Journal of Social History* (1972), 427.

15. "Constitution of the American Protestant Association" (Presbyterian Historical Society, Philadelphia: 1842).

16. "Annual Report of the American Protestant Association" (Presbyterian Historical Society, Philadelphia: 1843).

17. He had been given full jurisdiction as well as the right of succession because of

Conwell's physical and mental condition, and elevated to the Bishop of Arath in partibus, since, according to church doctrine, all bishops must have their own diocese. Those serving in administrative roles are given charge of a titular, or defunct, historical diocese, such as Arath. See Wolfgang Beinert and Francis Schussler Fiorenza, eds., *Handbook of Catholic Theology* (New York: Crossroad, 1995).

18. A series of letters from both Kenrick and Conwell to Rome sketch a strained, even violent relationship. Conwell wrote of Kenrick's actions on his arrival: "... he took forcible possession of my house, threw my furniture out of my parlour into the open hall, also several portraits attached to the wall, together with a desk belonging to the Jesuits inclosing sacred relics, where they remained for three weeks; the door being closed against me, the lock taken off and a new one put on the door. He claimed all the property attached to St. Joseph's as his own, and converted the house into a boarding and lodging house, obliging his boarders to pay him five dollars per week,—whilst in the meantime he accommodated them with my beds and furniture." Bishop Conwell to the Irish College, n.d., 1832, Papers of the Irish College, Philadelphia Archdiocese Historical Research Center.

19. James F. Connelly, *The History of the Archdiocese of Philadelphia* (Philadelphia: Philadelphia Archdiocese, 1976), 134.

20. Ibid., 156.

21. Ibid., 133–34.

22. Ibid., 166.

23. Ibid., 130–31.

24. Ibid., 156.

25. Ibid., 134.

26. Francis E. Tourscher, ed., *Diary and Visitation Record of the Rt. Rev. Francis Patrick Kenrick Administrator and Bishop of Philadelphia, 1830–1851* (Lancaster, PA: Wickersham Print Co., 1916), 50. Francis Patrick Kenrick to Propaganda Fide, 11 June 1830, quoted in Hugh J. Nolan, "Francis Patrick Kenrick, First Coadjutor Bishop," in *History of the Archdiocese of Philadelphia,* edited by James F. Connelly (Philadelphia: Archdiocese of Philadelphia, 1976), 113–208. 125.

27. This is a very complicated community. Richard Warren defines "pan-Americans" as "men and women with extensive ties to Latin America and the Caribbean." Some of these folks were slaves, some free, some of African descent, some were aiding colonizing projects, etc. To complicate matters further, some came to Philadelphia as Catholics, some as Protestants, some as followers of indigenous religions or hybrid movements during the decades of upheaval on the island that is now Haiti and the Dominican Republic. Some fled the island for a time and returned, some stayed and created larger and more visible communities in Philadelphia. See Warren's "Displaced 'Pan-Americans' and the Transformation of the Catholic Church in Philadelphia, 1789–1850," *Pennsylvania Magazine of History and Biography* CXXVIII, no. 4 (2004): 343 and John Davies, "Saint-Dominguan Refugees of African Descent and the Forging of Ethnic Identity in Early National Philadelphia," *The Pennsylvania Magazine of History and Biography* 134, no. 2 (April 1, 2010): 109–26, as well as his dissertation "Class, Culture, and Color: Black Saint-Dominguan Refugees and African–American Communities in the Early Republic" (University of Delaware, 1998).

28. Martin I.J. Griffin, "History of the Church of Saint John the Evangelist, Philadelphia," *Records of the American Catholic Historical Society of Philadelphia* 20 (1909):
360–61. (emphasis Griffin or Hughes).

29. *Catholic Telegraph*, April 28, 1832.

30. James Pyle Wickersham, *A History of Education in Pennsylvania, Private and Public, Elementary and Higher* (Lancaster, PA: Inquirer Publishing Co., 1886), 293.
Vincent P. Lannie and Bernard C. Deithorn, "For the Honor and Glory of God:
The Philadelphia Bible Riots of 1844," *History of Education Quarterly* 8 (Spring
1968): 47.

31. *Catholic Herald*, April 5, 1838.

32. "Common Schools," *Catholic Herald*, April 12, 1838.

33. "Education," *Catholic Herald*, March 21, 1839.

34. *Catholic Herald*, April 14, 1841.

35. Ibid., April 28, 1841.

36. Ibid., May 5, 1841.

37. Ibid., June 24, 1841.

38. Ibid., November 25, 1841. (Kenrick's emphasis and capitals).

39. *North American and Daily Advertiser*, December 11, 1841.

40. *Catholic Herald*, December 16, 1841.

41. Ibid., December 23, 1841.

42. Hugh J. Nolan, *The Most Rev. Francis Patrick Kenrick, Third Bishop of Philadelphia,
1830–1851* (American Catholic Historical Society, 1948), 198, 212–14, 293–95.
In his request, Kenrick contradicted himself regarding Protestants and Catholic
worshipping together; he showed great enthusiasm that Protestants were attend-
ing Catholic mass at Saint John the Evangelist, for instance. He also notes in his
diary that he said Mass in Protestant homes a number of times.

43. Ibid., 297.

44. Jan Shipps is the seminal historian of Mormonism in America. See also Matthew
Burton Bowman, *The Mormon People: The Making of an American Faith* (New
York: Random House, 2012); Patrick Q. Mason, *The Mormon Menace: Violence
and Anti-Mormonism in the Postbellum South* (New York: Oxford University Press,
2011); Philip L. Barlow, *Mormons and the Bible: The Place of the Latter-Day Saints
in American Religion* (New York: Oxford University Press, 1991); Jan Shipps,
Mormonism: The Story of a New Religious Tradition (Urbana: University of Illinois
Press, 1985); Richard L. Bushman, *Joseph Smith and the Beginnings of Mormonism*
(Urbana: University of Illinois Press, 1984).

45. Edwin S. Gaustad, *The Rise of Adventism: Religion and Society in Mid-Nineteenth-
Century America*, 1st ed. (New York: Harper & Row, 1974); Ronald L. Num-
bers and Jonathan M. Butler, *The Disappointed: Millerism and Millenarianism in the
Nineteenth Century*, 2nd ed. (Knoxville: University of Tennessee Press, 1993).

46. "The Full Particulars of the Late Riots With a View of the Burning of
the Catholic Churches, St. Michael's and St. Augustine's" (Philadelphia:
Library Company, 1844), 4. Available at http://www.archive.org/stream/
fullparticulars00phil#page/n3/mode/2up

47. *Native American*, May 6, 1844.

48. Some Catholic sources claim a Catholic, Patrick Fischer was the first to be killed
however, and that the shot was fired by a Native American. See Sister M. St.

Henry, "Nativism in America, 1840–1860" (master's thesis, University of Pennsylvania, 1936), 25.

49. *A Full and Complete Account of the Late Awful Riots in Philadelphia* (Philadelphia: Library Company, 1844) 6–7, 10. Available at http://catalog.hathitrust.org/Record/009606697.

50. "Native American Meeting," *Philadelphia Public Ledger,* May 8, 1844.

51. "Continuation of the Riots — More Bloodshed," *Philadelphia Public Ledger*, May 8, 1844.

52. Feldberg, *Philadelphia Riots,* 111.

53. *Public Ledger,* May 9, 1844; Thomas Cook Middleton, "The Very Rev. T.J. Donaghoe." *Records of the American Catholic Historical Society* 23 (1912), 77.

54. Feldberg, *Philadelphia Riots,* 112–13.

55. Ibid., 113–14.

56. Elizabeth Cowgill West, *Elizabeth C. West Journal of 1844,* Transcribed by Harry F. Langhorne, (Philadelphia: H.F. Langhorne, 1998).

57. "The Full Particulars," 130.

58. *Philadelphia Public Ledger*, May 10, 1844.

59. West, *Elizabeth C. West Journal of 1844.*

60. "The Riots and Some of Their Consequences," *Philadelphia Public Ledger,* May 11, 1844.

61. Francis Patrick Kenrick, "To the Catholics of the City and the County of Philadelphia" (1844), Archives of the Philadelphia Archdiocesan Historical Research Center.

62. *Philadelphia Public Ledger*, May 13, 1844.

63. St. Henry, "Nativism," 20.

64. Feldberg, *Philadelphia Riots,* 115–16.

65. St. Henry, "Nativism," 27.

66. "Grand Jury Presentment, Kensington Riots." Reprinted in *Records of the American Catholic Historical Society,* "A Selection of Sources Dealing with the Nativist Riots," Vol. 80 No. 2-3, (June-September 1969), 90; and Feldberg, 130.

67. "Address of the Catholic Lay Citizens of the City and County of Philadelphia, to Their Fellow-Citizens, in Reply to the Presentiment of the Grand Jury of the Court of Quarter Sessions of May Term 1844, in Regard to the Causes of the Late Riots in Philadelphia," (Philadelphia: M. Fithian, 1844), 9.

68. Susan G. Davis, *Parades and Power: Street Theatre in Nineteenth-Century Philadelphia* (Philadelphia: Temple University Press, 1986), 150–51. Ray Billington reports that the parades attracted seventy thousand people. Billington, *Protestant Crusade*, 227. Other accounts, such as Lannie and Diethorn's though, put the number at twenty thousand. Diethorn, "For the Honor," 83.

69. Davis, *Parades and Power,* 150.

70. Diethorn, "For the Honor," 80.

71. Davis, *Parades and Power,* 150.

72. "Riots at Southwark, Philadelphia," *Niles' National Register* (Baltimore), July 13, 1844.

73. Diethorn, "For the Honor," 83–85 and Ira M. Leonard and Robert D. Parmet, *American Nativism, 1830–1860* (New York: Van Nostrand Reinhold Company, 1971), 75.

74. Diethorn, "For the Honor," 87, and Nolan, *The Most Rev. Francis Patrick Kenrick*, 343.
75. Feldberg, *Philadelphia Riots*, 164–69.
76. Montgomery, "Shuttle and Cross," 427.
77. Agrarian communities were established in a number of rural places, the most noteworthy being the community in Benedicta, Maine. The German Catholic Brotherhood, founded in 1842, established St. Mary's, a colony in rural Pennsylvania, to protect German immigrants of Baltimore and Philadelphia from anti-Catholic violence. In the following letter to Propaganda Fide, Alexandre Czwitkowietz wrote of their project: "A great number of our German brothers of Baltimore and Philadelphia, seeing all the different sects with which our cities are populated, and the great danger for them and for their children of losing faith, proposed to form an exclusively Catholic community... I believe that I can see in the new establishment the future refuge where this infant Christianity sheltered from the corruption of the world and perversion of heresy, will increase in knowledge without losing virtue and will furnish generous vocations among which God will be pleased to choose Apostles for America. See Edward T. McCarron, "A Brave New World: The Irish Agrarian Colony of Benedicta, Maine in the 1830s and 1840s," *American Catholic Historical Researches* 105, no. 1-2 (1994). Many thanks to Jeffrey Marlett for bringing this to my attention.
78. Dale B. Light, "The Reformation of Philadelphia Catholicism, 1830–1860," *Pennsylvania Magazine of History and Biography* CXII, no. 3 (1988).
79. First, he did not have the funds during his tenure in Philadelphia to found an entire system of parochial education. Second, there is evidence that even when presented with financial contributions for education, he did not always use them. In 1845 for instance, he received a donation from the Sacred Congregation of Propaganda in Rome explicitly earmarked for the founding of Catholic schools in Philadelphia. He did not use it for schools though; it seems he thought that the money would be useless. Third, prior to Kenrick's bishopric a number of schools already existed: academies, parochial schools, and home schools. See Thomas J. Donaghy, *Philadelphia's Finest: A History of Education in the Catholic Archdiocese, 1692–1970* (Philadelphia: American Catholic Historical Society, 1972), 60. Many scholars claim that the Catholic school system in Philadelphia was explicitly the work of Kenrick though. James Burns calls him a "zealous educationalist" in his history of education in the archdiocese, and he disagrees with the analysis that establishing a Catholic school system in Philadelphia was a difficult undertaking for the bishop. Michael Feldberg concludes his study of the 1844 riots with the unambiguous pronouncement: "Bishop Kenrick abandoned his fight for the Catholic Bible in the public schools and turned instead to constructing a parochial school system. This was part of that broad effort … to create a complete set of separate but equal parallel institutions designed to insulate the Irish Catholic population from dependence on or contact with native Protestant institutions, such as the public schools or the Protestant charity hospitals, in which sectarian proselytizing was the rule." See Feldberg, *Philadelphia Riots*, 172.
80. Nolan, *Most Reverend Francis Patrick Kenrick*, 385–91.
81. Henry Leffman, *The Consolidation of Philadelphia* (Philadelphia: City History Society of Philadelphia, 1908), 30.

82. *On Scripture and Tradition, Councilium Tridentinum, Diariorum,* Session IV, April 8, 1546. Henry Bettenson, ed., *Documents of the Christian Church* (New York: Oxford University Press, 1967), 261–62.

83. David Brion Davis has asserted, "We have not sufficiently appreciated that for many American Protestants, the Reformation, even more than the Revolution, was the model of a timeless, archetypal experience that had to be reenacted, in almost ritualistic fashion, if freedom was to be preserved." *The Slave Power Conspiracy and the Paranoid Style* (Baton Rouge: Louisiana State University Press, 1969), 75–76. See also Hunter, "Before Pluralism," 39.

84. This first Catholic English translation was produced by exiled British Catholics who had fled the reign of Queen Elizabeth I and established a college in Douay, France. Under the instruction of Cardinal William Allen, the scholars based their translation on the Sixto-Clementine Vulgate. Allen suggested in a 1578 letter to Dr. Vendeville, regius professor of canon law at the University, that the reason for Bible study was to keep pace with the Protestant reformers, or "heretics" as he called them. In the same letter he also maintained the role of the biblical scholarship at Douay was so the "evil"—the corrupt Protestant translations—might be "remedied." Dr. Gregory Martin, professor of Hebrew and scripture interpretation, undertook the main translator's role and published the New Testament in 1582. In 1609 the Old Testament translation was completed and published in Douay, and hence, the proper title of the entire Bible is the Rheims-Douay. In 1749, London Bishop William Challoner began to revise the text—which had been fairly widely criticized for obsolete language and being too literal—and it was Challoner's revision, completed in 1772, that became the popular scripture used by English-speaking Catholics until the twentieth century. See Gerald P. Fogarty, *American Catholic Biblical Scholarship* (New York: Harper and Row, 1989), 5; Roland H. Worth, *Church, Monarch, and Bible in Sixteenth Century England: The Political Context of Biblical Translation* (Jefferson, NC: McFarland, 2000), 133–37; Bernard Ward, "Douai," in *Catholic Encyclopedia* (Robert Appleton Co., 1909); Lewis Lupton, *England's Word: King James Bible,* 4.

85. See Fogarty, *American Catholic Biblical Scholarship,* 4–7, and Hugh J. Nolan, ed., *Pastoral Letters of the American Hierarchy, 1792–1970* (Huntington, IN: Our Sunday Visitor, 1970), 28.

86. Nolan, ed., *Pastoral Letters,* 93.

87. Cameron MacKenzie highlights the different language used in Protestant scripture and how it "obscure[d] the sacred origins of words in favor of secularized" words. He suggests a number of important examples of this distinction: the Catholic use of "Sabbath" versus the Protestant "day of rest;" the Catholic "neophyte" as opposed to the Protestant "young scholar;" and the Douay terms "heaven" and "paraclete" versus the Protestant "sky" and "comforter." See *The Battle for the Bible in England, 1557–1582* (New York: Peter Lang, 2002), 203–4.

88. As we saw above, only "The Truth Unveiled" pamphlet mentioned that rioters passed a German church without harming it. The writer must have been referring to St. Peter the Apostle, which was located three blocks from the riots and was the only German church being built in 1844. In May however, the steeple had not yet been constructed, so a more likely explanation for why it was passed by the rioters is that they did not see it or know it was there, especially since a number of them were from other sections of the city. There are also numerous

Protestant sources supporting the fact that all Catholics and city churches were targeted. The writer of the "Full Particulars" pamphlet stated on Friday, May 10th, "... The military are still under arms, and are stationed at every Roman Catholic Church, Asylum, Seminary and the Jesuits' college on Race near the Schuylkill." Major General Patterson provided the clearest testimony that Philadelphia's non-Irish Catholic churches were in danger. In his "Orders No. 4" of May 9th, he dispatched units to Saint Mary's and Holy Trinity. He would not have done unless they were in danger. See "The Truth Unveiled"; Middleton, "T.J. Donaghoe," 76; and Tourscher, ed., *Diary*, 188–92.

89. *Philadelphia Public Ledger*, May 9, 1844.

90. Middleton, "Rev. Donaghoe," 76.

91. Sister M. Gonzaga, "Letter, May 9, 1844," *Records of the American Catholic Historical Society of Philadelphia* 80, no. 2-3 (1969): 109.

92. There were at least two German-speaking lodges: one in San Francisco and another in Philadelphia. In the early 1850s, the *New York Times* noted that most members of the APA were foreign-born. "Terrible Riot and Bloodshed, Dreadful Scenes on Newark, and Additional Accounts," *New York Times*, September 6, 1854.

93. There was a long history of religiously-motivated violence in Philadelphia. Irish Protestants and Irish Catholics for instance, marched and rioted in July of 1831, which in Ireland, was (and is) the month when commemorations of the 1689 Battle of the Boyne mentioned above were held. *Public Ledger*, May 9, 1844.

94. "The Full Particulars," 128.

95. "The Truth Unveiled," 22. (Capitals and emphasis theirs.)

95. *Philadelphia Public Ledger*, May 8, 1844 and May 9, 1844; Feldberg, *Philadelphia Riots*, 100.

97. Ibid. Interestingly, his family converted to Roman Catholicism after his death. See Martin I.J. Griffin, "Conversations of a Native American Rioter's Family," *American Catholic Historical Researches* 28 (1911).

98. *Philadelphia Public Ledger*, May 7, 1844, and May 14, 1844.

99. Also see Katie Oxx, "Considerate Portions: The Complex Religious Ecology of Early National Philadelphia" (Ph.D. diss., Claremont Graduate University, 2006).

100. In addition to the works mentioned below, two dissertations analyze the riots. Alexandra Griswold examines how Protestants "understood their own belief system ... [and] what they understood about the Catholics and their belief system." Catholicism is not interrogated in the same fashion but rather it is viewed as a monolith. See "An Open Bible and Burning Churches: Authority, Truth and Folk Belief in Protestant—Catholic Conflict—Philadelphia, 1844" (Ph.D. diss., University of Pennsylvania, 1997), 38. Daniel Crosby asserts that the riots were more substantial "not only physically, but in their cultural significance—than the earlier riots, because they encapsulated and were in some sense the logical result of a theological conflict." The other non-religious factors which scholars have blamed for the riots reflected "underlying religious hostility." See "A Christian Nation: Evangelical Protestantism and Religious Conflict in Antebellum Philadelphia" (Ph.D. diss., Washington University, 1997), 127, 129.

101. A number of other works from various disciplines analyze them in addition to the few I'll highlight here. Elizabeth Geffen situates them in the context of

the violence in Jacksonian Philadelphia, though she admits the city "has been fantastically successful in concealing its wild side from the rest of the world." She traces a number of conflicts, such as those that occurred frequently on the Christian Sabbath, or during "long, hot summers," and those between Protestant Irish and Catholic Irish. Like Feldberg, she examines the disorganized law enforcement agencies—"clubs" would be a more appropriate term for them —and how their incompetence caused controllable scuffles to become full-scale riots. The Bible riots, for Geffen, were caused by the already uncomfortable urban conditions plus Kenrick's "most unfortunate" request for his flock to read from their authorized Bible translation or at least be excused from reading the King James Version. Sam Bass Warner defines the riots as a combination of the effects of the depression that struck Philadelphia in the 1830s, the weakness of institutional order, and the identification of the Irish as a "legitimate target" in his widely acclaimed study of Philadelphia. He asserts that the interplay between the "elements of the big-city era" were what lead to so much violence in Philadelphia between 1834 and 1844. He acknowledges that many social clubs and labor organizations were born during this era, but he concludes they were not of much help in stemming the isolation and despair the burgeoning urban space perpetuated. The desperate need for social services went unmet, even as ethnic politics began to take root. Dennis Clark attributed the riots to a combination of the "highly emotional issue of religion" and like Warner, the problematic (or nonexistent) institutions for civil order. Clark saw the riots as predominantly Irish-Protestant versus Irish-Catholic. He emphasized that Orange Order members were deeply involved: William Craig and John McManus called the meeting in Nannygoat Market and Patrick Fisher was one of the first men to be killed. (The Orange Order is a fraternal and political organization named after and committed to the memory of William III of Orange, who in 1689 defeated Catholic James II at the Battle of the Boyne. The Order has been associated with sectarian violence in Ireland and to a considerably less extent, the United States, since its founding.) See Geffen, "Violence in Philadelphia"; Dennis Clark, *The Irish in Philadelphia; Ten Generations of Urban Experience* (Philadelphia: Temple University Press, 1973); Sam Bass Warner, Jr., *The Private City: Philadelphia in Three Periods of Its Growth* (Philadelphia: University of Pennsylvania Press, 1968).
102. Feldberg, Philadelphia Riots, ix.
103. Ibid., 78–79.
104. Ibid., 4.
105. Ibid., 13–14.
106. Gary B. Nash, *First City: Philadelphia and the Forging of Historical Memory*, ed. Daniel K. Richter, *Early American Studies* (Philadelphia: University of Pennsylvania Press, 2002), 175.
107. Before the American Revolution, only about one-fifth to one-fourth of Irish immigrants were Catholic. Between 1783 and 1819, two-thirds were Presbyterian and of the other third, most were Anglican; the remainder were Catholic. Through 1826, the vast majority of immigrants were Ulster Protestants, although Catholic numbers were on the rise. Over the period from 1827–1844, Catholics became a slim majority, although as Miller notes, "most were neither destitute nor desperate." Kerby A. Miller, *Emigrants and Exiles: Ireland and the*

Irish Exodus to North America (New York: Oxford University Press, 1985), 170, 196–200.

108. Montgomery, "The Shuttle and the Cross," 421.

109. Ibid., 439.

110. Lannie and Diethorn, "For the Honor," 46.

111. Ibid., 95.

112. Ibid., 72.

113. Tracy Fessenden, "The Nineteenth-Century Bible Wars and the Separation of Church and State." *Church History: Studies in Christianity and Culture* 74:4 (December 2005): 784–811.

114. Tracy Fessenden, "Christianity, National Identity, and the Contours of Religious Pluralism," in Catherine A. Brekus and W. Clark Gilpin, eds., *American Christianities: A History of Dominance and Diversity* (Chapel Hill: The University of North Carolina Press, 2011).

115. Fessenden, "Bible Wars." See also Botham, *Almighty God Created the Races* for a similar argument on interracial marriage law.

4 Destruction of the "Pope's Stone"

1. Editors, 9/11 Families for a Safe and Strong America, "9/11 Families Reject Towering Mosque Planned for Ground Zero Site," http://www.911familiesforamerica. org/?p=3993.

2. John F. Weishampel, *The Pope's Stratagem: "Rome to America!" An Address to the Protestants of the United States, Against Placing the Pope's Block of Marble in the Washington Monument* (Philadelphia and Baltimore: Weishampel, John, 1852).

3. See David Bodenhamer, John Corrigan, and Trevor Harris, eds., *The Spatial Humanities: GIS and the Future of Humanities Scholarship* (Indianapolis: Indiana University Press, 2010), especially pages 14–15 for an explication of the spatial aspects of American nationalism.

4. Roger Finke and Rodney Stark, *The Churching of America, 1776–2005: Winners and Losers in our Religious Economy* (New Brunswick: Rutgers University Press, 2005), 156–58; and Michael O. Emerson and Christian Smith, *Divided by Faith: Evangelical Religion and the Problem of Race in America* (Oxford: Oxford University Press, 2000), 34.

5. Emerson and Smith, *Divided by Faith,* 36; Forrest G. Wood, *The Arrogance of Faith: Christianity and Race in America from the Colonial Era to the Twentieth Century,* 1st ed. (New York: Knopf, 1990), 309.

6. The data on proslavery Christianity is staggering and repulsive. Twenty-five thousand Methodists, for instance, owned over two hundred thousand slaves. Of these slave owners, twelve hundred were clergy. For a nuanced perspective on both abolitionist and proslavery Christianity, see Charles Irons. He attests that neither was the eighteenth century as integrated nor the nineteenth as segregated as many scholars have written. See Emerson and Smith, *Divided by Faith,* 36, and Charles F. Irons, *The Origins of Proslavery Christianity: White and Black Evangelicals in Colonial and Antebellum Virginia* (Chapel Hill: University of North Carolina Press, 2008), 12–14.

7. Andrew Preston, *Sword of the Spirit, Shield of Faith: Religion in American War and Diplomacy,* 1st ed. (New York: Alfred A. Knopf, 2012); Robert Wal-

ter Johannsen, Sam W. Haynes and Christopher Morris, *Manifest Destiny and Empire: American Antebellum Expansionism* (College Station: Texas A&M University Press, 1997); Frederick Merk and Lois Bannister Merk, *Manifest Destiny and Mission in American History: A Reinterpretation* (Cambridge: Harvard University Press, 1963); Conrad Cherry, *God's New Israel: Religious Interpretations of American Destiny* (Englewood Cliffs: Prentice-Hall, 1971).

8. William Jason Wallace, *Catholics, Slaveholders, and the Dilemma of American Evangelicalism, 1835–1860* (Notre Dame, IN: University of Notre Dame Press, 2010), 23–25.

9. Ibid., 26 and 36.

10. Ibid., 71–88. Wallace notes the connection evangelical writers made between the physical enslavement of African-Americans and the "mental slavery" of Catholicism.

11. See Randall M. Miller et al., *Religion and the American Civil War* (NY: Oxford University Press, 1998) and Mark A. Noll, *The Civil War as a Theological Crisis* (Chapel Hill: University of North Carolina Press, 2006).

12. Dale T. Knobel, *America for the Americans: The Nativist Movement in the United States* (New York: Twayne, 1996), 68–69, 73, 83. I'm going to use "Native American/American Republican Party" to refer to this group; scholars often use one name or the other, which can be very confusing to readers.

13. David Harry Bennett, *The Party of Fear: From Nativist Movements to the New Right in American History* (Chapel Hill: University of North Carolina Press, 1988), 48.

14. Knobel, *America for the Americans,* 82–83.

15. Ibid., 85–87.

16. Ibid., 78–79.

17. Ibid., 81. It should be noted however, that Bennett also claims, "The new aliens bore so many burdens and presented so many problems they would have been assailed even if every one was a good Protestant." Bennett, *Party of Fear,* 85.

18. Bennett, *Party of Fear,* 92–95.

19. Ibid., 81.

20. John Hughes, *The Decline of Protestantism, and its Cause* (New York: E. Dunigan & Brother, 1850). Available at http://archive.org/details/trueprotestanism00illm.

21. Bennett, *Party of Fear,* 89. Historian David Endres notes that while both eminent historians of American Catholicism Peter Guilday and James Connelly analyze the visit, its effect on "American notions of free speech, citizenship, and the rights of the foreign born" remain unexamined. See Endres, "Know-Nothings, Nationhood, and the Nuncio: Reassessing the Visit of Archbishop Bedini," *U.S. Catholic Historian* 21, no. 4 (Fall 2003), 2; and James F. Connelly, *The Visit of Archbishop Gaetano Bedini to the United States of America: June 1853–February 1854* (Universita Gregoriana, 1960); and Peter Guilday, *Gaetano Bedini: An Episode in the Life of Archbishop John Hughes, 1853–1854* (New York: United States Catholic Historical Society, 1934). A few historians of an earlier generation do mention the event though. See for instance Oscar Handlin, *Boston's Immigrants 1790–1880: A Study in Acculturation* (Cambridge: Belknap Press of Harvard University Press, 1979), 382, and Ray Allen Billington, *The Protestant Crusade 1800–1860: A Study of the Origins of American Nativism* (Chicago: Quadrangle Books, 1938).

22. Endres, "Know Nothings," 2.

23. This of course, would tap in to the historical imagination of Protestants who

clung to Martin Luther's criticism of Johann Tetzel, papal representative in Wittenberg and the most famous indulgence-salesman in history, who Luther memorialized as final catalyst in his conversion process.

24. Endres, "Know Nothings," 8–11.
25. Ibid., 13.
26. Bennett, *Party of Fear*, 89.
27. Billington, *Protestant Crusade*, 312–13.
28. See the detailed record "Summary," *Prints & Photographs Online Catalog,* Library of Congress, http://www.loc.gov/pictures/item/2008661538.
29. Nathan Glazer and Cynthia R. Field, *The National Mall: Rethinking Washington's Monumental Core* (Baltimore: Johns Hopkins University Press, 2008), 179.
30. He continues, "Certainly, the monuments and memorials and the neoclassical architecture of the capital express the grandeur of the American experiment and the power of patriotic inspiration." See Edward Tabor Linenthal, *Sacred Ground: Americans and their Battlefields* (Urbana: University of Illinois Press, 1993), 2.
31. Pamela Scott, "This Vast Empire:" The Iconography of the Mall, 1791–1848," in *The Mall in Washington, 1791–1991,* edited by Richard W. Longstreth (Washington, DC: National Gallery of Art, 1991), 37.
32. He had originally intended to have thirteen such axes to symbolize the original colonies. Ibid., 38–39.
33. Kenneth R. Bowling, *The Creation of Washington, D.C.: The Idea and Location of the American Capital* (Fairfax, VA: George Mason University Press, 1991), 223. Scholars reference Jefferson's extensive European travels as profoundly shaping his ideas about public urban space.
34. Michael J. Lewis, "The Idea of the American Mall," in *The National Mall: Rethinking Washington's Monumental Core,* eds. Nathan Glazer and Cynthia R. Field (Baltimore: The Johns Hopkins University Press, 2008), 13.
35. Ibid.
36. Ibid., 14.
37. *Resolution of the Joint Committee Appointed to Prepare Measures to Honor the Memory of General George Washington, that $100,000 be Appropriated for the Purpose of Erecting a Marble Monument to Washington, 05/08/1800, Records of Joint Committees of Congress* (1800).
38. Kirk Savage, *Monument Wars: Washington, D.C., the National Mall, and the Transformation of the Memorial Landscape* (Berkeley: University of California Press, 2009), 50.
39. Louis Torres, "To the Immortal Name and Memory of George Washington:" *The United States Army Corps of Engineers and the Construction of the Washington Monument* (Washington, DC: Historical Division, Office of Administrative Services, Office of the Chief of Engineers, 1985), 8.
40. Savage, *Monument Wars*, 55.
41. *HR 347: An Act to Authorize the Officers and Managers of the Washington National Monument Society to Erect a Monument to the Memory of George Washington on the Public Mall,* Second Session of the Twenty Fifth Congress sess., Journal of the Senate, (1838).
42. Torres, *"To the Immortal Name,"* 8; Scott, "This Vast Empire," 47–49.
43. Torres, *"To the Immortal Name,"* 11.
44. Savage, *Monument Wars,* 55.

45. Ibid., 45. See also cultural geographer Wilbur Zelinsky's *Nation Into State*, in which he claims, "In every sovereign country of the modern world, the workings of the state have set their mark upon the land." This will be discussed below viz. nationalism and civil religion, but it is important to note here that slavery was as much a "working of the state" as any other aspect of American culture, and as such, left indelible scars on the landscape. See *Nation into State: The Shifting Symbolic Foundations of American Nationalism* (Chapel Hill: University of North Carolina Press, 1988), 175.

46. James Eveleth Griffith, *History of the Washington Monument, from its Inception to its Completion and Dedication* (Holyoke, MA: J. E. Griffith, printer, 1885), 18.

47. Griffith, *History of the Washington Monument, 18, and Judith M. Jacob, The Washington Monument: A Technical History and Catalog of the Commemorative Stones* (Lowell, MA: National Park Service, U.S. Dept. of the Interior, 2005), 3.

48. Savage, *Monument Wars*, 66 and 74.

49. James Chamberlayne Pickett, *Prospectus of the National Monument, a Weekly Journal, to Be Published in Washington, Under the Sanction of the Washington National Monument Society* (Washington, DC: J.C. Pickett, 1851).

50. *Barre Patriot*, July 9, 1852.

51. *Weekly Eagle*, March 25, 1852.

52. See George Washington, "Farewell Address to the People of the United States," http://www.earlyamerica.com/earlyamerica/milestones/farewell/text.html.

53. *Philadelphia Public Ledger* and *Philadelphia Inquirer*, January 30, 1852; *Pennsylvania Freemen*, February 5, 1852.

54. *The Weekly Eagle* of Brattleboro, Vermont reported this additional information in "Tribute to Washington By the Pope," on February 9, 1852. They claimed the editor of the Frederick, Maryland *Examiner* had allegedly read the letter. The *United States Service Journal* also reported on this but quoted Kimmel, "The Pope has directed two large stones—the one to be taken from the Capital—the other from the Coliseum—to be prepared and to be presented by him to the Washington Monument." See William Ward Tompkins, *United States Service Journal: Devoted to the Army, Navy, and Militia*, Volumes 4–6, 1851.

55. Letter, Lewis Cass, Jr. to Secretary of the Washington National Monument Society, Washington, December 14, 1851, quoted in "The Pope's Stone," *Columbia*, MLK Library, Washingtoniana Collection, Washington, DC Public Library.

56. "A Stone for the Monument," *Barre Gazette*, Feb 13, 1852.

57. Letter, George Watterston to Lewis Cass, February 4 1852, reprinted in "Pope's Contribution," *Public Ledger*, February 6, 1852.

58. Griffith, *History of the Washington Monument*, 66.

59. *New York Times*, Feb 27, 1852.

60. *Public Ledger*, Feb 27, 1852.

61. Ibid., March 9, 1952.

62. John F. Weishampel, "The Pope's Stratagem."

63. George Stewart, Letter to Washington Monument Society, June 25, 1852, "Letters Received Concerning Memorial Stones for the Monument, compiled 1849-1888," Textual Records from the Washington National Monument Society, Textual Archives Services Division, National Archives, Washington, DC.

64. Ibid., July 16, 1852.

65. Not every line of each petition was signed, but of those that were, approximately

forty names were listed. See "Letters Received Concerning Memorial Stones for the Monument.

66. Babbitt Letter, Ibid., Sept 8, 1852.

67. Emphasis theirs. Anonymous, "Citizens of New Jersey Petition to The Washington Monument Association," Textual Records from the Washington National Monument Society. Series 42: Records of the Office of Public Buildings and Public Parks of the National Capital, 1790–1992, National Archives, Washington, DC.

68. *Alexandria Gazette*, October 20, 1853; *Daily National Intelligencer*, November 4, 1853.

69. Griffith, *History*, 66.

70. Ibid.

71. This was common for nativist groups to do at the time for ceremonial events.

72. "The Pope's Stone: How the Pontiff's Gift was Stolen and Sunk," *Washington Post*, September 30, 1883; Griffith, *History*, 66.

73. "The Pope's Stone," *Washington Post*, September 30, 1883; "More About the Pope's Stone," Ibidem., October 3, 1883.

74. "The Destruction of the Pope's Block," *Farmer's Cabinet*, March 16, 1854, and "Destruction of the Pope's Offering to Washington," *North American*, March 8, 1852.

75. Griffith, *History,* 67.

76. *Washington Post*, September 30, 1854; the *Christian Watchman and Reflector* (1851–1861), March 9, 1854, actually claims it was "smashed."

77. *Pittsfield Sun*, April 18, 1854.

78. Ibid., June 28, 1855.

79. *New York Observer and Chronicler,* March 16, 1854. The "despot of the seven hills" is a reference to the Christian New Testament Book of Revelation, chapter 17. In the scriptural chapter, the writer imagines a "great harlot ... wearing purple and scarlet and adorned with precious stone and pearls" who sits "upon seven hills" (New American Bible, Revelation 17:1–4). According to the text, the harlot leads people to idolatry and will be judged and defeated by the "lamb." The passage has been used to justify a particularly vile—if unsophisticated—strain of anti-Catholicism, with the Bishop of Rome interpreted as the harlot, the "great whore of Babylon," and the lamb as Jesus.

80. *Barre Patriot*, July 21, 1854. *The Patriot* claimed the prayer had been published in the *U.S. Catholic Miscellany*, the largest and oldest Catholic paper in the country.

81. Frederick L. Harvey, *Monograph of the Washington National Monument*, Authorized ed. (Washington, DC: Judd & Detweiler, 1885), 56. Harvey had an intimate view of the history of the monument; he was Secretary of the Joint Commission for its completion.

82. Jacob, *Washington Monument*, 3.

83. Harvey, *Monograph of the Washington National Monument*, 58.

84. *New York Times*, February 23, 1855.

85. *Pittsfield Sun,* March 8, 1855.

86. Harvey, *Monograph of the Washington National Monument,* 60.

87. *Pittsfield Sun*, March 8, 1855.

88. Jacob, *Washington Monument*, 4.

89. Harvey, *Monograph of the Washington National Monument*, 69; Jacob, *Washington Monument*, 4; Torres, "To the Immortal Name," 27.

90. George Olszewski, *A History of the Washington Monument, 1844–1968, Washington, D.C.* (Washington, DC: Office of History and Historic Architecture, Eastern Service Center, 1971), 2.

91. Harvey, *Monograph of the Washington National Monument*, 73.

92. Charles Noble, "Boy's Life in Washington Seventy Years Ago," *Washington Post*, January 24, 1926.

93. Letter, Washington National Monument Society Committee to [Blank], November [Blank] 1867, Washington National Monument Society Office. National Archives, Washington, DC.

94. "S" (Special correspondent to the *New York Times*), "Great Demonstration of the Know Nothings at the Capital," *New York Times,* September 27, 1854.

95. "The Newark Riots," *New York Times*, September 18, 1854; "The Newark Riot — Letter from Bishop Bayley," Ibid., September 13, 1854.

96. "The Newark Riot," *New York Times*, September 7, 1854.

97. "The Newark Riots," *New York Times*, September 8, 1854. For a full description of the incident, see Augustine J. Curley, "The 1854 Attack on Saint Mary's Church, Newark: A Typical Know-Nothing Incident," *American Benedictine Review* 61, no. 4 (12, 2010), 387–406.

98. Billington, *Protestant Crusade*, 421.

99. Jacob, *Washington Monument*, 4.

100. Savage, *Monument Wars*, 108.

101. Ibid., 116.

102. "Dedication of the Washington National Monument" http://www.archive.org/ stream/dedicationofwash00unit#page/n7/mode/2up.

103. Jacob, *Washington Monument*, 4.

104. Sadly though, in the summer of 2011, an earthquake—an incredible rarity for the East Coast—struck Washington, DC and the Monument suffered extensive structural damage. As of this writing, it remains closed.

105. See the *Ellensburg Daily Record,* November 26, 1982, and Judith Jacob's description of the stone. Judith M. Jacob, *The Washington Monument: A Technical History and Catalog of the Commemorative Stones* (Lowell, MA: National Park Service, 2005), 16.

106. The District of Columbia was "produced," in other words, in the late eighteenth century through a fusion of its physical form (both the "natural" topography and the "built environment"), the idea of it as penultimate symbol of "America," and the ways humans lived in and experienced it and as each of these aspects informed and influenced one other. For more on this, see Henri Lefebvre, *The Production of Space* (Oxford: Blackwell, 1991).

107. Bowling, *Creation*, 224.

108. Jeffrey Meyer defines baroque in terms of the "rectangles, circles, and diagonals, the grand vistas, the dramatic highlighting of monumental buildings, and the emphasis on movement" in L'Enfant's design. See *Myths in Stone* (Berkeley: University of California Press, 2001), 8.

109. Robert N. Bellah, "Civil Religion in America," *Daedalus* 134, no. 4 (Winter 1967), 100. See also Art Remillard's *Southern Civil Religions: Imagining the Good*

Society in the Post-Reconstruction Era (Athens and London: University of Georgia Press, 2011).

110. Ibid., 105.
111. John F. Wilson, "The Status of Civil Religion'" in Elwyn A. Smith, *The Religion of the Republic*. (Philadelphia: Fortress Press, 1971), 296.
112. Zelinsky, *Nation Into State*, 180.
113. Ibid.
114. Edith L. B. Turner, "The People's Home Ground," in *The National Mall: Rethinking Washington's Monumental Core*, edited by Nathan Glazer and Cynthia R. Field (Baltimore: The Johns Hopkins University Press, 2008), 70.
115. Zelinsky, *Nation Into State*, 183.
116. Ibid., 233.
117. Kirk Savage, *Standing Soldiers, Kneeling Slaves: Race, War, and Monument in Nineteenth-Century America* (Princeton: Princeton University Press, 1997), 19.
118. See Karal Ann Marling, *George Washington Slept Here: Colonial Revivals and American Culture, 1876–1986* (Cambridge: Harvard University Press, 1988) for a keen discussion of the multifarious depictions of him, biblical and otherwise, and the historical uses of these images.
119. In one illustration, Washington is a shepherd surrounded by grazing sheep in front of the monument. The 1902 Senate Committee presented this image in their report, "The Improvement of the Park System of the District of Columbia." See Savage, *Monument Wars*, 18–19.
120. See Wilson, "Status," 4. Jeffrey Meyer took this a step further and connected JFK's eternal flame as consequence of this (unconscious?) notion of him as the American holy spirit. Washington himself seemed to lend credence to these upholders of a biblical worldview. He praised religion as a necessary moral backbone to society, and at his inauguration in New York City in 1789, he began the now-sacrosanct tradition of using the Bible to be sworn in. See Conrad Cherry, *God's New Israel: Religious Interpretations of American Destiny* (Englewood Cliffs: Prentice-Hall, 1971), 14, and Katie Oxx, "Considerate Portions: The Complex Religious Ecology of Early National Philadelphia" (Ph.D. diss., Claremont Graduate University, 2006), especially chapter 1.
121. Henry Beebee Carrington, *The Obelisk and Its Voices; or, The Inner Facings of the Washington Monument with Their Lessons* (Boston: Lee and Shepard, C. T. Dillingham, 1887); Rudolph De Zapp, *The Washington Monument: An Authentic History of its Origin and Construction, and a Complete Description of its Memorial Tablets* (Washington, DC: The Caroline Publishing Co, 1900); Ina Capitola Emery, *The Washington Monument: Complete Guide and History* (Washington, DC: 1909); John C. Goodridge, *Will the Washington Monument Stand?* (New York: [s.n.], 1885); Griffith, *History of the Washington Monument*; Harvey, *Monograph of the Washington National Monument*; J. P. Irvin and Alfred Downing, *Concerning Washington and His Monument* (Washington, D.C: [s.n.], 1875).
122. Olszewski, *History of the Washington Monument*; Torres, *'To the Immortal Name'*; Jacob, *Washington Monument*.
123. Bowling, *Creation*, 294.
124. Savage, *Monument Wars*, 4.
125. See also Savage, *Standing Soldiers*, 270.
126. Savage, *Monument Wars*, 76.

127. Meyer, *Myths in Stone*, 3–4.

128. Ibid., 10.

129. Ibid., 11.

130. Seth C. Bruggeman, *Here, George Washington was Born: Memory, Material Culture, and the Public History of a National Monument* (Athens: University of Georgia Press, 2008), 260.

131. David Chidester and Edward Tabor Linenthal, *American Sacred Space* (Bloomington: Indiana University Press, 1995), 15.

132. See the forthcoming article: Katie Oxx, "The 'Pope's Stone:' Contested Narratives and the Destruction of Sacred Space."

Documents

1. 1786–1842, first Bishop of Charleston, South Carolina.

2. Philemon Scank was the pseudonym of Kentucky Catholic apologist Reverend George Elder (1793–1838).

Bibliography

Aarim-Heriot, Najia. *Chinese Immigrants, African Americans, and Racial Anxiety in the United States, 1848-82*. Urbana: University of Illinois Press, 2003.

Ahlstrom, Sydney E. *A Religious History of the American People*. New Haven and London: Yale University Press, 1972.

Aho, James Alfred. *This Thing of Darkness: A Sociology of the Enemy*. Seattle: University of Washington Press, 1994.

Albanese, Catherine L. *Sons of the Fathers: The Civil Religion of the American Revolution*. Philadelphia: Temple University Press, 1976.

Allerfeldt, Kristofer, and Jeremy Black. *Race, Radicalism, Religion, and Restriction: Immigration in the Pacific Northwest, 1890–1924*. Westport, CT: Praeger, 2003.

Anbinder, Tyler Gregory. *Nativism and Slavery: The Northern Know Nothings and the Politics of the 1850s*. New York: Oxford University Press, 1992.

Axtell, James. *The Invasion Within: The Contest of Cultures in Colonial North America*. New York: Oxford University Press, 1985.

Baltzell, E. Digby. *Puritan Boston and Quaker Philadelphia*. 3rd. ed. New Brunswick: Transaction, 1979.

Beckford, James A. *Religion and Advanced Industrial Society*. Vol. 23. London: Unwin Hyman, 1989.

Beinert, Wolfgang, and Francis Schussler Fiorenza. *Handbook of Catholic Theology*. New York: Crossroad, 1995.

Bellah, Robert N. "Civil Religion in America." *Daedalus* 134, no. 4 (Winter 1967): 40–55.

Bennett, David Harry. *The Party of Fear: From Nativist Movements to the New Right in American History*. Chapel Hill: University of North Carolina Press, 1988.

Bercovitch, Sacvan. *Puritan Origins of the American Self*. New Haven: Yale University Press, 1975.

Berger, Peter L. *The Desecularization of the World: Resurgent Religion and World Politics*. Washington, DC and Grand Rapids, MI: Ethics and Public Policy Center; W.B. Eerdmans Pub. Co., 1999.

Bilhartz, Terry D. *Urban Religion and the Second Great Awakening: Church and Society in Early National Baltimore*. Rutherford: Fairleigh Dickinson University Press, 1986.

Billington, Ray Allen. "Maria Monk and Her Influence." *The Catholic Historical Review* 22, no. 3 (October 1, 1936): 283–296.

———. "The Burning of the Charlestown Convent." *New England Quarterly* 10, no. 1 (March 1937): 4–24.

———. *The Protestant Crusade 1800–1860: A Study of the Origins of American Nativism.* Chicago: Quadrangle Books, 1938.

Bisson, Wilfred J. *Countdown to Violence: The Charlestown Convent Riot of 1834.* New York: Garland, 1989.

Bloch, Ruth H. "Religion and Ideological Change in the American Revolution." In *Religion and American Politics From the Colonial Period to the 1980s*, edited by Mark A. Noll, 44–61. New York: Oxford University Press, 1990.

Bodenhamer, David, John Corrigan, and Trevor Harris, eds. *The Spatial Humanities: GIS and the Future of Humanities Scholarship.* Indianapolis: Indiana University Press, 2010.

Bonomi, Patricia U. *Under the Cope of Heaven: Religion, Society and Politics in Colonial America.* New York: Oxford University Press, 1986.

Botham, Fay. *Almighty God Created the Races: Christianity, Interracial Marriage, & American Law.* Chapel Hill: University of North Carolina Press, 2009.

Bouanani, Moulay Ali. "Propaganda for Empire: Barbary Captivity Literature in the U.S." *Journal of Transatlantic Studies* 7, no. 4 (Winter 2009): 399–412.

Bowling, Kenneth R. *The Creation of Washington, D.C.: The Idea and Location of the American Capital.* Fairfax, VA: George Mason University Press, 1991.

Boyer, Paul S. *Urban Masses and Moral Order in America, 1820–1920.* Boston: Harvard University Press, 1978.

Bushman, Richard L. *From Puritan to Yankee: Character and the Social Order in Connecticut, 1690–1765.* Cambridge, MA: Harvard University Press, 1967.

Butler, Jon. "Enthusiasm Described and Decried: The Great Awakening as Interpretive Fiction." *Journal of American History* 69, no. 1982–3 (1982): 305–325.

———. "Historiographical Heresy: Catholicism as a Model for American Religious History." In *Belief in History: Innovative Approaches to European and American Religion*, edited by Thomas Kselman, 286–302. Notre Dame: University of Notre Dame, 1991.

———. "Religion in Colonial America." In *Religion in American Life: A Short History*, 1–145. New York: Oxford University Press, 2011.

Butler, Jon, Grant Wacker, and Randall Herbert Balmer. *Religion in American Life: A Short History.* 2nd ed. New York: Oxford University Press, 2011.

Butler, Jonathon. *Awash in a Sea of Faith: Christianizing the American People.* Cambridge, MA: Harvard University Press, 1990.

Callahan, Richard J. *New Territories, New Perspectives: The Religious Impact of the Louisiana Purchase.* Columbia, MO: University of Missouri Press, 2008.

Carroll, Michael P. *American Catholics in the Protestant Imagination: Rethinking the Academic Study of Religion.* Baltimore: Johns Hopkins University Press, 2007.

Chang, Derek. *Citizens of a Christian Nation: Evangelical Missions and the Problem of Race in the Nineteenth Century.* Philadelphia: University of Pennsylvania Press, 2010.

Cherry, Conrad. *God's New Israel: Religious Interpretations of American Destiny.* Englewood Cliffs: Prentice-Hall, 1971.

Chidester, David, and Edward Tabor Linenthal. *American Sacred Space.* Bloomington: Indiana University Press, 1995.

Chidester, David. *Patterns of Power: Religion and Politics in American Culture.* Englewood Cliffs: Prentice Hall, 1988.

Clark, Dennis. *The Irish in Philadelphia: Ten Generations of Urban Experience.* Philadelphia: Temple University Press, 1973.

Cohen, Daniel A. "Alvah Kelley's Cow: Household Feuds, Proprietary Rights, and the Charlestown Convent Riot." *New England Quarterly* 74, no. 4 (December 2001): 531–579.

———. "Miss Reed and the Superiors: The Contradictions of Convent Life in Antebellum America." *Journal of Social History* 30 (Fall 1996): 149–184.

———. "Passing the Torch: Boston Firemen, 'Tea Party' Patriots, and the Burning of the Charlestown Convent." *Journal of the Early Republic* 24, no. 4 (Winter 2004): 527–587.

———. "The Respectability of Rebecca Reed: Genteel Womanhood and Sectarian Conflict in Early America." *Journal of the Early Republic* 16 (Fall 1996): 419–461.

Connelly, James F. *The History of the Archdiocese of Philadelphia.* Philadelphia: Archdiocese of Philadelphia, 1976.

———. *The Visit of Archbishop Gaetano Bedini to the United States of America, June 1853–February 1854.* Rome: Pontificia Universita Gregoriana, 1960.

Coppa, Frank J. *The Modern Papacy Since 1789.* New York: Addison Wesley Longman, 1998.

Corrigan, John, Art Remillard, and Tracy Leavelle. "French and Spanish Missions in North America." *Electronic Cultural Atlas Initiative,* n.d. http://ecai.org/na%2Dmissions/.

Cott, Nancy F. *The Bonds of Womanhood: "Woman's Sphere" in New England, 1780–1835.* 2nd ed. New Haven: Yale University Press, 1997.

Cox, Harvey Gallagher. *Religion in The Secular City: Toward a Postmodern Theology.* New York: Simon and Schuster, 1984.

Crosby, Daniel Lee. "A Christian Nation: Evangelical Protestantism and Religious Conflict in Antebellum Philadelphia", 1997.

Curley, Augustine J. "The 1854 Attack on Saint Mary's Church, Newark : a Typical Know-Nothing Incident." *American Benedictine Review* 61, no. 4 (2010): 387–406.

Curran, Thomas J. *Xenophobia and Immigration, 1820–1930.* Boston: Twayne Publishers, 1975.

Curry, Thomas J. *The First Freedoms: Church and State in America to the Passage of the First Amendment.* New York: Oxford University Press, 1986.

D'Agostino, Peter R. *Rome in America: Transnational Catholic Ideology from the Risorgimento to Fascism.* Chapel Hill: University of North Carolina Press, 2004.

Daniels, Roger. *Coming to America: a History of Immigration and Ethnicity in American Life.* New York: Perennial, 2002.

Davies, John. "Class, Culture, and Color: Black Saint-Dominguan Refugees and African-American Communities in the Early Republic." PhD diss., University of Delaware, 1998.

———. "Saint-Dominguan Refugees of African Descent and the Forging of Ethnic Identity in Early National Philadelphia." *The Pennsylvania Magazine of History and Biography* 134, no. 2 (April 1, 2010): 109–126.

Davis, David Brion. *The Fear of Conspiracy: Images of un-American Subversion from the Revolution to the Present.* New York: Cornell University Press, 1971.

————. *The Slave Power Conspiracy and the Paranoid Style*. Baton Rouge: Louisiana State University Press, 1969.

Davis, Susan G. *Parades and Power: Street Theatre in Nineteenth-century Philadelphia*. Philadelphia: Temple University Press, 1986.

DePalma, Margaret C. *Dialogue on the Frontier: Catholic and Protestant Relations, 1793–1883*. Kent, OH: Kent State University Press, 2004.

Diethorn, Bernard C., and Vincent P. Lannie. "For the Honor and Glory of God: The Philadelphia Bible Riots of 1844." *History of Education Quarterly* 8 (spring 1968): 44–106.

Diouf, Sylviane. *Servants of Allah: African Muslims Enslaved in the Americas*. New York: New York University Press, 1998.

Dolan, Jay P. *The American Catholic Experience: A History from Colonial Times to the Present*. Garden City: Doubleday, 1985.

Donaghy, Thomas J. *Philadelphia's Finest: a History of Education in the Catholic Archdiocese, 1692–1970*. Philadelphia: American Catholic Historical Society, 1972.

Donohue, Patrick. *The Charlestown Convent, Its Destruction by a Mob on the Night of August 11, 1834 with a History of the Excitement Before the Burning, and the Strange and Exaggerated Reports Relating Thereto, the Feeling of Regret and Indignation Afterwards, the Proceedings of Meetings, and Expressions of the Contemporary Press : Also the Trials of the Rioters, the Testimony and the Speeches of Counsel : with a Review of the Incidents and Sketches and Record of the Principal Actors and a Contemporary Appendix*. Boston: New England News Company, 1870.

Dorsey, Bruce. *Reforming Men and Women: Gender in the Antebellum City*. Ithaca, NY: Cornell University Press, 2002.

Douglas, Ann. *The Feminization of American Culture*. New York: Avon Books, 1978.

Duncan, Richard R. "Catholics and the Church in the Antebellum Upper South." In *Catholics in the Old South: Essays on Church and Culture*, edited by Randall M. Miller and Jon L. Wakelyn. Paperback. Macon, GA: Mercer University Press, 1999.

Dunn, Mary Maples, and Richard S. Dunn. "The Founding, 1681–1701." In *Philadelphia: A 300-Year History*, edited by Russell F. Weigley, 1–32. New York: W.W. Norton & Company, 1982.

Dwight, Theodore. *Open Convents, or Nunneries and Popish Seminaries Dangerous to the Morals and Degrading to the Character of a Republican Community*. New York: Van Nostrand, 1936.

Emerson, Michael O., and Christian Smith. *Divided by Faith: Evangelical Religion and the Problem of Race in America*. Oxford: Oxford University Press, 2000.

Endres, David J. "Know-Nothings, Nationhood, and the Nuncio: Reassessing the Visit of Archbishop Bedini." *U.S. Catholic Historian* 21, no. 4 (Fall 2003): 1–16.

Farrelly, Maura Jane. *Papist Patriots: The Making of an American Catholic Identity*. New York: Oxford University Press, 2012.

Feagin, Joe R. "Old Poison in New Bottles: The Deep Roots of Modern Nativism." In *Immigrants Out! The New Nativism and the Anti-Immigrant Impulse in the United States*, edited by Juan F. Perea. New York: New York University Press, 1996: 13-43.

Feldberg, Michael. *The Philadelphia Riots of 1844: A Study in Ethnic Conflict*. New York: Greenwood Press, 1975.

Felder, Cain Hope. "Race, Racism and Biblical Interpretation." In *Stony the Road We Trod*, edited by Cain H. Felder. Minneapolis: Fortress Press, 1991: 127–145.

Fell, Marie Léonore. *The Foundations of Nativism in American Textbooks, 1783–1860*. Washington, DC: Catholic University of America Press, 1941.

Fenton, Elizabeth A. *Religious Liberties: Anti-Catholicism and Liberal Democracy in Nineteenth-century U.S. Literature and Culture*. New York: Oxford University Press, 2011.

Fessenden, Tracy. *Culture and Redemption: Religion, the Secular, and American Literature*. Princeton: Princeton University Press, 2007.

———. "The Convent, the Brothel, and the Protestant Woman's Sphere." *Signs* 25, no. 2 (2000): 451.

———. "The Nineteenth-Century Bible Wars and the Separation of Church and State." *Church History: Studies in Christianity and Culture* 74, no. 4 (December 2005): 784–811.

Finke, Roger, and Rodney Stark. *The Churching of America, 1776–2005: Winners and Losers in Our Religious Economy*. 2nd ed. New Brunswick: Rutgers University Press, 2005.

Fogarty, Gerald P. *American Catholic Biblical Scholarship*. New York: Harper and Row, 1989.

Fong, Jack. "American Social 'Reminders' of Citizenship After September 11, 2001: Nativisms and the Retractability of American Identity." *Qualitative Sociology Review* 4, no. 1 (2008): 69–91.

Foote, Kenneth E. *Shadowed Ground: America's Landscapes of Violence and Tragedy*. Revised ed. Austin: University of Texas Press, 2003.

Foster, Charles I. *An Errand of Mercy: The Evangelical United Front, 1790–1837*. Chapel Hill: University of North Carolina Press, 1960.

Fox-Genovese, Elizabeth, and Eugene D. Genovese. *Slavery in White and Black: Class and Race in the Southern Slaveholders' New World Order*. Cambridge and New York: Cambridge University Press, 2008.

Franchot, Jenny. *Roads to Rome: The Antebellum Protestant Encounter with Catholicism*. Berkeley: University of California Press, 1994.

Gates, Henry Louis. *"Race," Writing, and Difference*. Chicago: University of Chicago Press, 1986.

Geffen, Elizabeth M. "Violence in Philadelphia in the 1840s and 1850s." *Pennsylvania History* 36 (1969): 381–410.

Genovese, Eugene D. *Roll, Jordan, Roll: The World the Slaves Made*. New York: Vintage Books, 1976.

Gjerde, Jon, and S. Deborah Kang. *Catholicism and the Shaping of Nineteenth-century America*. New York: Cambridge University Press, 2012.

Gjerde, Jon. *Major Problems in American Immigration and Ethnic History: Documents and Essays*. Boston: Houghton Mifflin, 1998.

Glazer, Nathan, and Cynthia R. Field. *The National Mall: Rethinking Washington's Monumental Core*. Baltimore: Johns Hopkins University Press, 2008.

Goldschmidt, Henry, and Elizabeth McAlister, eds. *Race, Nation, and Religion in the Americas*. New York: Oxford University Press, 2004.

Gollar, C. Walker. "The Alleged Abduction of Millie McPherson and Catholic Recruitment of Presbyterian Girls." *Church History: Studies in Christianity and Culture* 65 (1996): 596.

Griffin, Martin I. J. "Conversations of a Native American Rioter's Family." *American Catholic Historical Researches* 28 (1911): 189.

———. "History of the Church of Saint John the Evangelist, Philadelphia." *Records of the American Catholic Historical Society of Philadelphia* 20 (1909): 350–405.

Griffin, Susan M. *Anti-Catholicism and Nineteenth-century Fiction*. Cambridge: Cambridge University Press, 2004.

Griffith, James Eveleth. *History of the Washington Monument, from Its Inception to Its Completion and Dedication, and Mr. Robert C. Winthrop's Address on the Occasion of the Laying of the Corner Stone, July 4th, 1848, Together with a Great Many Interesting Facts Connected with the Construction of This Highest Structure of Human Hands, Also a Graphic Description and Complete Program of the Dedication Ceremonies, February 22, 1885*. Holyoke, MA: J. E. Griffith, printer, 1885.

Griswold, Alexandra F. "An Open Bible and Burning Churches: Authority, Truth and Folk Belief in Protestant-Catholic Conflict in Philadelphia, 1844." PhD diss., University of Pennsylvania, 1997.

Guilday, Peter. *Gaetano Bedini: An Episode in the Life of Archbishop John Hughes, 1853–1854*. New York: United States Catholic Historical Society, 1934.

Gutjahr, Paul. *An American Bible: A History of the Good Book in the United States, 1777–1880*. New ed. Stanford: Stanford University Press, 2002.

Hall, David D. *Worlds of Wonder, Days of Judgment: Popular Religious Belief in Early New England*. Cambridge, MA: Harvard University Press, 1990.

Hamburger, Philip. *Separation of Church and State*. Harvard: Harvard University Press, 2002.

Hamilton, Jeanne. "The Nunnery as Menace: The Burning of the Charleston Convent, 1834." *U.S. Catholic Historian* 14, no. 1 (Winter 1996): 35.

Handlin, Oscar. *Boston's Immigrants, 1790–1880: A Study in Acculturation*. Rev. Cambridge, MA: Belknap Press of Harvard University Press, 1979.

Handy, Robert T. *A Christian America: Protestant Hopes and Historical Realities*. New York: Oxford University Press, 1984.

Hansot, Elizabeth, and David Tyack. *Managers of Virtue: Public School Leadership in America, 1820–1980*. New York: Basic Books, 1982.

Harle, Vilho. *The Enemy With a Thousand Faces: The Tradition of the Other in Western Political Thought and History*. Westport, CT: Praeger, 2000.

Hatch, Nathan O. *The Democratization of American Christianity*. New Haven: Yale University Press, 1989.

Heimert, Alan. *Religion and the American Mind: From the Great Awakening to the Revolution*. Cambridge: Harvard University Press, 1966.

Henry, Mary Saint. *Nativism in Pennsylvania with Particular Regard to Its Effect on Politics and Education, 1840–1860*. Philadelphia: Dolphin Press, 1936.

Henry, Stuart C. *Unvanquished Puritan: a Portrait of Lyman Beecher*. Grand Rapids, MI: W. B. Eerdmans Pub. Co, 1973.

Higham, John. *Strangers in the Land*. 1st ed. New Brunswick: Rutgers University Press, 1955.

Hofstadter, Richard. *The Paranoid Style in American Politics, and Other Essays*. New York: Vintage Books, 1967.

Howe, Daniel Walker. *What Hath God Wrought: The Transformation of America, 1815–1848*. New York: Oxford University Press, 2009.

Hudson, Winthrop S. *Religion in America*. New York: Charles Scribner's Sons, 1965.

Hunter, Judith Amanda. "Before Pluralism: The Political Culture of Nativism in Antebellum Philadelphia," Yale University, 1991.

Husain, Ed. "Forgotten History: US Founding Fathers and Muslim Thought." *The Arab Street*, March 6, 2012. http://blogs.cfr.org/husain/2012/03/06/forgotten-history-u-s-founding-fathers-and-muslim-thought/.

Irons, Charles F. *The Origins of Proslavery Christianity: White and Black Evangelicals in Colonial and Antebellum Virginia.* Chapel Hill: University of North Carolina Press, 2008.

Irving, Katrina. *Immigrant Mothers: Narratives of Race and Maternity, 1890–1925.* Urbana: University of Illinois Press, 2000.

Isani, Mukhtar Ali. "Cotton Mather and the Orient." *The New England Quarterly* 43, no. 1 (1970): 46–58.

Jacob, Judith M. *The Washington Monument: a Technical History and Catalog of the Commemorative Stones.* Lowell, MA: National Park Service, U.S. Dept. of the Interior, Northeast Region, Design, Construction, and Facility Management Directorate, Architectural Preservation Division, 2005.

Jaschik, Scott. "Religious Revival." *Inside Higher Ed* (December 21, 2009). http://www.insidehighered.com/news/2009/12/21/religion.

Jenkins, Philip. *The New Anti-Catholicism: The Last Acceptable Prejudice.* Oxford: Oxford University Press, 2003.

Kaplan, Amy. "Manifest Domesticity." *American Literature* 70, no. 3 (September 1998): 581–607.

Kidd, Thomas S. *God of Liberty: A Religious History of the American Revolution.* First Trade Paper ed. New York: Basic Books, 2012.

Kirlin, Joseph Louis J. *Catholicity in Philadelphia from the Earliest Missionaries down to the Present Time.* Philadelphia: J. J. McVey, 1909.

Knobel, Dale T. *America for the Americans: The Nativist Movement in the United States.* New York and London: Twayne Publishers; Prentice Hall International, 1996.

———. *Paddy and the Republic: Ethnicity and Nationality in Antebellum America.* 1st ed. Middletown, CT: Wesleyan University Press, 1986.

Lannie, Vincent P. *Public Money and Parochial Education: Bishop Hughes, Governor Seward, and the New York School Controversy.* Cleveland: Press of Case Western Reserve University, 1968.

Leavelle, Tracy. "Geographies of Encounter: Religion and Contested Spaces in Colonial North America." *American Quarterly* 56, no. 4 (2004): 913–943.

Lefebvre, Henri. *The Production of Space.* Oxford: Blackwell, 1974.

León, Luis D. *La Llorona's Children: Religion, Life, and Death in the U.S.-Mexican Borderlands.* 1st ed. Berkeley: University of California Press, 2004.

Leonard, Ira M., and Robert D. Parmet. *American Nativism, 1830–1860.* New York: Van Nostrand Reinhold Company, 1971.

Levy, Leonard W. *The Establishment Clause: Religion and the First Amendment.* 2nd revised ed. Chapel Hill: The University of North Carolina Press, 1994.

Lewis, Michael J. "The Idea of the American Mall." In *The National Mall: Rethinking Washington's Monumental Core*, edited by Nathan Glazer and Cynthia R. Field. Baltimore: The Johns Hopkins University Press, 2008: 11-26.

Light, Dale B. "Class, Ethnicity, and the Urban Ecology in a Nineteenth Century City Philadelphia's Irish, 1840–1890", Temple University, 1979.

———. *Rome and the New Republic: Conflict and Community in Philadelphia Catholicism*

Between the Revolution and the Civil War. Notre Dame: Notre Dame University Press, 1996.

———. "The Reformation of Philadelphia Catholicism, 1830–1860." *Pennsylvania Magazine of History and Biography* CXII, no. 3 (July 1988): 375–403.

Lindley, Susan Hill. *"You Have Stepped Out of Your Place:" A History of Women and Religion in America.* Paperback. Louisville, KY: Westminster John Knox Press, 1996.

Linenthal, Edward Tabor. *Sacred Ground: Americans and Their Battlefields.* 2nd ed. Urbana: University of Illinois Press, 1993.

Lord, Robert H. "Religious Liberty in New England: The Burning of the Charlestown Convent." *Historical Records and Studies United States Catholic Historical Society* 22 (1932): 7.

Lupton, Lewis. *England's Word: King James's Bible.* London: The Olive Tree, 1993.

MacKenzie, Cameron. *The Battle for the Bible in England, 1557–1582.* New York: Peter Lang, 2002.

Mannard, Joseph C. "Protestant Mothers and Catholic Sisters: Gender Concerns in Anti-Catholic Conspiracy Theories, 1830–1860." *American Catholic Studies* III (Spring/Winter 2000): 1-21.

———. "The 1839 Baltimore Nunnery Riot: An Episode in Jacksonian Nativism and Social Violence." *Maryland Historian* 11 (spring 1980) 13-27.

Marling, Karal Ann. *George Washington Slept Here: Colonial Revivals and American Culture, 1876–1986.* Cambridge, MA: Harvard University Press, 1988.

Marty, Martin E. *Righteous Empire: The Protestant Experience in America.* New York: The Dial Press, 1970.

Marx, Karl, and Friedrich Engels. *The Marx-Engels Reader.* Edited by Robert C. Tucker. 2nd revised & enlarged. New York: W. W. Norton & Company, 1978.

Massa, Mark S. "The New and Old Anti-Catholicism and the Analogical Imagination." *Theological Studies* 62, no. 3 (September 2001): 549.

Massa, Mark Stephen. *Anti-Catholicism in America: The Last Acceptable Prejudice.* New York: Crossroad Pub, 2003.

Mathews, Donald G. "The Second Great Awakening as an Organizing Process, 1780–1830: An Hypothesis." *American Quarterly* XXI, no. 1 (1969): 23–43.

May, Henry F. *The Enlightenment in America.* New York: Oxford University Press, 1976.

McCarron, Edward T. "A Brave New World: The Irish Agrarian Colony of Benedicta, Maine in the 1830s and 1840s." *American Catholic Historical Researches* 105, no. 1–2 (1994): 1-15.

McGarvie, Mark Douglas. *One Nation Under Law: America's Early Struggles to Separate Church and State.* DeKalb, IL: Northern Illinois University Press, 2005.

McGowan, Catherine. *Convents and Conspiracies: A Study of Convent Narratives in the United States, 1850–1870,* 2009.

Mead, Sidney Earl. *The Lively Experiment: The Shaping of Christianity in America.* New York: Harper and Row, 1963.

Meyer, Jeffrey F. *Myths in Stone: Religious Dimensions of Washington, D.C.* 1st ed. Berkeley: University of California Press, 2001.

Michaels, Walter Benn. *Our America: Nativism, Modernism, and Pluralism.* Durham: Duke University Press, 1995.

Miller, Kerby A. "Class, Culture, and Immigrant Group Identity in the United States:

The Case of Irish-American Ethnicity." In *Immigration Reconsidered*, edited by Virginia Yans-McLaughlin. New York: Oxford University Press, 1990: 96-129.

———. *Emigrants and Exiles: Ireland and the Irish Exodus to North America*. New York: Oxford University Press, 1985.

Miller, Randall M. "A Church in Cultural Captivity: Some Speculations on Catholic Identity in the Old South." In *Catholics in the Old South: Essays on Church and Culture*. Macon, GA: Mercer University Press, 1999: 29-37.

Miller, Randall M., and William A. Pencak, eds. *Pennsylvania: A History of the Commonwealth*. Centerville, PA: Pennsylvania State University Press, 2002.

Miller, Randall M., Harry S. Stout, and Charles Reagan Wilson, eds. *Religion and the American Civil War*. New York: Oxford University Press, 1998.

Miller, Randall M., and Jon L. Wakelyn, eds. *Catholics in the Old South: Essays on Church and Culture*. Macon, GA: Mercer University Press, 1983.

Montgomery, David. "The Shuttle and the Cross: Weavers and Artisans in the Kensington Riots of 1844." *Journal of Social History* (1972), Vol 5, number 4, 411-446.

Moore, R. Laurence. *Religious Outsiders and the Making of Americans*. New York: Oxford University Press, 1986.

Moorhead, James H. "Prophecy, Millennialism, and Biblical Interpretation in Nineteenth-Century America." In *Biblical Hermeneutics in Historical Perspective: Studies in Honor of Karlfried Froehlich*, edited by Mark S. Burrows and Paul Rorem. Grand Rapids, MI: W. B. Eerdmans, 1991: 291-302.

Morgan, Edmund S. *Roger Williams: The Church and the State*. New York: W. W. Norton & Company, 2007.

Mulkern, John R. *The Know-Nothing Party in Massachusetts: The Rise and Fall of a People's Movement*. Boston: Northeastern University Press, 1990.

Nash, Gary B. *First City: Philadelphia and the Forging of Historical Memory*. Philadelphia: University of Pennsylvania Press, 2002.

Newcomb, Steven T. *Pagans in the Promised Land: Decoding the Doctrine of Christian Discovery*. Golden, CT: Fulcrum Publishers, 2008.

Nolan, Hugh J. "Francis Patrick Kenrick, First Coadjutor Bishop." In *History of the Archdiocese of Philadelphia*, edited by James F. Connelly, 113–208. Philadelphia: The Archdiocese of Philadelphia, 1976.

———. *Pastoral Letters of the American Hierarchy, 1792–1970*. Huntington, IN: Our Sunday Vistor, 1971.

———. *The Most Rev. Francis Patrick Kenrick, Third Bishop of Philadelphia, 1830–1851*. Philadelphia: American Catholic Historical Society, 1948.

Noll, Mark A. *America's God: From Jonathan Edwards to Abraham Lincoln*. Oxford: Oxford University Press, 2002.

———. "The Bible in American Culture." In *Encyclopedia of the American Religious Experience*, edited by Charles H. Lippy and Peter W. Williams New York: Charles Scribner's Sons, 1988: Volume 3, 1075-1088

———. *The Civil War as a Theological Crisis*. Chapel Hill: University of North Carolina Press, 2006.

———. "The Image of the United States as a Biblical Nation, 1776–1865." In *The Bible in America: Essays in Cultural History*, edited by Mark A. Noll and Nathan O. Hatch. New York: Oxford University Press, 1982: 39-58.

Nord, David Paul. *Faith in Reading: Religious Publishing and the Birth of Mass Media in America*. New York: Oxford University Press, 2004.

Olszewski, George J. *A History of the Washington Monument, 1844-1968, Washington, D.C.* Washington, DC: Office of History and Historic Architecture, Eastern Service Center, 1971.

Oxx, Katie. "Considerate Portions:" *The Complex Religious Ecology of Early National Philadelphia, 1827–1845,* Vol 5, number 4, 411–446, 2006.

———. "'Sprung Forth as If By Magic:' Saint John the Evangelist Catholic Church as a Model for a Spatial Analysis of Early National Philadelphia." *American Catholic Studies* 119, no. 4 (Winter 2009): 53-72.

Pagliarini, Marie Anne. "The Pure American Woman and the Wicked Catholic Priest: An Analysis of Anti-Catholic Literature in Antebellum America." *Religion and American Culture: A Journal of Interpretation* 9, no. 1 (Winter 1999): 97–128.

Perea, Juan F., ed. *Immigrants Out!: The New Nativism and the Anti-immigrant Impulse in the United States.* New York: New York University Press, 1997.

Pew Research Center for the People and the Press. *Religion and Politics: Contention and Consensus.* Pew, 2003. http://www.people-press.org/2003/07/24/religion-and-politics-contention-and-consensus.

Pickett, James Chamberlayne. *Prospectus of the National Monument, a Weekly Journal, to Be Published in Washington, Under the Sanction of the Washington National Monument Society. The Monument Is Intended to Be a Literary, Agricultural, and Miscellaneous Paper.* Washington, DC: J.C. Pickett, 1851.

Rable, George C. *God's Almost Chosen Peoples: A Religious History of the American Civil War.* Chapel Hill: The University of North Carolina Press, 2010.

Richey, Russell E., and Robert Bruce Mullin. *Reimagining Denominationalism: Interpretive Essays.* New York: Oxford University Press, 1994.

Roy, Jody M. *Rhetorical Campaigns of the Nineteenth-Century: Anti-Catholics and Catholics in America.* Lewiston, NY: Edwin Mellen Press, 1999.

Rugoff, Milton. *The Beechers: An American Family in the Nineteenth Century.* 1st ed. New York: Harper & Row, 1981.

Sandeen, Ernest R. *The Roots of Fundamentalism: British and American Millenarianism, 1800–1930.* Chicago: University of Chicago Press, 1968.

Sassi, Jonathan D. *A Republic of Righteousness: The Public Christianity of the Post-Revolutionary New England Clergy.* New York: Oxford University Press, 2001.

Savage, Kirk. *Monument Wars: Washington, D.C., the National Mall, and the Transformation of the Memorial Landscape.* Berkeley: University of California Press, 2009.

———. *Standing Soldiers, Kneeling Slaves: Race, War, and Monument in Nineteenth-century America.* Princeton: Princeton University Press, 1997.

Schrag, Peter. *Not Fit for Our Society: Nativism and Immigration.* Berkeley: University of California Press, 2010.

Schultz, Nancy L., and Nancy Natale. *Lifting the Veil: Remembering the Burning of the Ursuline Convent.* Multimedia Installation at the Somerville Public Library, Massachusetts, 1997.

Schultz, Nancy Lusignan. *Fire and Roses: The Burning of the Charlestown Convent, 1834.* New York: Free Press, 2000.

———. "Introduction." In *Veil of Fear: Nineteenth-Century Convent Tales,* edited by Nancy Lusignan Schultz. West Lafayette, IN: Purdue University Press, 1999.

Schultz, Nancy Lusignan, ed. *Veil of Fear: Nineteenth-Century Convent Tales.* West Lafayette, IN: Purdue University Press, 1999.

Scott, Pamela. "'This Vast Empire:' The Iconography of the Mall, 1791–1848." In

The Mall in Washington, 1791–1991, edited by Richard W. Longstreth. Washington, DC: National Gallery of Art, 1991.

Sehat, David. *The Myth of American Religious Freedom*. Oxford: Oxford University Press, 2011.

Shea, William M. "Biblical Christianity as a Category in Nineteenth-Century American Apologetics." *American Catholic Studies* 115, no. 3 (2004): 1–21.

———. *The Lion and the Lamb: Evangelicals and Catholics in America*. New York: Oxford University Press, 2004.

Sklar, Kathryn Kish. *Catharine Beecher: A Study in American Domesticity*. New Haven: Yale University Press, 1973.

Smith, Ben, and Jonathan Martin. "Obama Plan: Destroy Romney." *Politico* (August 9, 2011). http://politi.co/qpP85m.

Stout, Harry S. "Ethnicity: The Vital Center of Religion in America." *Ethnicity* 2 (1975): 202-224.

Stout, Harry S., and D. G. Hart, eds. *New Directions in American Religious History*. New York: Oxford University Press, 1994.

Suggs, Jon-Christian. "Romanticism, Law, and the Suppression of African-American Citizenship." In *Race and the Production of Modern American Nationalism*, edited by Reynolds J. Scott-Childess, 67–95. Wellesley Studies in Critical Theory, Literary History, and Culture. New York: Garland, 1999.

Sweet, William Warren. *The Story of Religion in America*. New York: Harper & Brothers, 1939.

Swierenga, Robert P. "Ethnoreligious Political Behavior in the Mid-Nineteenth Century: Voting, Values, Cultures." In *Religion and American Politics From the Colonial Period to the 1980s*, edited by Mark A. Noll, 146–171. New York: Oxford University Press, 1990.

Torres, Louis. *"To the Immortal Name and Memory of George Washington:" The United States Army Corps of Engineers and the Construction of the Washington Monument*. Washington, DC: Historical Division, Office of Administrative Services, Office of the Chief of Engineers, 1985.

Tourscher, Francis E. *Diary and Visitation Record of the Rt. Rev. Francis Patrick Kenrick Administrator and Bishop of Philadelphia, 1830–1851, Later, Archbishop of Baltimore; Translated and Edited by Permission and Under the Direction of His Grace the Most Rev. Edmond F. Prendergast*. Lancaster: Wickersham Print Co., 1916.

———. "Marc Antony Frenaye - A Sketch." *Records of the American Catholic Historical Society of Philadelphia* XXXVIII, no. 2 (1927): 132–143.

———. *The Hogan Schism and Trustee Troubles in St. Mary's Church Philadelphia, 1820–1829*. Philadelphia: The Peter Reilly Company, 1930.

———. *The Kenrick-Frenaye Correspondence: Letters Chiefly of Francis Patrick Kenrick and Marc Antony Frenaye, Selected from the Cathedral Archives, Translated, Arranged, and Annotated as Sources and Helps to the Study of Local Catholic History, 1830–1862*. Lancaster: Wickersham Printing Company, 1920.

Turner, Bryan S. *Religion and Modern Society: Citizenship, Secularisation and the State*. Cambridge and New York: Cambridge University Press, 2011.

Turner, Edith L. B. "The People's Home Ground." In *The National Mall: Rethinking Washington's Monumental Core*, edited by Nathan Glazer and Cynthia R. Field. Baltimore: The Johns Hopkins University Press, 2008: 69-78.

Tuveson, Ernest Lee. *Redeemer Nation: The Idea of America's Millennial Role*. Chicago: University of Chicago Press, 1968.

Tweed, Thomas A., ed. *Retelling U.S. Religious History.* Berkeley: University of California Press, 1997.

Volo, James M., and Dorothy Denneen Volo. "Louisiana Purchase." *Encyclopedia of the Antebellum South.* Santa Barbara, CA: ABC-CLIO, 2000. http://www.xreferplus.com.ezproxy.sju.edu/entry/abcas/louisiana_purchase.

Wacker, Grant. "Religion in Nineteenth-Century America." In *Religion in American Life: A Short History,* edited by Jonathon Butler, Grant Wacker, and Randall Balmer, 155–310. New York: Oxford University Press, 2011.

Wallace, William Jason. *Catholics, Slaveholders, and the Dilemma of American Evangelicalism, 1835–1860.* Notre Dame, IN: University of Notre Dame Press, 2010.

Ward, Bernard. "Douay Bible." *Catholic Encyclopedia.* New York: Robert Appleton Co., 1909.

Warner, Sam Bass. *The Private City: Philadelphia in Three Periods of Its Growth.* Philadelphia: University of Pennsylvania Press, 1968.

Warren, Richard A. "Displaced 'Pan-Americans' and the Transformation of the Catholic Church in Philadelphia, 1789–1850." *Pennsylvania Magazine of History and Biography* CXXVIII, no. 4 (2004): 343–366.

Weber, David J. *The Spanish Frontier in North America.* The brief ed. New Haven: Yale University Press, 2009.

Weigley, Russell F. *Philadelphia: A 300-Year History.* 1st ed. Philadelphia: Barra Foundation, 1982.

Wickersham, James Pyle. *A History of Education in Pennsylvania, Private and Public, Elementary and Higher, from the Time the Swedes Settled on the Delaware to the Present Day.* Philadelphia: Inquirer Publishing Co., 1886.

Wills, Garry. *Under God: Religion and American Politics.* New York: Simon and Schuster, 1990.

Wilson, Bryan R. *Religious Toleration & Religious Diversity.* Santa Barbara: Institute for the Study of American Religion, 1995.

Wilson, John F. "The Status of Civil Religion." In *The Religion of the Republic,* edited by Elwyn A. Smith. Philadelphia: Fortress Press, 1971: 1-21.

Wood, Forrest G. *The Arrogance of Faith: Christianity and Race in America from the Colonial Era to the Twentieth Century.* 1st ed. New York: Knopf, 1990.

Wood, Gordon S. *Empire of Liberty: A History of the Early Republic, 1789–1815.* 1st ed. New York: Oxford University Press, 2009.

———. "Religion and the American Revolution." In *New Directions in American Religious History,* edited by Harry S. Stout and D. G. Hart. New York: Oxford University Press, 1997: 173-205.

Worth, Roland H. *Church, Monarch, and Bible in Sixteenth Century England: The Political Context of Biblical Translation.* Jefferson, NC: McFarland, 2000.

Young, Robert J. C. *Colonial Desire: Hybridity in Theory, Culture and Race.* New York: Routledge, 1995.

Zapp, Rudolph De. *The Washington Monument: An Authentic History of Its Origin and Construction, and a Complete Description of Its Memorial Tablets.* Washington, DC: The Caroline Publishing Company, 1900.

Zelinsky, Wilbur. *Nation into State: The Shifting Symbolic Foundations of American Nationalism.* Chapel Hill: University of North Carolina Press, 1988.

Ziff, Larzer. *Puritanism in America: New Culture in a New World.* New York: Viking Press, 1973.

Index